An Irrational Hatred of Luton

An Irrational Hatred of Luton

The classic account of one fan's obsession
with West Ham United

Robert Banks

First published in Great Britain 1995 by Independent UK Sports
Publications

This edition published in Great Britain in 2010 by
Biteback Publishing Ltd
Heal House
375 Kennington Lane
London
SE11 5QY

ISBN 978-1-84954-050-6

10 9 8 7 6 5 4 3 2 1

A CIP catalogue record for this book is available from the British
Library.

Set in Georgia and Bell Gothic
Printed and bound in Great Britain by CPI Cox & Wyman, Reading, RG1 8EX

For Elaine

Luz do meu dia. Te amo.

Contents

Foreword

I read *Irrational* when it first came out in the mid-nineties. It's a bit like *Fever Pitch*, but better because it's about West Ham not Arsenal. No disrespect to the Arse, but a book about your team is special. I've always been a Happy Hammer, or to be more accurate a Hammer. If I wanted to be happy I should have picked another team.

Except you don't pick your club, it usually picks you. Growing up in Clayhall in East London, I didn't have much choice. Robert Banks did. He was from across the water in Kent and picked West Ham because he liked claret and blue. The strange allure of those classic colours would affect his whole life.

West Ham shirts are beautiful: the claret like the blood Julian Dicks and Alvin Martin spilled in pursuit of attractive football; the blue like the sky our bubbles nearly reach, before fading and dying. I'm pretty sure that's what the shirt maker had in mind when he designed them a hundred years or so ago. You might prefer to believe the story that the club won a set of Aston Villa shirts as settlement for a bet over a running race. I do not.

Either way our shirts are a design classic, but they should come with a health warning stamped on them, like on a packet of cigarettes: 'Watching West Ham United can seriously damage your health. Before pulling on this shirt, please note that you can never change your mind. You can never support another team. You are opting for a life of frustration and despair where fortunes will always be hiding, even if you have looked everywhere. But, and this is the killer bit, there will be just enough hope and glory to keep you hanging in there. You will be part of the best group of supporters in the country. You will have the best song. And there will be a belief that just around the corner the greatest days are still to come.'

Having read this warning you can then opt to purchase the shirt or move along the rail and buy a shirt of a different colour. You could buy an Arsenal shirt if you never want to experience the pain of relegation. You could buy a Manchester United shirt, especially if you have a southern accent. Or you could buy a Tottenham shirt for. . . well I can't really think of a reason why you'd want to buy a Tottenham shirt.

Most West Ham fans are born into the faith and wouldn't want it any other way. It's rare for people to convert to the Hammers in later life. We don't have many glory hunters at the Boleyn Ground.

Yet the claret and blue is the only club shirt in England entitled to an embroidered gold star above the club crest. We won that World Cup for England in 1966 and don't let anyone ever tell you different. We choose not to wear the gold star on our shirts, because we don't like to go on about it. You'll hardly ever hear a West Ham fan boasting about Moore, Hurst and Peters and that day at Wembley. If, however, a fellow football fan brings it up casually, at a wedding reception perhaps, we are prepared to chat about it for a couple of hours, just to put them straight on the details.

The attraction of those beautiful colours and the invisible star proved too much for the young Robert Banks in Kent. He ignored the health warning and bought the shirt. He could have been a Crystal Palace fan. He must be kicking himself now.

I remember the print in my original copy of *Irrational* was incredibly small. I would have given up if it hadn't been such a good read. It was a strain on the eyes and also the heart, because I identified with so much of what he wrote. I'd been a passenger on the same roller coaster ride.

The highs and lows of our lives coincided exactly. 1975, 1980 and 1986 were the peaks on the biorhythm charts of our lives. Our heroes were Brooking, Cottee and McAvennie. Our villains were Macari, Ince and Hackett.

Like me Robert spent the eighties lurching from one disastrous relationship to another. He interviewed a succession of potential Mrs Bankses, including at least two Karens. I remember thinking Karen II sounded like half a football score.

The front cover of the original *Irrational* summed it up. Robert is wearing a West Ham shirt, holding a can of beer with a pretty woman on his lap. She's wearing thigh high boots, another reason I persisted despite the small print. It almost certainly added to the eye strain. He's in his element, but she clearly doesn't want to be there. Women, like football clubs, can break your heart. I know that only too well.

In 1998 I became the West Ham United stadium announcer. I was so proud to be the voice of the club. After ten years in the job I was given the push, the day before the start of the 2008/09 season. I felt as though I'd been chucked by a girlfriend. But it was worse than that, because I've been in love with West Ham United since I was six. That hollow feeling was something I thought I'd never experience ever again. I'd finally met the woman of my dreams and we'd been married at the Boleyn Ground. Yet here was the club telling me they didn't want me any more. I was deeply touched by the supporters who mounted a campaign for my reinstatement and midway through the season I returned. I'm now in my thirteenth season as MC Hammer and still proudly wearing that invisible gold star.

Irrational is a love story. Despite the Karens and others, it's about Robert's love for West Ham United. It doesn't have a happy ending and Colin Firth is unlikely to play Robert in the book of the film. If you love the beautiful game, you will identify with one man's love for his chosen team, even if he did pick them for the beautiful colours.

Jeremy Nicholas
Broadcaster, Speaker, MC, Hammer
London, 2010

Acknowledgements

Iain Dale, Jonathan Wadman and Katy Scholes at Biteback.

My family again for their constant support.

Jeremy Nicholas for doing the foreword.

To everyone who bought this book the first time around.

Que sera sera. . .

West Ham United 2 Fulham 0 – 3.5.75

F.A. Cup Final

When I was just a little boy, I asked my mother, what will it be? Will it be Arsenal, Will it be Spurs? Here's what she said to me: 'Shut up and eat your dinner.'

Well, it wasn't quite like that. It would be tempting to relay wonderful stories of being taken along to the 1975 Cup Final by my father, a fellow long suffering West Ham supporter, and that at the tender age of six I became smitten with the boys in claret and blue. It wasn't like that at all, and I can't change those facts even for the purposes of a book. Dad wasn't a West Ham fan and I didn't go to the 1975 Cup Final. As hard as I try, I cannot conjure up wonderful memories of the year. In fact I hardly remember anything about 1975 but then, I was only six years old. The Bay City Rollers were quite big; their flares and platform heels were even bigger. Mud were at number one with the old Buddy Holly song 'Oh Boy!' (Nothing new, even then.) My sister Sylvia was at that age, fourteen or so, when she was beginning to cause us all headaches – my parents because she'd go out until all hours (Up to ten o'clock at some stages – can you believe it?) and for me and my eldest sister, Lynn, because we were always in the room when Dad shouted at her.

Despite generally hazy memories of the time, I clearly remember the 1975 Cup Final. It made an indelible mark on my life, mainly, of course because as a direct result I ended up supporting West Ham United. This was in the days before I developed a sense of wanting the underdog to win. Had I been a few years older, I might well be a Fulham supporter today. I don't come from the East End. My family doesn't hail from the East End. My father's family have their roots in Hertfordshire, and my mother's family have always been in the Beckenham area of Kent. If place of birth dictates your football team, I ought to support Crystal Palace or Watford. The reason, purely and simply, that I began to support West Ham was because I liked the colour of their jerseys.

1975 was a bad year for disasters. The Moorgate tube crash claimed thirty-four lives and gave me nightmares. The people of Britain voted to stay in the common market – there was to be no greater fix in English history until Manchester United were seeded for the 1994 European Cup. Inflation hit 25% – remember that? No, neither do I, but I wouldn't like to see it again, thanks. I do remember Mum buying a packet of cornflakes that had about six different labels on it because the price went up at least once a week. Nostalgia is OK, but it wasn't all great music and cheap beer. Dutch Elm disease took hold, and worse than all the above put together, I started supporting West Ham United.

You might think that liking claret and blue as a colour combination is a pretty feeble reason for supporting a football team, but when you are six years old, it's good enough for anybody. That Saturday afternoon, Sylvia had sneaked out to see one of her boyfriends, and I think Lynn was probably studying away upstairs for some exams. I had been out during the morning for a quarter of lemon bon-bons and a copy of *Buster* (That's the comic, not the film starring Phil Collins). This was the Saturday ritual. I had thirty pence pocket money, and that is largely what it was spent on.

The room being empty; just me and Dad, we settled down to watch the match. 'Who do you want to win, son?' He probably said. Forgive me if I forget the exact dialogue, but I had not then developed my photographic memory.

'Errr. West Ham.'

'Why?' he undoubtedly said.

'Umm. Not sure. I just do,' I possibly said.

'Me too,' he might have said.

'Why?' I probably didn't say, because I have never been that curious about anything. However, it is convenient for the opening chapter of this book.

'Oh, I have a mate at work who supports them. Bob Morey. I think he's gone along today. Watch closely, you might see him.' Apart from the fact that I had no idea what Bob Morey looked like, and the fact that he wasn't actually there, I thought I stood a pretty good chance of spotting him in the 100,000 crowd.

Bob Morey had a lot to answer for. It was he, along with Dad, who took me to my first game at Upton Park, and then cunningly sloped off into the background, never mentioning West Ham again until he phoned me out of the blue in 1994 wanting my membership number to get tickets for the last game of the season. He was like the drug pusher giving away the first fix to get you hooked, except he then disappeared and left me scratching at the floor. It was he who got me well and truly smitten, and he who holds the real blame. If Dad had said 'Why not support Fulham today?' things might have been so different. I was always keen to please Dad, but when it came to cup finals, we generally supported opposite sides to make life interesting. This, apart from the 1980 final was the only time we agreed on the same team.

The more observant reader will by now have ascertained that my father was not an ardent West Ham fan at the time. He has since been converted, but it has been a long and painful process. He supported Crystal Palace passively, and would often relate to me tales of how he used to sell programmes at Selhurst Park in the days when the team wore Black and White, and they were nicknamed 'The Glaziers' after the famous palace of glass. He said that even in those days they used to call Millwall fans 'The Bottle Boys' because they always brought a bottle or two to throw when things got a bit boring. At Palace, of course, this happened quite frequently.

I contented myself with my lemon bon-bons and a mug of tea and watched the game. Dad always encouraged me to watch football, right from an early age, and there came the other link with West Ham. It must have been shortly before the West Ham cup final victory that England played Scotland at Wembley in the Home Internationals. Trevor Brooking had a blinding game, and Dad always singled him out as the best player on the pitch.

'He's got two feet,' he would say. 'All the best players in the world have got two feet.' Being young, and not fully aware, I thought that all players had two feet, otherwise they tended to fall over. This, I later learned, was not the case. Fortunately I was still too young to have developed my cynical and smutty sense of humour, and I did not snigger to myself and say 'He's got two feet? How does he get it in his shorts? No wonder he runs a bit crooked.'

All I recall about the game itself was David Coleman's commentary on the BBC. We always watched the cup final on the BBC – always. No exceptions. In 1975, and right up to 1986 the Cup Final was shown live on both ITV and BBC. Dad always chose BBC. Coleman's voice puzzled me. He sounded confused and behind the action. He sounded as though he was about to burst into tears or have a nervous breakdown. I can't claim to remember what he said, but his tone of voice will remain with me forever. I can't claim to remember much about the game, either. The video sits proudly on the shelf at home, and it gets the occasional airing. Second half goals from Alan Taylor brought the cup to Upton Park and I celebrated by having another lemon bon-bon. When you become enthralled by something at the age of six there is very little anyone can say or do to make you change your mind, you will always be secretly fascinated by it or them.

It was at this stage in my tender beginnings that I also met the wonderful Helen. Not on May 3rd 1975, but around that time. The skinny little blonde girl with pig tails and a holier-than-thou attitude was to fascinate me and frustrate me for the next, ooh, five years, until she left me for another school. She re-surfaced again, quite by chance, in 1991. The pigtails had gone, but the fascination remained as she continued to look down her pretty little nose at me. It was terminal. Far too late to be reclaimed, as I recall those early days, my own version of the Doris Day song reverberates around my head. I wrote it specifically about my feelings towards the wonderful Helen and the not quite so wonderful West Ham United: 'Que Sera Sera, Whatever will be will be, You're doomed for eternity, Que Sera Sera.'

For Ever and Ever. . .

Anderlecht 4 West Ham United 2 – 5.5.76

European Cup Winners' Cup Final

One year on. The football season came and went and West Ham managed a highly disappointing eighteenth place. As Cup winners the previous year, hopes were high of another good cup run, but a third round draw at home to Liverpool put paid to that. In the fourth round of the League Cup, West Ham drew 0–0 at White Hart Lane, earning a replay. If you can imagine 38,443 people inside Upton Park then you were probably there. Spurs won 2–0 after extra time. Even a two-legged Anglo-Italian Cup winners tournament against Fiorentina ended in failure. It was a typical season of highs and lows – raised hopes and unfulfilled promises.

I had a very happy life around this time. Shortly after the 1975 Cup final I celebrated my seventh birthday. Seven is a nice age to be. You don't have the pressures of being a teenager or an adolescent, and yet you are fully able to communicate and remember. Some people say that being a baby is the best time of your life, but I disagree. Who wants to be molly coddled, with no right of reply, no ability to do anything except cry, puke and sit in your own poo? No thanks. At this time I was at Balgowan Infants School in Beckenham. What a great life! You went to school at about nine, mucked about with crayons and paint, not to mention the sand-pit, and got to play football three times a day with a ropey old tennis ball before being collected by your mother and taken home for tea at three thirty. Only building site workers and Quantity Surveyors are afforded such luxury in adult life. The football in the playground took on a magical importance. Each of us pretended to be our favourite player – and it's no use any of you reading this saying 'I never used to do that!' If you played, you did it. In my case, I made my only deviation from the West Ham faith, and used to pretend to be Gordon Hill, the former Manchester United and Derby County winger, except that unlike Gordon, I didn't leave defenders trailing in my wake with the ball still miraculously glued to my feet. More often than not, I used to try and play a one-two off a concrete flower tub and would end up in the flower tub with the ball nowhere to be seen.

My best friend was Neil Dobson. He supported West Ham, or Aston Villa; he wasn't quite sure because he couldn't tell the difference. Even at the age of seven, he was a bright footballer, and everyone wanted to have him on their team. Of course, he later went on the play for the school, the County, and have trials with Leyton Orient before tragically having to quit at the age of twenty-five after surviving a brain haemorrhage suffered while working in Germany. Throughout our teenage years we went to Upton Park together, but at this stage of our lives he had to endure constant ribbings about his mum looking like the Queen, and the fact that his handwriting was so neat. He sent me a Christmas card in 1976 which said 'Happy Christmas Robert. I hope you get better at football.' This was his way of being nice, and I accepted that, along with the fact that I would probably never be good enough to play for Balgowan Juniors, let alone West Ham United and England.

After many brief encounters with concrete flower tubs, I decided to try and work on my game. Saturday afternoons were spent in the garden kicking a ball against the wall, trying to control it with my left foot and kick in with my right, then vice-versa. At about four forty, the shout would come from the back room. 'Results!' I would rush in and sit down in front of the TV. Again, it was always the BBC and their Teleprinter rather than Dickie Davies and his magic hairstyle on ITV's *World of Sport*. I think this was purely because Dad wanted to avoid the wrestling at all costs. Also, there was a kind of manic anticipation about watching results come up letter by letter – a sadistic pleasure for a West Ham fan. Throughout the winter of 1975/76 the results came in, some of which weren't too bad. Stoke 1 West Ham 2 the printer flashed. . . West Ham 0 Liverpool 4 it flashed again. . . West

Ham 0 Everton 1 it flashed on April 24th, and the season was over. As I only generally saw the results on a Saturday, I had somehow managed to miss out on the fact that we had reached the final of the European Cup Winners' Cup. I feel very bitter about this because as a fan, you want to be involved in these things, and I missed out because I was asleep. Looking back at the videos and the programmes it must have been great to see us pull back such deficits against European clubs on Winter's nights at Upton Park, particularly the quarter final against Den Haag from Holland, in which West Ham trailed 2–4 from the first leg, but won the second 3–1 to go through on the away goals rule. Similarly, the semi final against Eintracht Frankfurt produced a 1–2 defeat in the first leg in Germany, but a brilliant performance at home to win 3–1.

I remember the final – or the night of the final – quite well. It was played in Anderlecht's Heysel stadium in Brussels, a fact which I thought was rather unfair, as Anderlecht were the opposition. Dad pointed out that the stadium to hold the final was picked before the tournament began, and there was no fiddling involved. Also, he said that when West Ham got to the final before in 1965, they had played at Wembley, which was nearly home advantage. Two vivid memories remain from that night. The first was West Ham's disgusting new strip. Fortunately it was modified slightly for the next season, but it was an Admiral strip with a blue yoke and huge collars with Admiral badges on. The West Ham badge was right in the centre and looked truly awful.

The second was the unfairness of it all. Anderlecht were by far the better side and despite going 1–0 up we didn't really stand a chance. Dutch World Cup stars Robbie Rensenbrink and Ari Haan were on top form. As Francois Van der Elst (later to join West Ham) rounded Mervyn Day to slot home the fourth, I think it was Coleman again who shouted 'Foooouuurrr–two!' It was only a few years later that I learned that the West Ham side had nearly all been suffering badly with upset stomachs and played on through considerable discomfort. This match enhanced my now growing sense of support for the underdog. Why should it be that Anderlecht should have home advantage and better players? Come on West Ham – you show them!

It was an instinct which had floundered only a week earlier, when I had staked my reputation as a football expert at school on the line by declaring that Manchester United would beat Southampton in the Cup final by eight goals to nil. No-one seemed to disagree with me, and so I was particularly upset when Bobby 'off-side' Stokes slammed the winner passed Alex Stepney. I was sure that if Gordon Hill hadn't been substituted, United would indeed have won by eight. It's very strange, but if Manchester United were playing Southampton in the cup final today, I know who I would be rooting for.

Having established my faith in the underdog, West Ham United were now my team. The years that followed immediately after the Cup Winners' Cup defeat in Brussels were highly unproductive and ended in relegation in 1978. For two years we were underdog to everybody, even in cup matches. Just as I was underdog to Steven Scott for the affections of the wonderful Helen, I began to realise that this was my role in life. Now that Helen saw me as nothing more than a football hooligan, she went off with Steven Scott, who had a new bike, a big tree house, and could burp the tune of 'God Save the Queen.' Like West Ham at Heysel, I didn't stand a chance. The long hot summer came and I found myself drawn away from football and into music.

My tearaway sister had developed her own version of head-banging called 'Rocking'. This usually took the form of sitting in an arm chair, putting a record on very loud and hitting your head against the back of the chair in time to the music. It had to be music that could easily be 'rocked' to. Anything by Mud, Sweet, The Rubettes or Alvin Stardust was generally acceptable, as was 'Crocodile Rock' by Elton John. I am sure that 'Rocking' made me the man that I am today. It gave one a terrific sense of well being. After a session of rocking, you could stand up and find that you were too dizzy to walk. An early form of intoxication, which invariably had no more damaging side effect than a sore head. That year, a record by Slik made number one, which couldn't be rocked to, but was still played over and over again until the record wore out. It had bells, and a church organ and sounded a bit of a dirge, but it was appropriate, maybe not immediately, but certainly for my future with West Ham: 'I dedicate to you All my love My whole life through, I'll love you Forever and ever.'

You're the One that I Want. . .

West Ham United 3 Chelsea 1 – 25.3.78

In the same way one remembers losing their virginity, it ought to be with a glow of thrilling reflection that one remembers their first live football match. For me, it was a strange experience, and one which irritatingly, considering my ability to recall most useless information, has largely slipped from my memory.

Bob Morey lived somewhere down in the very bowels of the Kent countryside, and had to make very deliberate efforts to attend a home game. When Dad told him I was showing an interest, he made the mistake of saying 'We must take him to a game some time, then. . .' This didn't happen for a long time, and despite the efforts of a neighbour, Mr Chidley, to get me to support Palace and go along to see them with him, it was almost three years from my initial fascination taking root, that I finally managed to see a game at Upton Park.

I will always feel guilty about Mr Chidley though. He stopped me and my sister in the street one Saturday and asked me if I wanted to go and see Crystal Palace against Chelsea that afternoon. I rudely replied that I'd get a better view on the box, a fact that my dear sister lost no time in telling my mother. It was the only time I have ever seen her really angry. She apologised to Mr Chidley for my behaviour, but I still didn't really see what I had done wrong. After all, seeing Crystal Palace live was probably going to be about as exciting as a day's shopping in Bolton, with less to show for at the end of it. Watching it with Mr Chidley would double the boredom, and I didn't think my mother would be too keen on the idea anyway. It turned out that I was right, but she was upset that I had been so rude. My sister had no doubt embellished the story with a few carefully chosen adjectives, which added to the severity of my sentence.

'Does that mean I have to go with him, then?' I asked as I was packed off to go and apologise.

'No, of course not,' Mother said. 'I wouldn't force you to go anywhere you didn't want to.' This was a lie. She forced me to go to my sister's wedding in 1984 when West Ham were at home to Aston Villa. My mother would have made a good referee – no consistency. I'd get a red card and an early bath for rudeness, yet only a yellow card and a talking to for pinching soft bread from the middle of the loaf; thereby forcing Dad to have holey sandwiches. My guilt piled up over a number of years, and I decided to take Mr Chidley to a game one day, only to find that he was ill in hospital. He died of cancer a few days later, and while I never regretted not going to see Crystal Palace against Chelsea, it taught me to be polite when rejecting offers. A lesson a few women I know might like to heed.

March 25th 1978 was Easter Saturday. It was the day of the Boat Race; one that Cambridge will want to forget. Not only did they lose, they sank. Pocket money had gone up to fifty pence a week (Well, that was a Labour Government for you. Inflation was rife and I had trouble keeping pace. I tried to get it index-linked, but Dad was having none of it.) I don't know how much a quarter of lemon bon-bons was, but it must have burned a substantial hole in my weekly income. Dad said that he and Bob Morey were going to Upton Park to watch West Ham against Chelsea, and did I want to go? I remember thinking 'You're going where? You're asking me what?' Perhaps he thought he might get a Mr Chidley type reaction, but I leapt at the chance and Bob Morey arrived from his Kentish home in time for us to get the train to London. It was a tortuous journey. We took a train to Victoria and got on the District Line all the way to Upton Park. I knew no better then, and blindly followed, but travel always seems to take twice as long when you are nine years old. Of course, we know a much more direct route by public transport now.

It's like that Billy Bonds interview, or any interview with a player who has been to Wembley on more than one occasion. They always say: 'You let it all go by you on the first occasion. On the second visit, you take it all in more and take notice of things; remember them, savour them.' I always thought this was a bit daft. I mean, after all, these were grown men, surely they can remember the day, but now when I think of this significant event in my life I really remember very little about it, except the smell of horse manure, the big crowd, and the noise they made every time a goal was scored. On this occasion it happened three times, although I have to quickly refer to a book to see that Trevor Brooking, Bill Green and Patsy Holland scored West Ham's goals, after Bill Garner had put Chelsea ahead. All I vividly recall was that the Chelsea goalkeeper took a bad knock, and the spindly frame of Tommy Langley took over in goal. I also remember walking away from the game disappointed that I hadn't seen Pop Robson score a goal.

Bryan 'Pop' Robson was a bit of a cult figure to me. This small balding man seemed to be able to run rings around defences, and they were always very keen on showing his goals on *The Big Match* on a Sunday afternoon, when we settled down after our roast dinner, followed by peaches and custard and too much cream soda. Looking back, it seems that West Ham were nearly always on *The Big Match* but I'm sure that wasn't the case. It helped that *The Big Match* was run by London Weekend Television rather than a national organisation like the BBC and that we were the top London Club in the Second Division for almost as long as we were down there. Crystal Palace stole our thunder in 1980, but then we had the cup run to make up for it. Just as we now think that John Motson is a Manchester United supporter, I was convinced in those days that Brian Moore was a West Ham fan. He always grinned with delight when talking about a win, and looked sullen and sombre when describing a defeat. I almost expected him to refer to West Ham as 'we'. Perhaps he liked us so much because he shared a hairdresser with Pop Robson. I could never work out why Robson was called 'Pop'. I assumed it was down to some disagreeable personal habit he had, but later found out it was because he looked old enough to be everybody's dad. Why then, does every player by the name of Robson seem to be called 'Pop'? I heard Ron Atkinson refer to the other Bryan Robson – the crap one who played for England a couple of times – by that name the other day and it made me cringe. There was only one 'Pop.' Some of the goals he scored were unbelievable, and he'd run all day for the team. He was in his second spell at West Ham when I saw him play, and unlike Frank McAvennie a few years later, he seemed able to recapture the form that had made him a hero in the first place.

It occurred to me that this was what I wanted. This was the way I wanted to spend my Saturday afternoons, up to my neck in horse manure, beef burgers, peanuts and coke. It was simple in those days. You could pay on the door and get in without too much bother, there was no sponsorship, and our most expensive player was David Cross, who had cost two weeks pocket money and a packet of crisps from WBA. And yet I didn't go to another game for just over five years. I am always galled by this fact, as it was second only to the mid-sixties period as the most successful in the club's history, with the FA Cup in 1980, promotion and League cup final in 1981 and a healthy start back in the top flight. A number of things stopped me going back for more after my initiation. Firstly, my parents were reluctant to allow me to go to football in the first place. This was an attitude I could not understand at the time. Now though, I can see their point of view. I certainly wouldn't let a nine year old son of mine go to football alone or with his mates. Dad wasn't keen on live football after so many years of armchair support, and while Bob Morey would have been able to take me he now went even less frequently due to the arrival of children in his life. Mr Chidley wouldn't go to Upton Park unless Crystal Palace were playing there and I wasn't allowed to go alone with my friends. My parents were almost successful in weaning me off my childhood addiction, but it came back to me in September 1983 in a big way. With the new found freedom that earning a bit of extra money brings, I was able to make my own arrangements to go out on a Saturday afternoon or a Wednesday night. Meanwhile the armchair support continued, in between impersonations of John Travolta and a deep and to this day lasting crush on Olivia Newton-John. Oooh Oooh Ooooh Honey!

Revolution!

Blackburn Rovers 1 West Ham United 0 – 5.5.79

The boys were on a roll – downwards. It was difficult for me to keep in touch with this game, as I had been on a week's holiday with the school to Butlins at Minehead of all places. I enjoyed the week, but never thought about going back to a holiday camp. They are full of people telling you what to do. You could get that at home a lot cheaper.

This day was significant. Not only did it mark the end of a season ending like a damp squib, with a 0–0 draw at Cardiff and a 1–2 defeat at Millwall to follow, but this very day, 5 May 1979 was one day after Margaret Thatcher became Prime Minister. Again, the sense of wanting the underdog to win inspired me, and I was pleased that she had won – it seemed that she was the West Ham of the political world; no-one gave her a chance, but she didn't care, and no woman had ever been Prime Minister before. Go on Maggie! I thought. You show 'em. Politics meant nothing to me then.

The long faces of the teachers that Saturday morning said it all. 'She's done it,' they muttered to each other with a glazed expression. It was as though the button had been pressed, and a nuclear holocaust was about to follow; as though they already knew that the National Curriculum, Public Sector pay cuts and Baker Days were already on the way. They looked shell shocked. Their holiday was over in more ways than one. I thought it was brilliant.

I couldn't understand why they were all so upset. From my uneducated and naive viewpoint it seemed that a new broom was needed to sweep clean. We had one day rail strikes, public employee strikes and lorry driver strikes. I hoped that Mrs Thatcher wouldn't do too much for the lorry drivers just yet, as it meant that we could have days off during the winter when the central heating oil didn't arrive. The rubbish had piled up in the streets as the dustmen went on strike. Houses burned down while the army tried to put fires out during the fireman's strike. The Yorkshire Ripper had killed his eleventh victim – surely Maggie would sort him out? She probably wouldn't have been able to do anything about the Welsh though. They had won the Rugby Union triple crown for the third year in a row, and were becoming boring.

Someone, I can't recall who, had heard the football results on the coach radio and gloated. We had the most expensive goalkeeper in the world in £565,000 Phil Parkes, but still it seemed we would not win promotion.

'Remember this day,' my Crystal Palace supporting teacher, Mr Harper told me. 'It will go down as one of the darkest days in English history.'

'Come on,' I replied, as only a precocious ten year old can. 'It was only one-nil.'

I'm into Something Good. . .

West Ham United 1 Arsenal 0 – 10.5.80

F.A. Cup Final

In the two years that separated my first game at Upton Park and the team reaching the cup final for the second time in six years many changes had taken place in the life of the young Master Banks. (How pleased I was that my surname wasn't Bates.) The vital importance West Ham United had was not so nagging. Like any addict separated from his drug for a prolonged period, the craving declines. This did not stop me watching the results service at 4.40pm on a Saturday and groaning at a poor result and whooping at a good one. It didn't stop me wearing that awful Admiral replica shirt during games of football in the park. Neil Dobson was still head and shoulders above everyone else as a player, but he didn't write comments in my Christmas cards any more. This was partly due to the fact that I had improved as a player, and partly because we did a display on the wall at school for Guy Fawkes night, and Neil had been asked to write out the famous rhyme due to his superb handwriting. He wrote: 'Remember, remember the fifth of November, gunpowder trees and in plot.' We were quits after that. Neil still followed West Ham, and was now able to distinguish them from Aston Villa due to our distinctive, if somewhat disgusting new shirts. We were joined as fans by Paul Cole, a lad I identified with due to his similar, diminutive stature. With us both being small for our age, we had to stick together, and while the rest of the class supported Liverpool, Manchester United or Arsenal, we resolutely remained Hammers fans.

In September 1979 we all moved together up to the big school. Kelsey Park School for Boys, again in Beckenham. It was something of a culture shock to move from being the most senior pupils at junior school to the lowest of the low at the comprehensive. Kelsey Park was a nightmare building, slung together in the early 1970s, it had a capacity for about 1000 boys. Its modern buildings were supplemented by mobile classrooms permanently anchored to the spot close to the playgrounds. The smell of those rooms remains with me to this day, a mixture of chalk, rubber and mud. Towards the end of the first year there was a buzz of expectation among the West Ham contingent which had been added to by boys from other local schools, Derek 'Close' Shave, Graham 'Lanky' Holland, Lee 'Bish' Bishop, Dave 'Fat' Saddler, Martin 'Barney' Barnard and Neil 'Stain Tooth' Daniels. By the quarter final stages, small transistor radios found their way into classrooms for the draw. Derek, or 'Close' as he was rather unimaginatively known, was the first to spread the news that we had been drawn at home to Aston Villa.

Despite listening to the draw on the radio, it never occurred to any of us to listen to the game on the radio or try and track progress during the game. It was always the done thing to wait until 4.40pm and watch the results as they popped up. I was allowed to wait up and watch our 1–0 win over Villa which was shown on Match of the Day the same night. A rather dodgy penalty award, but calmly despatched by Ray Stewart. Two days later, we got the draw we wanted, against Everton in the semi-final to be played at Villa Park. The other semi was between Liverpool and Arsenal, and as was well documented, went to four games before Arsenal finally came out on top.

The game against Everton was played in glorious sunshine in our local park. It finished 14–3 to West Ham and Robert Banks scored a hat-trick. It was watched by an indifferent crowd of three people and one dog. Apart from the crowd, the location, the score and the teams it could have been the very same game as that which finished 1–1 at Villa Park. We all ran back to Paul's house after our game to hear the news, and felt curiously deflated, despite the fact that Everton were a first division side and that we had come back from a goal down.

The replay was at Elland Road, Leeds, and again went into extra time. Bob Latchford's goal cancelled out Alan Devonshire's opener.

Frank Lampard then scored a brilliant diving header. He jogged across the penalty area and danced around the corner flag.

We didn't get to see this marvellous goal until *Football Focus* the following Saturday, but it was worth the wait. West Ham were in the FA Cup final. Once the other semi had been decided, we knew we would be playing Arsenal, and all the games in the park became West Ham v Arsenal, in an attempt to try and predict the outcome. The smart money at school was on Arsenal, as they were in their third Cup Final in a row, and were in the final of the Cup Winners' Cup as well.

Paul came over to my house and we watched the game with me and my dad. To put up token resistance, Dad said he wanted Arsenal to win, but I knew he really wanted West Ham. Not only was our team in the cup final, but our team was the underdog! Sheer heaven.

I was worried about Mum and Dad. They knew very well that I had an ambition to become a writer. Yet, at no stage did they even attempt to get a divorce, to throw things at each other or beat me severely. Most people would say 'and a jolly good job, my son', but not for a writer. A writer needs to have a past – a history of strife, something to make him bitter and angry. My dad didn't even go to the pub on a Sunday and come home late for lunch. The most controversial thing he used to do was to comb his hair over the kitchen sink and leave all the bits in the washing up. Hardly a capital offence is it? Their marriage wasn't without incident, but it never affected us kids. Therefore, when cup final Saturday came around, as one of the few occasions in the year when there was a bit of live footie on the box, Mum withdrew gracefully to bed with a Daphne du Maurier and a Crunchie Bar, leaving 'The Boys' to watch the match on the telly undisturbed.

Arsenal wore their yellow away kit on 10 May 1980, as they had done in the previous two cup finals. This was boring. Even more boring, from my point of view, was the fact that West Ham wore their all white away kit. For me, part of the glamour of the cup final is the colour of the shirts, and for me, yellow and white just didn't work. I accepted that one team had to wear an away strip, but if it had to be us, why couldn't Arsenal have worn their red shirts? I wasn't too upset that we didn't have to wear those rotten Admiral claret and blue shirts.

The game itself got off to a flyer. I remember Pikey had a shot that fizzed across the goal and Paul and I drew our breath sharply. Then Devonshire broke down the left, got to the by-line and put in a cross which Pat Jennings could only palm on to Stuart Pearson, who slammed it back towards goal. A bit of pinball ensued, finally ending up on Trev's head. 1–0. I remember Stuart Pearson looked as though he had just given birth as he walked back to the centre circle – that was him gone for the rest of the game. West Ham battled on bravely to get the win. Who could ever forget 'little' Paul Allen at seventeen years, still at the time of writing the youngest ever player to appear in an FA Cup final, ruthlessly pulled down by Willie Young when clean through. The fact that Allen stood about as much chance of scoring as Long John Silver was neither here nor there. That tackle effectively ruined Willie Young's career, as no-one ever mentioned anything else, and all we got out of it was a free kick. Today, five players would have been sent off for that tackle. Allen of course went on to claim that he was 'Happy to be a Hammer for life' – I have the press cutting to prove it. Moments later he signed for Spurs. Judas!

Naturally, the day ended in high celebration. Paul and I went out on our bikes to buy a celebratory round of sweets. As we left the shop he grabbed two 'Texan' bars from the shelf and stuffed them under his shirt. He grinned as he handed me one of them outside, and I accepted it with doubtful gratitude. Why had he done that? I was confused. From the highest of highs I was cast into a pit of uncertainty. Dad always said if he caught me stealing he would thrash me to within an inch of my life, a threat which I always took great care to heed. Was I really into something good?

Imagine. . .

Blackburn Rovers 0 West Ham United 0 – 13.12.80

December 9th 1980 will be etched on my memory for ever. It was a Tuesday. I know that without referring to any old diaries or school books. On December 9th 1980, one of my heroes died.

Mr Clark, our maths teacher, who I liked and respected, despite the fact he was a Villa fan, was late for double maths. Obviously, we didn't actually care about that fact, but he walked into the room with a tear in his eye that morning. The classroom was silenced so quickly it was as though the plug had been pulled out. 'Boys,' he said, his voice trembling, 'I'm sorry I'm late. I've just heard about John Lennon.' To most of the boys in the room, this meant nothing. They, like me, were about eighteen months old when The Beatles split up, and if it wasn't anything to do with Duran Duran or OMD then it didn't really matter. I had 'different' tastes in music, and Beatles records were good records to 'Rock' to, as my sister and I had experimented with *Magical Mystery Tour*, and I loved the music of The Beatles. At the age of ten, I first heard *Rubber Soul* and felt that if I was only ever able to own one album, this would be it.

'Sir?' I ventured.

'Yes?' He looked up from the floor.

'What have you heard about John Lennon?' A snigger came from the back of the room.

'He's dead. He's been shot. Murdered. Now then. Quadrilateral Equations!'

I couldn't believe it. For the first time I had heard about someone dying and it hurt me. Not just an 'Oh well, that's a shame – still, he had a good innings' reserved for family funerals. This was a tragedy. An amazing talent swiped from us at the age of forty. I stopped at my friend's house on the way home, as I always did. His mum always gave us a glass of milk and a Kit-Kat to help us along until tea time (Suburban life doesn't get any more exciting than that, I'm afraid) 'Have you heard about John Lennard?' said Lanky's mum. I was angry that someone old enough to remember him, and who probably bought Beatles records when they first came out, should get his name wrong. I wanted to say 'It was Lennon you fool!' but all I said was 'Yes.' I didn't know what else to say. I didn't know if she would have approved of him. After all, he took drugs and stuff once. 'Still, I don't suppose he means a great deal to you, does he?' This attitude always made my blood boil, and was the first of many occasions which forced me to believe that I was actually meant to have been born in 1958 and not 1968. Had that been the case, I would have been just old enough to remember West Ham winning the Cup in '64, the Cup Winners' Cup in '65 and the World Cup in '66. (If you support another club and you're reading this, now is the time to throw your hands up in horror and say: 'It wasn't *just* Hurst, Moore and Peters, you know.' Well, for your information, it bloody well was, OK?) I would have been able to buy a copy of *Rubber Soul* when it first came out, not thirteen years later, and I would have been able to marry Diana Hopkins when the opportunity presented itself. I would have been able to sympathise with the rest of the mourners about the passing of Lennon and say 'I remember him'. It's not as daft as it sounds – Mum did have a child in 1958. It was stillborn. It should have been me – I inherited the soul. I have the body of a twenty-seven year old, but a mind ten years older.

What has all this got to do with West Ham sharing out a goalless draw at Ewood Park, I hear you cry! Well, very little really, except that on the evening of Lennon's death, they showed the film *Help!* as a tribute. Dad got annoyed because they shifted his favourite programme to accommodate it. After the film I went upstairs and decided to keep a diary. I put 'Imagine' on the record player and began to write. That was the first entry. The second entry came the following Saturday and read: 'West Ham drew 0–0 at Blackburn. I'm upset about John Lennon but I really think West Ham are going to win promotion this season.' That was the last entry for nearly four years.

I was right though. West Ham did win promotion and got two trips to Wembley that season as well. Both were against Liverpool. First was the Charity Shield, which we lost, and second, the League Cup Final. I was really pissed off about the League Cup Final because Neil Dobson's dad had got two tickets and the greedy sod took one for himself. Honestly! The match took place on a Saturday afternoon, before the days of sponsorship and Sunday afternoon TV. The highlights were shown on the Sunday *Match of the Day* special. A dull 0–0 draw was brought to life in extra time when Alan Kennedy scored for Liverpool, the goal was allowed despite Sammy 'off-side' Lee (No relation to Bobby 'off-side' Stokes) lying in the six yard area and moving his head out of the way to allow the ball into the net. Not interfering with play? Yeah, right and my Granny played centre half for Bolton. With a minute to go, Terry McDermott handled an Alvin Martin header on the line and Ray Stewart converted the penalty. A 1–1 draw, but we held the moral high ground, being a second division club and having conceded a highly dodgy goal. Highly dodgy.

The replay was the next Wednesday and was shown live on ITV from Villa Park. At last we got to wear Claret and Blue in a major final, even if it wasn't at Wembley. Our shiny new Adidas strip actually looked the business. Goddard scored and I hit my head on the wall. We had enjoyed so much success in recent months I was sure we would hold on. Of course, it all went belly-up. Was that a Bonds o.g.? Liverpool credit it to Alan Hansen, but I know who got the last touch. I was so upset I took the next two days off school, pretending to be ill. At least promotion was still on. Dobbo didn't even buy me a programme, from the Wembley game, the miserable git.

Paul's behaviour was beginning to worry me. He was a good mate to have at the age of twelve. He had an Australian mum who was a midwife and used to keep all sorts of weird things belonging to other women in the freezer. His dad was the funniest man I ever met – a real wag. They owned a big house which had been extended upwards to make it even bigger, and Paul knew all the best places to go on our bikes after school. We made a hideout at the nearby Harvington Woodland, which had a small river and a V-2 crater, ideal for mucking about in and generally getting up to no good. He had a brilliant collection of mucky books, which his older brother had given to him. To top it all he had a snooker table. All in all he was a good mate. But he was starting to steal things. By now he was nicking anything that wasn't bolted down; starting with sweets from the tuck shop at school, and rapidly graduating to library books, chairs, desks and computers. It was only a matter of time before he moved on to cars. He would have stolen the burning sun in the open sky given the chance. The thought of stealing things never really appealed to me, and I therefore decided to back away from Paul gradually, as I knew that one false move would see me strung up from the highest yard arm. I'm just one of those people – if I let the tax disk on my car go one day overdue I get a fine, whereas my neighbour has had three cars untaxed in the road since last July. I'm not bitter about this, at least I know where I stand. Paul had to go. He was moving into the expensive clothing market, and three Pringles and two pairs of Farrars later, he was caught. Still, I told him later, when I bumped into him in a pub: 'At least West Ham got promotion. Can you imagine what a bummer of a year it would have been otherwise?' 'Yes,' he said, bitterly. 'I can imagine.'

That period was a real up and down affair. We won the cup, we lost the cup, I lost John Lennon, I lost Paul. Both Steven Scott and I lost the wonderful Helen. Helen always said she hated me, but I knew deep down she loved me. She tried to make me jealous by going out with Steven Scott, but it didn't work – well, not on the surface, anyway. I tried to make her jealous by going out with Jennifer Cousins. That worked superbly, but Helen managed to hide it very well. In the end, obviously ripped apart by her love for me, she persuaded her parents to move to Hartley, and I didn't see her again for eleven years. Imagine that.

I Believe. . .

Tottenham Hotspur 0 West Ham United 4 – 2.9.81

We made it. Back in the top flight, but I still felt strangely removed from the success. Not so strange really, when you consider that having set myself up as a loyal supporter, devoted to the cause, I hadn't attended a game for over three years. I was starting to get a little bit of grief from the Spurs contingent at school. At the end of the previous season they had won the FA Cup beating Manchester City 3–2 in a memorable replay at Wembley, thus starting a period of three successive FA Cup Finals to be decided by replays. Spurs were cock-a-hoop, if you'll pardon the pun, and would be back at Wembley at the end of the season to win the cup again, against QPR. Those Spurs fans at school who were allowed to go to matches were licking their lips at the prospect of mauling the newly promoted Hammers. Mike Morris, for one, covered his exercise books in anti-West Ham graffiti for weeks before the game, saying that we would get slaughtered, Spurs were on top form and would be parading the cup before the game. Bye-bye West Ham. I prayed that we would get something out of the game, if only to keep Morris reasonably quiet, but I got more than I could possibly have hoped for.

One-nil up at half time, West Ham must have smelled blood, because they ripped Spurs to shreds in the second half, winning 4–0 with David Cross scoring all four goals. The feeling of smug satisfaction I gained as I walked into double French on the Thursday morning was unbelievable. I hadn't felt anything like it before. Up to that point it had always been personal – triumphs had been shared with friends, but we had never suffered abuse or even doubt before a game, to make the taste of victory that much sweeter. I took up my seat next to Morris, who had an angry look on his face. He had been to the game. He was not happy. 'Did they parade the cup before the game, Mike?' I asked.

'Yes, of course,' he said down his nose.

'Oh well, you got that bit right then.'

'Shut up!'

'I never said anything.'

'You were going to.'

'Four – Nil.' I said the words slowly, savouring each one as though it were a piece of Turkish Delight smothered in icing sugar. I saw his fist move, just as our French teacher interjected. 'Now then boys!' I spent the rest of the lesson scribbling '4–0' on my exercise book in a million different fonts and showing it to Mike Morris.

1981 was a funny year. Funny strange, not funny ha-ha. I use football matches to assimilate what was happening in my life and in the world, and it helps me greatly to remember where I was at any given time, what records were in the charts and what was happening in the news. On that day, Thursday 3 September 1981, I remember the first lesson of the day so clearly it could have been this morning. It was followed by Religious Education, in which we were set the task of writing an essay on why Bobby Sands, the IRA hunger striker, had died. It was too tempting to put 'Because he didn't eat anything for three months' or 'Because he was a prat'. I wrote a page of what I thought my teacher would want to read: Political struggle in Ulster, dying for his beliefs, etc. That was always the best thing to do in RE, and as I later found in Sociology. Speaking your mind rarely results in good exam marks.

Two Tone was in. I think The Specials had just been knocked off the number one spot with 'Ghost Town' but in our class, there was only one band to be interested in, and that was Duran Duran. This was not because we liked the music particularly, but because there was a boy in the class called Michael Durani. He only had to walk in the room to be met by a chorus of 'Girls on film!' He hated it, which was why we did it even more. Children are more cruel than any other creature in the world. That's a fact.

It was getting serious now. The following year I got a paper round and started earning the princely sum of £5.70 a week. That was good money in 1982, and apart from the benefits of never being late for school, I was able to read the sports pages of every newspaper in the shop before setting off, and every sports magazine too, if the lad setting up was a bit slow. The lad setting up was Richard Pusey. I was dead jealous of him because he was a Chelsea fan and went to every game, home and away, with his older brother. At that time, Chelsea languished in the old second division, a fact which I lost no time in pointing out to him, but he would always talk about the great adventures he'd had travelling around the country following the Blues. He was a year older than me, and had already seen West Ham on more occasions than I had, and he didn't even support them! Something had to be done about it. Passive support had been going on for too long. A year of nagging finally succeeded. 1983/84 was the start of the great adventure.

Red Red Wine. . .

West Ham United 3 Leicester City 1 – 6.9.83

We did it. We finally broke the shackles that had prevented us from going to matches and became members of the crew. It was a Wednesday night, towards the end of the summer holidays. Both Dobbo and I were about to start our fifth year at Kelsey Park, a year for taking vital exams and one in which we could have done without the extra distractions of football, but we could wait no longer. I felt that as impatient adolescents go, we did quite well to hang on as long as we did. We didn't even know we would be going until the actual day. We hadn't planned it, but the team had started the season so well, with a thumping 4–0 win over Birmingham City on the opening day, and then two away victories, at Tottenham again, much to Mike Morris's dismay, and at Everton, not a previously fruitful hunting ground for us. We had two new signings, Steve Whitton and Steve Walford, both of whom appeared to be playing well, Walford having scored the winner at Goodison Park. It was too tempting an idea to ignore. Newly promoted Leicester City under the lights at Upton Park. We were rather matter-of-fact about it as we informed our parents. I expected mine to go through the roof, but they accepted it with a calm assurance that bothered me. If they weren't so worried, why hadn't they let me go before?

We were actually quite scared. At the time, sections of the West Ham crowd had a bit of a reputation which preceded them. The infamous ICF (Inter-City Firm) were notorious on our away trips, often stopping off at towns en-route to do a bit of damage. We were totally inexperienced about such things, and kept a watchful eye out at all times. We made the same journey that I had made five years previously, train to Victoria then District Line all the way to Upton

Park. As we emerged from the tube station, I noticed several changes had taken place since my last visit, but felt unable to put my finger on them. There was certainly more of an atmosphere about the place – a hustle and bustle that follows a successful team, the talk full of expectation, the brisk business of programme sellers and hot-dog stands alike. I bought a programme, which for the first time had been increased in size from A6 to A5, something which has continued to this day. Previously, programmes had been a rather scrappy affair, and I had never really considered collecting them, but these were precious mementoes and I made every effort not to get mine creased. The front cover of the Leicester programme showed a picture of Alan Devonshire leaping over a Birmingham defender's lunging tackle. I've not seen a better photograph on the front page of a programme since then; it really fired up the imagination.

We took up a place behind the North Bank goal, right at the back. From this angle we were able to see most of the action without getting crushed. When the teams came out I was surprised by the loud roar that came up from all around us. When Bob Morey, Dad and I had been in the East Stand five years earlier, it had all seemed so much more sedate and quiet, only reaching a crescendo when a goal was scored. Now, it appeared to be going on all the time.

The team that night was: Parkes, Stewart, Walford, Bonds, Martin, Devonshire, Whitton, Cottee, Swindlehurst, Brooking, Pike. I will never forget it. The team wore the brand new strip from Adidas, a claret body with white V-neck, blue sleeves and a blue band across the chest. I look back at this kit with deep affection. When I see clips of the team in action wearing that strip it always brings back happy memories. Leicester, on the other hand, ironically, sported a hideous Admiral strip. You will think I have got it in for Admiral. That is not the case, but you have to admit they made some pretty grotesque kits – witness the England 1982 World Cup shirt. No wonder we didn't win it that year.

Leicester had a young unknown in their side by the name of Gary Lineker. Despite the burden of having to wear this hideous green shirt with yellow stripes, he managed to bag the first goal of the evening. The first goal West Ham conceded that season, the second goal I ever saw West Ham concede. It all went quiet except for the far right hand corner of the ground, which strangely erupted in a sea of blue and white; of waving arms (and legs) and grown men kissing each other. I remember thinking what a long journey home they had afterwards, and was glad, not for the last time in my football career, to be with the majority. The fact that Leicester had scored did not bother us. Chelsea had gone ahead in the last match I attended, and we had won 3–1. No problem. Nor did it seem to bother the rest of the crowd, who started to shout louder and louder encouragement. Shortly before half time, we got our reward, Steve Walford firing in from the edge of the box: 1–1. We didn't move from our spot at half time, at least not voluntarily, but we found by the time the second half started that we had in fact moved a good few feet forward. A crowd of 22,000 inside Upton Park in those days was 'comfortable.' No more than that. The most frightening experience I ever had at Upton Park was in a crowd of 35,000 for the game against Arsenal the following season. The capacity was reduced every year by the police and by ground 'improvements'. It was hard to imagine, even when the West Stand had terracing, how 43,000 might have crammed in.

The second half began in the same fashion as the first had ended. Goals from Tony Cottee and Dave Swindlehurst wrapped up a 3–1 win, and we walked contentedly back to the tube station, carried along on a wave of emotion. This was a good place to be. We were still cautious – looking over our shoulders for a possible assailant with a Stanley knife. It seems ridiculous now, but we really did believe that danger lurked on every corner.

Dobbo started to collect the away programmes as well, but began to feel the pace around Christmas time. He sold them to me, and for a few seasons I collected them as well, but again this can become a crippling financial commitment, so I now only gather programmes from the games I have attended away from Upton Park. I still, at the age of twenty-seven, collect every home programme, whether I attended the game or not. It is not a question of them 'possibly being worth something one day' because I would never part with them. It is the most precise and concise way to record a season, even if the editorial, in the light of my fanzine experience, is somewhat slushy.

With game number two under the belt, I went to school to start the fifth year as a seasoned professional. The next game West Ham played was the following Saturday, against Coventry City. I can't remember why I didn't go, but I remember listening to reports on LBC, totally shocked that Coventry had taken a 2–0 lead. I knew we could come back from 1–0 down, but 2–0? Coventry had won 3–0 at Upton Park the previous year thanks to a hat-trick from Steve Whitton, the main reason why we bought him. By half time, we were 3–2 up and at full time we had wrapped up a comfortable 5–2 win, Whitton getting two, this time for us, and Swindlehurst a hat-trick. This was child's play. Five games, five wins, fifteen points and daylight at the top of the first division. West Ham were going to win the league for the first time in their history, and I was going to be there to see it.

At school, things changed. I had always thought of myself as the perfect pupil, conscientious, hard working and diligent. But something happened after I started going to football, and I'm convinced that it was because I started going too late in life. Had I been a regular at the age of ten, it wouldn't have mattered what Mike Morris said about Spurs, I wouldn't have felt compelled to hit him. It wouldn't have mattered what my English teacher said to me, I would have agreed that it was not a good idea to read 'The Hammer' in class rather than the course book *To Kill a Mockingbird*. Things went rapidly downhill at school, but fortunately, I had built up enough credit with the teaching staff not to be too severely punished. Those boys who had caused grief right from the start and were now trying to put things right had a problem because their every move was watched. I held a position of trust, and abused it. At least I had learned enough in my first four years to scrape through my exams with seven 'O' level passes all at grade C. That was my parents' only concern. They knew I was in trouble when I sloped off upstairs one evening to 'revise' and Mum brought me a cup of tea to find me writing a match report.

Our next game was away at WBA. I didn't consider going, we never did. The travel was always a bit pricey. I wasn't concerned when we went 1–0 down, because I knew this team could come back, even though WBA scored in the eighty-first minute, I was sure we would come back. We didn't. Still, not to worry, we were still top! The next game was at Upton Park against Notts County, who had been up at the top with us for the early part of the season, but then fell away alarmingly. Their demise was further hastened when we thumped them 3–0, Goddard, Brooking and Stewart scoring.

Neil had bought a fog horn, and took delight in leading the crowd on the North Bank into hand clapping with carefully timed bursts. We were in our element. Not only were we now watching games, but we led the crowd as well. It was only a matter of time before we became celebrities. I bought myself a hat; one of those eight panelled affairs with a peak – what a plonker – and West Ham consolidated their position on the top of the tree with the three points against County. The sun shone, the team played well and I was a true Hammers fan.

Karma Chameleon. . .

West Ham United 10 Bury 0 – 25.10.83

I don't know what went wrong that night, but West Ham made damn sure it never happened again. Dobbo had already bought his replica shirt, which seemed to cost a fortune then, but compared to today's prices was dirt cheap at £10.95. He paid an extra pound to have 'Avco Trust' emblazoned across the front of it, but I bought mine the night of the Bury match and decided to leave it plain. That band of blue across the chest should not be tampered with, I thought. This was where the superstitions started to creep in. I thought that if I spent a similar amount of money in the Hammers Shop before each game, we would win by an equally large margin. I now know a lot better of course, but still carry out other ridiculous rituals before matches, just in case.

Things hadn't been going too well since we beat Notts County. We lost the next league game, away at Stoke, 1–3. The following Wednesday we squeaked a win away at Bury in the first leg of the second round of the 'Milk' Cup as it was now embarrassingly known, then lost 1–3 again, this time at home to Liverpool. That game remains with me to this day as one of the worst experiences of my life. It rained from eight in the morning to ten in the evening without even thinking about stopping. The team were hopelessly outclassed by a side that would go on to win the League and the Milk Cup that season, and humiliate us at Anfield. We were 2–0 down at half time with goals from Michael Robinson. We stood right at the front of the North Bank, while everyone else cowered at the back trying not to get wet, but we didn't care, we wanted to feel the glory. Unfortunately, there wasn't a lot of it about, as Liverpool took a 3–0 lead with Robinson completing his hat-trick. Craig 'Magic Boots' Johnson was sent off, before we managed to pull one back, but we were outside the ground when Devonshire scored. That was the first and last time I ever left a match early. I'll move towards the back by all means, but never walk out before the final whistle has gone. To compound our misery that day, London Bridge station was closed and we had to get an East London Line train to New Cross and change there. Fortunately, Millwall were not at home, but we got on the wrong train at New Cross and ended up in Kidbrooke, with someone throwing up all over Dobbo's jacket. Days like that are, fortunately, few and far between. If only you had days where everything went 'right' in the same proportions to balance it out, it might be easier to accept. However, I digress.

Following the Liverpool debacle, we drew at home 0–0 with Norwich. This was a disappointing result because we should really have beaten a team like Norwich, who were nothing special. A point also meant that both Manchester United and Liverpool were able to overtake us and we finished the afternoon in third place. I didn't go to the game as I had to bottle forty pints of home brew. I had developed a highly inflammable form of cider, simply by adding yeast to cartoned apple juice. You had to be careful how you took the lid off, or it would have your eye out. You also had to be careful not to hold a naked flame near the bottle or one of the belches that would inevitably follow.

The game against Bury has now gone down in Upton Park folklore, and I am just grateful that I was there that night among a meagre crowd of 10,896 to witness it for myself. It was a combination of inept defending by Bury and competent attacking play by West Ham that led to the demolition. We were 5–0 up at half time, although Bury had missed a penalty at 1–0 which might have knocked their confidence a bit. I remember saying to Dobbo, 'It should be ten then!' We should have known that things just don't work that way in football. How many times have you seen a team race into a 3–0 lead at half time and finish the game 3–0 or 3–1? Tonight, it worked logically. Tony Cottee, still not regarded as a first team regular, but in the side as a replacement for the injured Paul Goddard, got four. Trevor Brooking and Alan Devonshire two each and Alvin Martin and Ray Stewart one each. It was a feature of our big wins that our main striker, our feared target man, rarely got on the scoresheet. This was the case with Dave Swindlehurst, who had four men on him, leaving the other members of the team to pick up the rewards. We were happy. The North Bank chanted 'We want eight!' when it was 7–0, and the team duly obliged. Then we chanted 'We want nine!' and so on, until we ran out of time. The newspapers were full of it the next morning – 'West Ham hotshots just Bury 'em alive!' 'Ten out of ten Hammers!' 'West Ham Blitz Bury!' It was the biggest ever margin of victory in a League Cup match, an aggregate score of 12–1. Liverpool equalled it a few years later by winning 13–2 over Fulham, but the record for margin of victory is still held jointly with them.

The Bury management team had taped the game as part of a training exercise. They probably called it 'How NOT to defend'. The BBC approached them and asked if they could use the tape to show the goals on *Football Focus* the next Saturday. Bury told the BBC politely to get stuffed. They must have agreed to letting us have access to it though, because within a few weeks, the recording was available in the club shop on video. I always regret not buying a copy of that. I understand the quality was appalling, but nevertheless it was a significant day in the history of the club. Dobbo and I considered going to Watford the next Friday for the league match. The BBC were showing it live as part of their new fangled live TV experiment, with ITV showing a game on a Sunday, and the BBC on a Friday evening. We decided, or rather, finances dictated, that we watch the game at home, only to find that we were the victims of another strike, and the game was blacked out. Just as well, I hear, as the game was a dire 0–0 draw. How could that happen, when the team were red hot on the previous Tuesday? The harsh reality of being a West Ham supporter was beginning to hit home. Nothing made sense.

Uptown Girl...

West Ham United 1 Manchester United 1 – 27.11.83

Fortune swung back in our favour. Following the bore draw at Watford, West Ham won their next four matches to bring them back into contention. A win over Manchester United, live on Sunday afternoon TV, would have seen us back on top of the pile.

The next game after Watford was the league match at home to Ipswich Town. This was the first indication that a bit of 'bandwagon jumping' might be going on. The other West Ham fans at school, seeing what a generally good time me and Dobbo were having on a Saturday, wanted a slice of the action. Martin Barnard joined us for the Ipswich game. There was a group of five of us for the match against Manchester United, a group which grew and grew until ten of us went to the match at Highbury at the end of the season. While we were to be applauded for our recruitment drive, I was disappointed that, as usual, something I felt I had discovered had been hi-jacked and taken over by others. As it happened, almost all of us left school at the end of June, and as I moved largely in different social circles, it provided a useful means of keeping in touch with former school friends. As the Ipswich game was 'Barney's' first, Dobbo and I as seasoned campaigners of five games, played a little trick and wrote to Bill Remfry, the legendary 'Bubbles Time' disc jockey, who read out dedications and played records (usually by Abba) before every game. He read out our letter, which welcomed young Martin Barnard to his first game on his fifth birthday. The range of expressions on Barney's face that afternoon demonstrated the versatility of the human race.

The following game was attended for the last time, by Dobbo and myself alone. It was the next round of the Milk Cup which saw us drawn at home to Brighton and Hove Albion. They had been relegated the previous season, and had been at Wembley in May, only just missing out on cup final victory over Manchester United. Gordon Smith missed a sitter in the last minute of extra time, which would have given them a 3–2 win. John Motson's commentary of that incident inspired the title of the Brighton fanzine: 'And Smith must score. . .' Of course, that was their only chance. Manchester United were not so charitable in the replay, and won 4–0. We met some Brighton fans on the tube and had a chat with them. When I recall how nervous we had been of opposition fans just a few months earlier, it was amazing progress for us. Despite Brighton's cup pedigree, we remained quietly confident that we would win easily. It didn't work out that way. We struggled to win 1–0, Swindlehurst scoring again to take his total for the season to eleven. We were most relieved.

The hype surrounding the Manchester United game was such that it was taking on the importance of a cup final. Our form going into it was excellent. We beat bottom club Wolves at Molineux 3–0. The journalists on the Sunday papers were having orgasms over our performance. 'It should have been eight.' 'Devonshire cream whips sad Wolves.' The last headline inspired myself and Dobbo to do something rather silly. We knew that the Manchester United game was going to be on live TV, so we decided to make a huge cup final type banner so that we could be seen. If we got there early enough, we could hang the banner over the front wall and become overnight stars.

Dobbo's handwriting expertise was useful. We used a white sheet and carefully cut out claret and blue letters from material and glued them on to the sheet. The banner read: 'DEVONSHIRE, THE CREAM OF UPTON PARK'. My sister saw this and, having acquired A-level needlework, set to work on it with her sewing machine to stop the letters from fraying. The finished article was a work of art. Not one of these hastily prepared 'Lyall Out!' banners, but the Leonardo da Vinci of football banners. We felt sure the TV cameras would give us air time.

The banner was completed as Swindlehurst banged in his twelfth goal of the season at Sunderland to put us within one point of leaders

Liverpool. The importance of the game was such that whoever won would go top – a draw would see Liverpool safe. The TV company were wetting themselves. They had a really important top of the table clash live. It was built up on *On the Ball* with Ian St John the previous Saturday. They showed footage of our 3–1 win over Manchester United the season before. For the first time in my football watching career, I was nervous.

Kick-off was due at 2.35pm, and we arrived at the ground at midday to get a good place for the cameras. We rushed onto the North Bank and ran to the front, slightly to the left hand side of the goal, unfurling our precious banner and hanging it over the wall in full view of the dozen or so people who were also in the ground. The wait was unbearable. The latest team news was that Bonds was still out after an injury sustained in the Ipswich game. Steve Walford moved across to centre back, and Frank Lampard came in at left back. I was still worried. Although Walford had started the season well, he had started to show worrying flaws in his game, such as lack of pace, inability to tackle, inability to head the ball. Nothing serious for a West Ham centre half, but I worried nonetheless.

To our dismay, after receiving lots of encouraging comments from programme sellers and lottery ticket sales girls, an ITV cameraman came and set up stall right in front of us. 'Oi!' Dobbo said, 'what about our fucking banner?' The cameraman just laughed and said: 'It's very nice,' and continued to set up his glorified camcorder. His director had given him instructions and he followed them to the letter. Our banner received about five seconds on the ITV network, not enough for it to be read properly. Despite the fact that Devonshire remained at Upton Park for another seven years, we could not bring ourselves to attempt to use it again, and it remains in the bottom of a drawer somewhere in Dobbo's bedroom.

The game progressed and was one of the best of the season thus far. United had Bryan Robson (not Pop, the crap one who played for England a few times) in good form, Ray Wilkins, Arnold Muhren, Frank Stapleton and Norman Whiteside. With Ron Atkinson in charge of United, we knew we were in for a good game. What worried me was that we might be humiliated live on TV.

Wilkins scored in the second half and I had my doubts. A couple of minutes later, a corner from the right was driven in by Trevor Brooking, and Swindlehurst headed past Gary Bailey. The North Bank went absolutely bananas. 1–1 was a fair result, but it left Liverpool sitting smugly at the top of the table, where they remained for the rest of the season. I scanned the video on returning home for evidence of our banner. Deflated, I looked forward to our fourth round Milk Cup tie the next Wednesday against Everton at Upton Park. Usually, I wouldn't have gone to two games in such quick succession, but it was starting to take over. I remember Mum saying: 'You're not going again are you?' I was puzzled by this attitude. 'Of course I am.' I said. 'We're at home.'

As we had already won against Everton earlier in the season, I was convinced that a home game against them would be a mere formality. A good chance to see us rattle in a few goals. It turned out to be the first of many incidents where the game of football, and West Ham in particular, kicked me squarely in the bollocks.

Pipes of Peace. . .

Crystal Palace 1 West Ham United 1 – 28.1.84

I vowed to myself that I would make an effort to attend every FA Cup match in 1984. That would have been a little difficult, so I confined it to all those involving West Ham. League form had fluctuated after out live TV clash with Manchester United. Home form was steady, with home wins over Arsenal, Tottenham and WBA, and a Boxing Day defeat against Southampton. We won at Luton, but were beaten at Aston Villa, Nottingham Forest and Birmingham City. We also frittered away a 2–0 lead at Notts County to draw the game 2–2. The game against Spurs was rather special. It was New Years Eve 1983, and a large group of us gathered behind the North Bank goal, including Scabby Hefford the Spurs fan, and watched Tony Cottee repeat his debut trick and put West Ham 1–0 up. Gary Stevens equalised for Spurs before half time, but in the second half, West Ham took over with goals from Brooking, Martin and a strike from Ray Stewart that was so good, he hit it from all of thirty yards and Ray Clemence in the Tottenham goal didn't even move. I've never seen it again since – I don't think the cameras were there that day, but it must go down as 'Goal of the Decade.' To achieve the double over Spurs was something that didn't happen very often, and indeed hasn't happened since.

The game against Forest at the City Ground was overshadowed by the IRA Harrods bomb. My sister had gone up to town and had hinted that she might go to Knightsbridge. By the time she got home at 7.00pm, Mum and Dad were doing their pieces. Our inconsistent league form had seen us drop to fourth place, still only four points behind leaders Liverpool, and only one win away from second spot. However, we were not to know that we were about to embark on a disastrous run of games that cost us a place in Europe, which had been looking a certainty at Christmas.

The old adage about West Ham coming down with the Christmas decorations was never truer than in 1983/84, and by April we couldn't wait for the season to end.

There was still the FA Cup. I felt we were due a reasonable run because we had a naff draw in the 1983 competition, going out to Manchester United at Old Trafford in the third round. In 1984, we had what appeared to be a cushy number in the third round, at home to Wigan Athletic. Obviously expecting another Bury, 16,000 people turned up to witness the carnage. They were to be disappointed. We scraped through 1–0 with a Ray Stewart penalty, and Alan Devonshire picked up the knee injury that kept him out for over a year. John Lyall often referred to that incident and said that it cost us a place in Europe, but really, we were highly inconsistent before that injury, and it would have been a struggle even with Dev in the side. The Wigan side included teenagers David Lowe, who went on to play for Ipswich and Leicester, and Kevin Langley, who was later signed by Everton. They made life extremely difficult for us, the highlight of the afternoon was when the bloke behind us suddenly leapt in the air. Bournemouth had scored against Manchester United. Everard La Ronde, a former Hammers youth team player, was playing for Bournemouth. Once again, the holders had gone out in the third round.

The fourth round draw saw us paired against Crystal Palace at Selhurst Park. This worried me. Palace had a useful side at the time and had knocked out first division Leicester in the third round. There was a lot of needle surrounding the game. Alan Mullery, the Palace manager, had been sounding off in the press saying that Palace would win. Dave Swindlehurst, a former Palace player, was quoted in the press as saying that he planned to 'Hammer' his former pals. It all pointed towards disaster. At school too, there were a lot of idle threats flying about. The majority of boys at school supported Palace, as they were the local side, and not for the first time our group was outnumbered. The playground games of football did not take the form of West Ham v Palace games, as they had done for the Arsenal

Cup Final. This was too serious. We travelled to Upton Park after school one afternoon to get tickets. I still have my ticket. £2.50 to stand at the old Holmesdale End. With the introduction of all-seater stadia, in just over ten years, prices had increased tenfold at Palace – a very sorry state of affairs.

The day of the game arrived and we decided to walk to the game, cutting across the nearby disused sewage works to Upper Norwood, it was only a twenty minute stroll. This, of course was my first away match, and although the atmosphere was hostile, it had nothing on the partisan atmospheres at some other grounds I have experienced since. The feeling you experience when the opposition score a goal – the home side – is second only to being stripped naked and forced to stand in the middle of a city centre roundabout. You feel so helpless, unloved, unwelcome. It hurts. On the other hand, the experience of celebrating a goal away from home is that much sweeter, it makes up for it. When Swindlehurst bundled in the equalising goal that afternoon, I knew how those Leicester City fans must have felt when Gary Lineker put them ahead. The feeling of mutual happiness was almost tangible and we hung on for a replay at Upton Park the following Wednesday. We knew that we would win. There was no doubt. We had a little bit of trouble persuading the police to let us walk back the way we had come. They had trouble identifying with the notion that West Ham fans could live in Beckenham.

The replay at Upton Park was, as we had guessed, a formality, Bobby Barnes and Geoff Pike getting the goals in a 2–0 win, which allowed us, albeit temporarily, to hold our heads up high at school. It signalled a departure from the norm for us in that someone, I can't remember who, suggested that we watch the game from the South Bank instead of the North. We had always held the South Bank in some awe. It was the South Bank that did the majority of the singing and shouting, the pushing and shoving, and of course, the South Bank contained the majority of the visiting supporters within the little cage in the corner. This is where the majority of the singing started. Visiting supporters are always more vocal, as they have made the effort to come such a distance, they want to make themselves heard. That, in my opinion, is why so many away supporters sections were uncovered at that time, so the noise went straight up in the air and the team couldn't get any encouragement from them. That was apart from the obvious reason for leaving visiting fans uncovered – to get them frozen and, if possible, soaked. How many times have you met a rival supporter in a pub or club, who has said 'Oh, yes, I was at that game – we out-sang you that day.' And you say 'I didn't hear a bloody thing!' Being in among your own make the facts distort quite alarmingly. When all is said and done it is the noise that can be heard on the pitch that matters – it has to have a positive effect on the players. If the visiting team know that 2000 fans have travelled down from the North to watch them, and they are singing their hearts out, they are bound to step up their game a little. I was a great advocate for the idea of taking the roof off that particular section of the South Bank, but that might have looked a little obvious. At Selhurst Park, we sang our hearts out, but the noise dissolved into thin air, and despite the fact that I was deaf by the end of the day, several school friends who had tickets in the Arthur Waite stand, said that they could not hear us.

We decided to become South Bank regulars. The atmosphere was better and it was more of a laugh. The fog horn was better appreciated on the South Bank, and we got to know some of the other lads who regularly inhabited the same spot. We watched the next league game, a 3–0 win over Stoke, from the South Bank. We thought this might help – perhaps changing ends had helped the team's form. Another victory came away at Coventry, and the title challenge was looking good again. Our home match with Watford was postponed because of our fifth round cup tie at Birmingham, but we felt sure that as long as we stood on the South Bank, we would win.

I kept my promise and saw every FA Cup match in 1984. I joined the travel club along with Barney, Fat Sadds and Dobbo, and we travelled on the football special to St Andrews. Strangely though, we never for one moment felt that we would win. We were not to be disappointed.

Relax. . .

Birmingham City 3 West Ham United 0 – 18.2.84

At last I had something I could blame my parents for. Something to be bitter about, something to lodge a chip on my shoulder, something that would make me a successful writer. While my friends' parents were busy rowing, and getting divorces left, right and centre, Mr & Mrs Banks arranged their eldest daughter's wedding, thought about buying a new car, did the garden, decorated and were generally nice to each other. My mother got a part-time job in a baker's shop, but only once I had shown that I was capable of feeding myself, and tying my own shoelaces. Dad continued to be the major bread winner, had his tea on the table for him when he got home, then fell asleep in front of the TV while Mum did the washing up and the ironing. It was sickeningly happy and suburban.

I had no desire to run away from it. My friends were out almost every night, at the park, at the youth club, or the street corner. Only the tallest and bravest went to the pub. To me, it made perfect sense, but they couldn't work out why I generally chose to stay at home, read a book, play the guitar, dream my dreams. I didn't care. I got out when I wanted to. I would play football with them in the park on a Sunday, but saw no point in hanging around on a street corner on a freezing November night when there was a comfortable room at home with a constant supply of tea and biscuits. I didn't have a clue about fashion or girls, and wouldn't say boo to a goose; a fact that was to be rudely exposed.

If I was a psychiatrist, I would say that I loved going to football because there was safety in numbers. In a large group, you could shout abuse, be generally cruel and unfair to people and no-one cared. In fact, most people would agree with you. Four of us planned to go to Birmingham City for the fifth round FA Cup tie. We anticipated getting home at about nine, after which, myself, Fat Sadds and Dobbo were invited to join Barney at his parents' social club.

We got on the train at Euston, and clearly recall the trip taking ages. We were all convinced we were going to lose, because we had played a league match at St Andrews a few weeks earlier and had been thumped 3–0 without even looking like scoring. Everyone else on the train had the same opinion, but it didn't stop us all wanting to see the game. It was almost as though we had already lost as the train pulled into Small Heath station and we boarded the buses that would take us to the ground. It suddenly dawned on me. 'We might actually win – you never know.'

The negative thoughts of the crowd obviously transmitted themselves to the pitch, as a shocking display of lethargy and apathy resulted in the game being lost by the same margin as the league match: 3–0. The crowd decided to take matters into their own hands. Relations with the West Midlands Police had not been good from the off, when Fat Sadds got thrown out for making an 'obscene gesture'. We weren't quite sure what he was supposed to have done, but a kindly steward let him back in when the Police were looking the other way, saying that the coppers had a reputation for slinging visiting fans out every now and then for no apparent reason. It was a sign of boredom. If they were bored, there was certainly plenty to do later on in the game, as the third goal went in, we suddenly found we had a lot more room around us. West Ham fans flooded onto the pitch, in an attempt to get the game abandoned. It had a better chance of success than letting the team try to pull it around. St John Ambulance men were attacked with corner flags, the referee was hit, and the players all disappeared down the tunnel quicker than a ferret down a trouser leg. The interruption lasted about fifteen minutes, the mounted police clearing the pitch and making several arrests. The four of us watched the events, dumbstruck. We had never seen anything like it. We had heard stories of the escapades of Leeds supporters, and the riots that went on after games, or in the pubs in towns, but never during the game itself. We could not decide whether to be astonished, excited or horrified. It was probably a mixture of all three.

Perversely, the train didn't take so long on the way back. We quickly changed at Barney's house. 'You're going to wear that shirt, are you?' Barney said, pointing at my most comfortable cotton checked shirt.

'Why not?' I asked.

'No reason,' he laughed, putting on his Pringle jumper and adjusting his perm in the mirror, squeezing a few blackheads at the same time. When we got to the club, there were some other people from school there, we were allowed to drink and play pool and there was a disco, with girls. I didn't have A CLUE what to do, and I was getting on for sixteen. Surely this wasn't right? One of my friends had made his girlfriend pregnant by the time he was sixteen, and here I was too shy to even talk to one. My shirt earned me a new nickname at school – Bronco Billy. Fortunately it didn't stick, but for a few weeks I thought it was going to. They soon got fed up when they realised I wasn't rising to it, and went back to 'Barclays' which was much more acceptable to me, even though I later learned it had rhyming slang connotations. I told you how cruel kids could be.

When I got home, I thought about it. I liked women – I liked them a lot. I remember how I fell in love with Melanie McGuire and Wendy McCarthy, two friends of my sister. At seven and eight I wasn't afraid of women, but at fifteen I was terrified. Thinking about teenage pregnancies made me think I was better off where I was. Kissing and sex and all that stuff usually led to trouble. I'd read that, and the evidence was everywhere to see. I was much better off playing my guitar and writing songs about being in love than actually doing it. The nearest I had got to falling in love by the time I was sixteen was with a girl called Ruth Kendrick. I thought she was quite pretty and sent her a valentine card one year, but she never knew who it was from. Wendy McCarthy broke my heart when I was seven years old by turning me down. Writing this book has certainly dredged a number of pleasant and unpleasant memories up from the very dregs of my mind. Wendy was fourteen and was Sylvia's best friend. She accompanied us on our family holiday to Eastbourne, and I fell in love with her. She was seeing some bloke called Barry, who had a motorbike and a tattoo. I was sure that if I had a motorbike, and/or a tattoo I would have stood a chance. At seven and fourteen, the age gap was a little tricky to bridge. When I was twenty three, I met her at a party. I was relaxed and open with her, and we got along like a house on fire. Now it didn't seem so bad. My inexperience at the age of fifteen has not done me any harm, in fact, having two older sisters around for most of my formative years helped to make me a more helpful and understanding person (or so my shrink tells me). So I haven't really got anything to blame my parents for after all. Damn! I'm determined to find something before the end of this book.

The Reflex. . .

West Ham United 4 Tottenham Hotspur 1 – 18.5.84

Pat Holland Testimonial

By the time April ended, we couldn't wait for the season to finish. After the cup exit at Birmingham, the season virtually fell apart. Injuries didn't help – Alan Devonshire was already out of course, then Alvin Martin and Steve Whitton were involved in a car crash and both missed most of February and March. In an effort to bolster the defence, John Lyall (have I introduced you to John? He was the nice man who used to look after the team) signed Paul Hilton from Bury. It was a curious signing to say the least. The last game he had played at Upton Park he had been on the receiving end of ten goals. He made his debut the Tuesday after the Birmingham disgrace in a home game against Watford. Despite Dave Swindlehurst putting us 1–0 up in the first minute, we lost 2–4, and Watford looked irresistible. They were to knock Birmingham out of the cup in the next round, and went on to lose in the Final to Everton. Another defeat at Norwich followed, then a 'Blip.' A 3–0 win at Ipswich. This game took place shortly after my French oral exam. I was waiting outside the room waiting to go in. I was under strict instructions not to talk to anyone when 'Woolley' Woollard strolled up and asked me if I was going to Ipswich. Daft git. He thought we called him Woolley because his name was Woollard, but it wasn't; it was a reference to the consistency of his brain. He was another bandwagon jumper, who subsequently left the sinking ship and was last seen supporting Millwall via Chelsea and Arsenal. Having nearly caused me to fail an exam before entering the room, we went to Ipswich and saw a great win, Hilton, Cottee and a Terry Butcher o.g. notching for us. We failed to build on it, and could only manage a 1–1 draw at home to Wolves, who were already relegated, then got slaughtered 4–1 at Leicester. Things went from bad to worse. A superb first half performance against QPR was undone by Clive Allen, a constant thorn in our side, and we had to settle for a 2–2 draw. Liverpool sneaked past us 6–0 at Anfield. We were still in sixth place at this stage, and yet we crumbled at the hands of the champions. We were 4–0 down after just twenty minutes. My only consolation that day was that Aston Villa fans would be even more depressed having lost 1–5 at home to Nottingham Forest. Some consolation. On Cup semi-final day we inexplicably lost 1–0 at home to Sunderland. It was all going belly-up now. 'Pop' Robson was playing for Sunderland that day – his last appearance at Upton Park as a player. Our last win of the season was against Luton Town, 3–1 at home. The papers made a great deal of the win and said we were on course for Europe, whereas in fact, we failed to win another game, losing at home to Aston Villa, Nottingham Forest and Everton, away to Southampton and drawing away at Manchester United and Arsenal.

The last home game of the season was at home to Everton, re-arranged due to their involvement in the Milk Cup final. The match was of no footballing merit whatsoever, but it signalled the end of Trevor Brooking's career. The previous Saturday he had received his crystal decanter and all the plaudits, *The Big Match* gave special coverage to the game, which re-enforced my view that Brian Moore is a Hammers fan. I think Trevor thought he had got away with it. All the hype had been on the Saturday. He was expecting to finish the game against Everton, slip off and have a shower, then down to the BBC for a bit of pundit-practice. He wasn't allowed to do that. The crowd demanded that he re-emerge and do a few laps of honour. Eventually he was carried off, shoulder high by his adoring public. It was such a send-off that he didn't dare think about a comeback. He had made it clear right from the start of the season that this would be his last and he kept his word. I was pleased in a way. No-one likes to see a favourite player go on longer than he should, beyond the stage when he is able to produce the quality of play for which he was once famed.

Pat Holland had no choice but to pack up. One of the best players ever to come through the youth policy, Patsy was granted a testimonial game at the end of the season as a mark of gratitude for his loyal service to the first team, for whom he made his first appearance during season 1968/69, and 227 games later his last appearance came in 1981. His testimonial was on the Friday before the cup final and was played at Upton Park against Spurs. I went along with Stain Tooth and stood on the East Terrace for the first time. It was brilliant! I could see so much clearer, the steps were that much deeper, which meant I could see the game, not the back of somebody's head. It took me a while to convince everyone else that the East Terrace was the place to stand, but once they had all taken in a game there, they all agreed it was worth the extra pound for the better view. Being a long terrace along the side of the pitch, it meant that you could also 'change ends' at half time, and you weren't confined to one end and straining to see the home team attack the North Bank goal while you were stranded on the South Bank. You were free to move. West Ham won the game 4–1. Clive Allen, a QPR player at the time, played for us and scored two goals. Vince Hilaire, the former Palace and Portsmouth winger, also played for us, in one of the most impressive West Ham line-ups I had ever seen. Of course, eight years later, we signed Clive Allen, but by then it was far too late.

As the final whistle went, I realised that there would be no more West Ham for a few months, and therefore no excuse not to concentrate hard on my 'O' levels which were less than a month away. The European Championships were being held in France, but there was no England to cheer on, and so I did just that, got my head down and concentrated on my 'O' Levels. I was tired of school, and went for an interview with a local property company. I was offered the job on the spot, and decided to take it, as my initial desire to be a journalist was subsiding on the basis that I would require a degree in English. I'd had it with exams. I wanted to see the world. What I didn't know was that I would be taking exams every year for the next eight years, and it would have been a lot easier to stay at school, and go through the proper channels.

Given the chance to do it all again, there is one reason why I would still take the job. That reason is Diana Hopkins.

I Just Called to Say I Love You. . .

Chelsea 3 West Ham United 0 – 15.9.84

Seven 'O' levels later, a job at Baxter Payne & Lepper fell into my lap. (Why are you laughing?) Not content with working for a company with 'Lepper' in its name, the Senior Partner was a guy called John Thomas. D H Lawrence fans will know what I'm saying. On my first day, I wore my West Ham tie to the office. I was called to go out on an appointment with my new boss, and he noticed it straight away. 'That's a West Ham tie, isn't it?'

'Yes.' I thought, maybe he's a fan!

'I'm a Tottenham man, myself.' Oh bollocks.

The job I took on was that of Assistant Surveyor. The company did most things connected with property: sales, lettings, surveys, management – you name it. I assisted the Partner in charge of the Survey Department in mortgage valuations and structural surveys for those silly people who had decided to buy a house. We told them what was wrong with it and why they shouldn't buy it. I did that for three days a week. For the other two, I went to college, and took an ONC in Land Use.

Between starting at BP&L and going to college, the 1984/85 season kicked off. West Ham were widely being tipped to struggle – not quite relegation material, but things didn't look too good. Trevor Brooking had gone, Billy Bonds had decided to take a step back and Frank Lampard was on his last legs. Alan Devonshire was still injured, and we were relying heavily on the talent provided by the youth team.

The season opened with a 0–0 draw at home to Ipswich, a trend that was to continue in subsequent seasons. We managed to get Anfield out of the way early on, a 3–0 defeat was almost viewed as a good result after the slaughter that had taken place there the previous year. That was followed by a surprising 3–2 win at Southampton, with Goddard getting two goals, and Alan Dickens, one of the youth team products, the other. I say surprise, because Southampton had finished as runners up the previous season, and were expected to do very well. It knocked me backwards, because I didn't hear the result until later in the evening, and when I heard 'Southampton two. . .' I thought, 'Oh no!' Nice surprise.

The next game was an evening affair against Coventry City. Ray Stewart bagged a couple and Cottee the third in a 3–1 win, and everything looked rosy – nothing to worry about at all. Another win, this time over Watford, saw us go joint top with Arsenal on ten points, and all looked good for another sustained challenge. Things were looking good for the clash at Stamford Bridge against newly promoted Chelsea.

Now that I was working I had given up the paper round, but I still saw Richard Pusey occasionally. I did my best to avoid him after this game. It was the first time I had ever seen Chelsea play, and after being used to the layout at Upton Park, with the terraces so close to the pitch you can touch the players, Stamford Bridge came as a bit of a shock. The pitch was miles away! If I had known, I would have brought binoculars and a tent. I could have camped down over night and made an attempt to reach the pitch the following day. At least it was easy to distinguish the two teams, Chelsea in their Royal Blue and West Ham in an all white strip, with blue socks. The game started badly. Phil Parkes had been injured in pre-season training, and our reserve 'keeper, Tom McAlister, was in goal. He made spectacular saves, but I never had a great deal of confidence in him, and I don't think the rest of the team did either. For that reason, we looked edgy and insecure whenever Chelsea brought the ball into our half, which, let's face it, was for most of the game. Chelsea won a penalty, and Colin Lee took it. McAlister saved it. The referee, obviously unable to cope with that concept, ordered it to be retaken, and Lee scored. We managed to keep them out until mid way through the second half, but then Speedie and Nevin scored a couple of quick goals and we were dead and buried.

It is unfortunate that my lasting memory of the game will be for events off the pitch. We got to the ground at about 2.00pm and took up our position on the terrace. Chelsea were another of those teams that gave visiting supporters an uncovered terrace.

I remember standing there admiring the three tiered stand to my left, when suddenly, and without warning, all hell broke loose in the bottom tier. Police swarmed across the pitch from the other side to quell the trouble, but no sooner had they done so, then trouble broke out in the other stand. It was farcical, like watching a Keystone Cops movie in slow motion. In the paper the next day, we learned that the trouble had been serious, and a few people injured. I was to feel the full force of Chelsea fan's aggression later that season, but it brought home to me that our initial reservations about the safety factor at football matches may have been justified. Trouble continued throughout the game and afterwards. We kept our heads down and ran for Fulham Broadway tube station.

It was a violent time. The miners' strike had been going since March, and was just about to enter its battle stage; Scargill v Maggie as the first feature, followed by Miners v Police at every opportunity. In October, the IRA bombed the Tory Party Conference in Brighton. This was possibly the single most worrying act of terrorism ever carried out in Britain, as it was the closest anyone has ever come this century to murdering not only the Prime Minister, but the entire Cabinet as well. The previous April, a siege at the Libyan Embassy ended in the death of WPC Yvonne Fletcher, and in Africa, war and famine continued as it always had done. This time it was Ethiopia. A few years later it was Somalia. Currently it is Rwanda and Bosnia – nothing will ever change. Violence at football matches appears to have changed, thankfully. The signs were there during the miners' strike, when there were no police available to attend the Nottingham derby match between Forest and County. The match went ahead, controlled by stewards, and there wasn't a hint of trouble. Today, things appear to be a lot better, and there can be no denying that West Ham had more than their fair share of problems. I cannot profess to be an expert on these matters, but I have match programmes dating back as far as 1968 asking the 'North Bank Boys' to refrain from their violent activities. Interestingly, when the real problems started, such as in the Cup Winners' Cup game in Castilla, Spain, in 1980, they didn't bother with such requests, obviously realising that it was futile.

It hardly mattered that we had lost to Chelsea 3–0. All the papers were worried about was the violence. At first I thought this was a welcome diversion from the football, but I used to get teased at work about being a ring-leader, and sparking it all off. Following the two week course at college, I returned to BP&L to find things had changed somewhat. Mike had been 'moved upstairs' a phrase to strike fear into anyone's heart, to the Commercial Department, and we had two new secretaries. Kate Lawrence was a lively, bubbly character, who was larger than life and a wonderful person. She wore a pair of Denis Taylor type up-side-down glasses, which thoroughly reflected her character. She was (and still is) a very warm, sincere character and above all else a true friend. Diana was blonde, had a superb body for a thirty-two year old, and was charming as well as possessing a scathing wit. Sarcasm, parody, satire, she had the lot. She was absolutely beautiful. At least, I thought so. She possessed all the best bits of Olivia Newton-John and Jayne Mansfield. Think about it for yourself. She could recite most Monty Python sketches with me verbatim, which excluded us from the rest of the staff. We could go into our own little dream world. I loved her deeply, but not in a way that might have been considered a threat to her marriage. After all, I was sixteen – she was thirty two, old enough to be my mother. She was married with a young daughter, and living, happily so it seemed, in Gillingham. She supported Sunderland, the land of her father, and talked knowledgeably about the game, and about music. In fact, everything I had a remote interest in, she knew about. She was also a complete cricket fanatic, a devoted fan of Ian Botham, though I don't think that had anything to do with his cricketing capability. Diana and I worked as a great team, and it seemed inevitable that we would become firm friends. I was more surprised than anyone at the way it eventually turned out.

Do They Know It's Christmas?

West Ham United 2 Southampton 3 – 22.12.84

All the old jokes about West Ham coming down with the Christmas decorations weren't funny any more. This time, there was nowhere to fall. We were mid-table and only eight points above the relegation zone when Christmas approached. Another disaster like last year and it was goodbye Liverpool, hello Barnsley. Our form had not been too bad until December, when things started to go wrong rapidly, losing at home to WBA and away at Norwich, and only managing a 0–0 draw at home to Sheffield Wednesday. Having topped the league in September, we drew against Forest and then at Newcastle before beating Leicester 3–1 at Upton Park. This was the first game for which I ever wrote a full match report, on my BBC Computer at home. It was for my eyes only, and compared to the work I now produce, was naive and childish, but the tendency to take the piss was still there, in foetal form. We hammered Bristol City 6–1 in the Milk Cup, and were on a goalscoring high, when it all came off the rails at Old Trafford. We lost 5–1, and Alan Brazil had a field day for United; a good indication of how badly we played. Inconsistency was the name of the game. A mini revival followed, with a 3–1 win over Arsenal. This was the only home game I have ever attended where I have actually felt uncomfortable. The crowd on the South Bank was absolutely packed. So packed that I was being held off the ground by the pressure from other bodies. This was at the time when alcohol was still permitted on the terrace during the game, and I clearly remember dipping my hand in my pocket after the match to find half a pint of lager and a dog end floating around. The previous Saturday we had won 4–2 at Stoke, but a few days later managed only a 0–0 draw at second division Manchester City in the Milk Cup. In the replay, they beat us 2–1, an inconceivable result. I walked away from the game thinking that there ought to be a re-count, or at least a stewards' enquiry. Surely we could not lose to a team from a lower division? Not at Upton Park? Not while I was watching? Defeat at home to Everton ensued, followed by victory against Sunderland and a draw at Luton. We were totally confused, and realised painfully that it was all part of being a West Ham United supporter. You never knew where you stood. We could beat Liverpool one week, and lose to Oldham the next. Football, as Jimmy Greaves famously pointed out, is a funny old game, but surely it's not that funny.

My devotion to West Ham became a point of much amusement, both at work and at college. Fortunately I did not suffer alone at college, as I met a lad called Andy Russell, who lived in West London, but regularly travelled across the capital to watch West Ham. Lunchtime conversations took place in the pub. Although still only sixteen, as we were at college, we felt it was safe to go into pubs. Andy looked eighteen, and with my 'mature attitude' despite being short, I gave the air of someone of about twenty-seven. Pete actually was eighteen, but as a Charlton fan, had a mental age of about twelve. Brian was a Luton fan, and therefore needed to drink on a regular basis. Johnny 'B' Goodall remains the only WBA fan I have ever met face to face. The talk was always about football, nothing else ever entered the equation. At work, football wasn't important to most people, but they found my devotion quaintly fascinating. On Friday 21st December, the office was closing down for Christmas. This was my first Christmas party, and I wasn't sure what to expect. As the youngest male there, my presence was demanded by most of the women, and I had a great time. The powers that be had organised a system whereby we all wore badges with our names on, and a different symbol indicating which office we came from. The orders were issued that no more than two of the same symbol were to be seen together at any one time. No cliques, no office groups, no exclusions and definitely no exceptions. By mutual arrangement, we managed to change identities in order that we could talk to who we wanted to. We turfed one of the surveyors out of the broom cupboard, where he had managed to get half the way there with his secretary. His new year began at the Job Centre.

Diana was teasing me. She said she had polished her shoes especially so I could tell what colour knickers she was wearing by the reflection. I was shocked, delighted and frightened at the same time. How do you react to a statement like that? 'One day,' she said, a young lad like you will come and sweep me off my feet and we'll be blissfully happy together.'

'Seduce me,' I said.

'You'd run a mile,' she slurred.

'Try me,' I answered. She didn't. What a bummer.

I thought about Diana all the way through the game with Southampton, not intentionally ignoring my friends, but I was pretty distant. I thought about what she would be doing over Christmas, whether she'd be climbing on top of her obese husband, and if she did, whether she'd think of me. The crowd around me surged forward to greet West Ham's opening goal, a cracking shot from Tony Cottee after a slick one-two with Alan Dickens. Peter Shilton came in for some stick that afternoon. For some reason we were all calling him 'Tina'. I can't remember the exact story behind it, but it had something to do with an extra marital affair. I felt nothing but sympathy for him.

Steve Walford was beginning to work his way steadily into my West Ham United Worst XI of all time. Competition for places in the team is fierce, but 'Wally' will be there for some time to come. I understand he also appeared in 'all time worst XI's' for Norwich and Arsenal, his two previous clubs. It's a pity John Lyall didn't check that one out before buying him. That afternoon, he scored the best goal of his career. Unfortunately, it went into our own net. He lobbed McAlister from an impossible angle. I would have laughed if I hadn't already been crying. Southampton scored two more goals in the second half, and the game was up, not before Paul Allen surged through the midfield, the ball tied to his foot, and laid it across the six yard box to provide a chance for Cottee that he simply could not miss. The game appeared on *The Big Match* the next day, which now seemed to happen less frequently, and only when we got beaten.

Christmas came and went, the highlight being Boxing Day, which was spent crouched over a radio at my uncle's house listening to West Ham come back from 2–0 down to draw 2–2 at White Hart Lane. We were still Spurs' bogey team, and loved every minute of it. Tottenham were challenging for the title that year; they won at Anfield for the first time since the game had been invented and broke all sorts of other club records, but they still couldn't manage to beat us. The calendar year ended with a 2–1 win at Coventry, something we were learning to expect. New Years day was a disaster. We lost 3–1 at home to QPR and had Tony Gale stretchered off. Paul Brush opened the scoring for us in the first half, and Steve Potts made his debut. That's where the good news ended. Whitton had a goal disallowed which would have made it 2–0, then QPR took over. Gary Waddock scored a goal for Rangers that they still talk about in Shepherd's Bush.

The FA Cup campaign began with a convincing 4–1 win over Port Vale, Paul Goddard grabbing a hat-trick, then the weather intervened and we had no football for a few weeks. There is nothing worse than not being able to watch football because of the weather. You may have been looking forward to a game all week; if it's a big derby match, maybe for a month, only to have it whipped away from you without warning – well, without much warning. On at least two occasions I have got as far as Upton Park tube station before finding that a game had been postponed. West Ham are notoriously bad at making decisions. The installation of undersoil heating would help, both in this direction and in the avoidance of fixture backlogs. By the time we played Newcastle at Upton Park it was early February, and we turned up in eager anticipation, having been denied a glimpse of our heroes for so long. Although we took the lead through Paul Allen, the old frailties returned and we conceded a late equaliser to Chris Waddle.

Two days later, on the Monday evening, we took on Norwich City in the fourth round of the cup. There was something special about that evening. It is one of the few games which will stay with me for a very long time. Norwich went ahead in the first half and we were having another nightmare. In the second half, with West Ham kicking towards the South Bank, the atmosphere suddenly exploded into something quite electric, an atmosphere which despite many great evenings at Upton Park since, I have yet to experience again. Geoff Pike levelled with a brilliant volley, and within a couple of minutes we were ahead through a Ray Stewart penalty.

After the game, we took part in a massive conga down Green Street. For some reason, we surrounded a double decker bus and tried to kick it to death. The effect of the adrenalin was twenty times stronger than any alcohol. We were convinced, somewhat foolishly, that after this experience, we would win the FA Cup. After all, it appeared that a five year pattern was emerging: 1975, 1980, and, possibly 1985?

I Know Him So Well...

Wimbledon 1 West Ham United 1 – 4.3.85

By now I justifiably considered myself to be a veteran. I had been to Old Trafford, Highbury, St Andrews, Selhurst Park, Carrow Road, Griffin Park and Portman Road in pursuit of my beloved Hammers. Significantly, on my travels, I had only seen them win once, but the disease had taken hold, and that fact did not seem to deter me from going on my first mid-week away game at Wimbledon in the fifth round of the FA Cup.

Just as February had begun with two games in the space of three days, so did March. On the Saturday, we lost 1–2 at Highbury, after taking the lead through Tony Cottee. Everything was going according to plan until Alvin Martin had to go off to have stitches put in a head wound. While he had his back turned for no more than ten minutes, Arsenal scored twice, then shut up shop. On the Monday, we played away at Wimbledon in the cup. I have vivid memories of this game. I had been unable to concentrate at college that day, thinking about the football match that approached on the one hand, and about Diana Hopkins' thighs on the other. How I wanted to get between them!

Despite being the beginning of March, the weather was still bitterly cold; the central heating in the college refectory was on full blast and it contrasted sharply with the icy blasts of cold air that shot past every time someone opened the door, and the sickly hot chocolate we forced down our throats. It made the air dry and uncomfortable, but it was nothing compared to what was to follow that evening. I went with Close and Woolley. Wimbledon's ground was a complete pit; we had to scamper up a mud bank to get onto the terrace, and the whole place appeared to be falling apart. Even the tickets appeared to have been produced on an amateur printing kit. Wimbledon v Norwich or

West Ham they proudly stated. A few years later, as we waited for Liverpool and Everton to settle their three match FA Cup squabble, the same thing happened to us, but at least they looked professional!

The teams Wimbledon were producing at the time were inconsistent and relied heavily on the infamous 'long ball' tactics employed by manager Dave Bassett. They had dodged between fourth, third and second divisions ever since their election to the league in 1977. It was built up as a contest of contrasting styles; The Academy against The Crazy Gang. On paper, any result other than a huge win for West Ham would have been unthinkable.

The game kicked off and we never really looked to be in any trouble. Alan Devonshire made a welcome (if brief) comeback, which lasted a whole two games. I think about five balls were used during the game, due to hasty clearances and misguided long passes. At half time, the groundsman got out a ladder and climbed up onto the roof near the section of West Ham supporters, to fetch the balls out of the gutter. He should have known better, as some bright spark promptly removed the ladder, and left him stranded up there for the rest of the match. We took the lead through, who else, but Tony Cottee in the second half, and went very close with an effort from Neil Orr. Wimbledon were sporting their all red strip, and I'm not sure if it was this that confused the West Ham defence, but they allowed Stewart Evans to equalise a few minutes from the end, and all parties were relatively happy. Despite losing to Manchester City in the Milk Cup, we all felt that a replay against Wimbledon would not present a problem, we had dominated the game, and Wimbledon got a bit of extra cash. How could we have known that in three short years, Wimbledon would be lifting the FA Cup at Wembley, and would enjoy a consistently higher league placing than ourselves. Justice? Don't ask.

It's quite a long walk to Wimbledon Tube Station from Plough Lane, and we were provided with a heavy police escort to the station, where a special District Line train had been laid on. We sensed there might be trouble in store as we heard the sound of breaking glass up ahead, but it did not worry us unduly. Chelsea had been playing at home a few miles down the road, and their fans were not happy Hectors, as they had lost the second leg of their Milk Cup semi-final to Sunderland 3–2. The news of this brought cheers all around the station, but the smile soon fell from my face as a train loaded with snarling Chelsea fans pulled up on the other side of the platform. It was bad enough that this should happen in the first place, but the fact that Chelsea had just lost a semi final made it ten times worse. The entire compartment behind me rushed forward to greet their blue chums. As the Chelsea fans also rushed from their train, a pitched battle took place on the platform. I had been sucked into it, along with Woolley as the crowd had surged forward, and I was on my hand and knees, unashamedly trying to crawl to safety. I was not one to brag about victories over the opposition of this kind. I thought it all a bit stupid and mind-numbingly pathetic. Just as I was about to emerge from the darkness, a Doc. Marten caught me square in the face. I don't know what colours its owner wore, and I don't really care. I just wanted to get away. With blood pouring from my nose, I sought assistance from the ticket office. No-one could, or rather, would help me. Woolley refused point blank to lend me his scarf to bleed on. I had already soaked my own and I was beginning to look like an Arsenal fan, pasty, delirious and with a red scarf.

A policewoman sympathetically grabbed me by the arm and put me in a lock. 'Come on!' I said, 'I'm an innocent victim!' She looked me up and down and had to agree, and gave me her hanky. A St John Ambulance worker called Jane patched me up before the train left and I was allowed to go. The mood on the train was not friendly. Light bulbs were smashed, seats ripped up and slammed against the windows. At every stop, 'fans' with arms locked behind their backs, were marched off by transport police. The emergency cord was pulled twice, and I began to feel faint. I got no sympathy from Woolley, who thought it was all very exciting, but stopped short of joining in.

We met up with Close at Charing Cross, just in time to make the last train home. I managed to clean myself up and dispose of my bloodstained clothing before getting indoors, but fortunately Mum and Dad were both fast asleep. Although I had my independence at the age of sixteen, and was allowed to go more or less where I wanted when I wanted, I knew that if Mum and Dad knew what had happened on Wimbledon Station that night, they would worry every time I went to a football match. I knew that this was a one-off incident, which had occurred due to some unfortunate timing, but they wouldn't see it that way. I lay in bed but did not sleep, wishing that Diana would come and talk to me. Two obsessions in one young life was just not healthy, and the joke I had heard at school a few years earlier came to mind:

Q: What's the difference between light and hard?
A: You can get to sleep with a light on.

This was 1985. In 1985, cup replays took place within a few days, not ten days later if you are lucky, and by which time the first game has been forgotten. The Wimbledon replay took place on the following Wednesday; a game every other day since the Saturday, and Manchester United awaiting the winners just three days later. And you thought they played too much football today? Admittedly, the main reason for the pile up was the bad weather, but even so it was a farcical situation.

On the Wednesday night we brushed Wimbledon aside as though they weren't there. Devonshire was playing again, and a Cottee hat-trick together with goals from Dickens and Paul Allen, secured a 5–1 win and a trip to Old Trafford in the quarter-finals.

I couldn't go. I had flu. Unfortunately for West Ham, so had most of the team. A highly depleted squad took the trip up north, and by all accounts put up a superb show. The previous game at Old Trafford had produced six goals and ended in a 1–5 defeat. This game also provided six goals, but this time ended in a 2–4 defeat. The score doesn't give the full story however. Pikey had to come off after twenty-six minutes to be replaced by Paul Hilton. Mark Hughes scored and it looked as though the roof would cave in, but hard work saw us pull level when Allen crossed from the right and Graeme Hogg deflected the ball into his own net. Norman Whiteside put United 2–1 up before half time, and added a third, and another mauling looked on the cards, West Ham looked like a team suffering from flu. Then, Paul Allen pulled one back with five minutes to go and suddenly we were in with a shout. But in the last minute, Whiteside completed his hat-trick and United went on to win the trophy, beating Everton in the final. As with all these perverse footballing situations, we had to play United again six days later in the league match at Upton Park. The game was played on a Friday night because the BBC were keen to have us, but not so keen that they wouldn't shift Wogan to allow the whole game to be shown live. Seventy-five minutes were shown, during which we managed to salvage a little bit of pride by leading twice before drawing 2–2.

I was ill. Not just flu, but headaches and nausea too. I told myself it had nothing to do with the kick in the face I had received at Wimbledon, and that I was just lovesick, and desperately disappointed about West Ham's poor season. This had caused me to reach an all time low, and the flu had knocked me sideways. My brain accepted the fact and allowed me to recover in time to go on a trip away for a few days with the college to survey Dartford Heath. The place we stayed was just like a cross between a five star hotel and a borstal. The facilities were fantastic, but we weren't allowed to use any of them. Dartford Heath was more like Exmoor, cold, wet and inhospitable. We made up most of our figures. I sharpened up my table tennis, and we watched Gary Lineker score his first goal for England against the Republic of Ireland on TV. We ventured down to the local pub, but were thrown out for looking underage and nicking the bikers' favourite pinball machine. Life, at the age of sixteen, was just so unfair.

N-N-N-N-Nineteen. . .

Sheffield Wednesday 2 West Ham United 1 – 11.5.85

When I met Zoe, she was nineteen. As Diana's younger sister, it would have suited all parties if I had fancied Zoe instead. I was still sixteen, and feeling hornier than ever. Working every day with Diana increased my frustration even further, as she told me what she'd like to do to me, and jealously protected me from the advances of the other women within the office. I was her plaything. The original Toy Boy. The company I worked for were the oldest company of surveyors in the area, having been established in 1760. To celebrate their 225th anniversary, they held a big bash at a local golf club, and that's when Diana introduced me to Zoe. By now I was learning, and knew a little more about 'chatting up' rather than just plain conversation. Flatter them, talk about them, don't mention yourself unless they ask, above all, be charming and never mention football. The evening was a great success, and was the first time I thought that I really ought to buckle down and get some qualifications, if I was going to be a chartered surveyor. I was coming towards the end of my first year at college, and decided that, as soon as the cup final was over, I would concentrate on my exams. I didn't leave myself quite enough time, as I only just scraped through once again, but it was enough, and I was content with my career prospects. The job wasn't too difficult, got me out of the office a lot, and brought me into contact with people. What's more I had Saturdays free and had ample time to get to Upton Park for mid-week games. Life could not have been better – well, Diana could have left her husband and moved to Bromley, but you can't have everything.

Diana left her husband and moved to Bromley. She came into my office on the day she had made up her mind, crept up behind me and covered my eyes with her hands. 'Guess who?' she said, as she always did. I went through the names of every woman in the company before reaching her name, just as I always did. It was a well rehearsed routine. 'I'm leaving Alan,' she said, matter of factly.

'I'm sorry,' I lied.

'I'm not,' she said, her eyes sparkling. 'I'm renting a flat in Bromley – come and see it tonight!'

Life was perfect.

After the cup exit the team continued to hurtle relentlessly towards the relegation zone. Defeat in the last minute at Leicester and a 5–0 walloping at Watford sandwiched a characteristically unexpected win at Nottingham Forest. West Ham hadn't so much as scored a goal at Forest since Geoff Hurst struck in 1969, so for Goddard and Cottee to get one each in a 2–1 win was nothing short of a miracle. Over Easter, we frustrated Tottenham's title bid with a 1–1 draw and lost 2–4 at QPR. That was a strange game. Tom McAlister was clattered by Alan McDonald, broke two ribs and punctured a lung. The referee saw nothing wrong with the challenge, but McAlister was carted off the field, and in the days before substitute goalkeepers, Ray Stewart pulled on the green jersey. Cottee had only just equalised and we were looking good for a point, when QPR won a penalty. It was ironic that our ace penalty taker should have to face one from the other side. He couldn't stop it, and QPR got a fourth to leave the scoreline looking a little flattering. A vital win at Diana's Sunderland followed, loyalties divided, but not enough to stop me yearning for a Hammers victory – there's only so much crawling you can do, after all.

Luton Town have never been one of my favourite sides. They came to Upton Park on April 27th not totally out of danger themselves, and bumped and scraped their way to a 0–0 draw. The reason this sticks in my mind was that the gentleman standing directly behind me said every five minutes 'Come on West Ham, you can beat this second division shit!' I wouldn't have minded if he had said it once. Twice would have been acceptable, three times I could have coped, but he literally said it every few minutes. By the end of the game I was praying for a relaxation of the gun laws, and, as I cannot focus my hatred on this individual, I focused it on Luton Town Football Club.

As any self respecting lovesick moody adolescent will admit, growing up and writing poetry go together. With me, it was songs, as I now knew more than three chords on the guitar, I wrote a dirge about Luton Town entitled 'Lost at Home' the chorus of which went along these lines:

And in life's rosy garden
The beer is warm
My love has flown
The Hammers lost at home. . .'

The final rendition of the chorus had the additional line 'Again, 5–0 to Luton Town or someone equally crap.' Billy Bragg should look out. I have never quite come to terms with Luton Town being allowed to continue in the league, and probably never will.

Barney and I took the train to Rolfe Street to see the game against WBA at The Hawthorns. We couldn't believe our luck when we saw they were only charging £3.50 for a seat, so we sat down and watched our side get demolished 5–1. Strangely, I do not have an irrational hatred of WBA, despite the fact that of all the teams someone at college in London could have supported, my mate Johnny 'B' Goodall supported WBA.

The Mayday Bank Holiday game against Norwich now took on extra significance. Norwich were up to their necks in it as well, and a win would put us in a strong position. They battled bravely, and I really felt for them when Bobby Barnes scored our winner in the eighty-first minute. There are some teams I hate: Liverpool, Arsenal, Luton Town and Manchester United are but four, however, there are some teams I have quite a soft spot for, and have no real objection to, unless they should dare to beat us. Norwich are one of those teams. The others are Nottingham Forest, Ipswich Town, Manchester City and QPR. Don't ask me why, it just happens that way. Two days later we were summarily despatched 3–0 by the soon to be champions, Everton.

The firm's 225th anniversary do immediately preceded our vital game at Sheffield Wednesday. We were in trouble; just one place and five points above the relegation zone, although we did have games in hand on all the clubs below us and most of those above us, due to the long cup run. On the Saturday, I went through my usual ritual when not attending a game, tuning the radio in to LBC and listening to the match reports, biting my nails down to the elbows. Some wag at LBC, who was probably fired on the spot, said 'Things are hotting up at Valley Parade, Bradford. There's a fire in the main stand. We'll bring you more news as we get it. . .'

Bradford City were playing Lincoln City in a third division match at Valley Parade. Somehow the main stand, an ancient wooden structure, caught fire and went up like a tinder box. I switched on the TV to see the tragedy unfold live. I felt sick as I watched the flames engulf the entire stand, people wandering around like lost souls, searching for friends and relatives, some of whom would still be in there. Fifty-five people died and many more were disfigured for life, scarred both mentally and physically. The pictures remain with me today, and make my stomach lurch every time I think about it. The expression 'There but for the grace of God go I' would have been appropriate, except that when things like that happen, it is very difficult to believe that God exists. Of course, there was absolutely no reason whatsoever why I should have been at that game, but it need not necessarily have been Bradford – it could have happened anywhere, and that's what was so frightening. The minute's silence at our next home game against Stoke was impeccably observed. It touched everyone very deeply.

On the same day, a fan was killed at the Leeds v Birmingham game, and I began to think about my future with the game. It was a temporary disillusionment, but after the events at Wimbledon, and the form of the team, it called into question the whole rationale behind watching live football. Of course we beat Stoke 5–1 and all doubts were dispelled, but the fact that they had appeared in the first place showed that there was something desperately wrong with the game.

Later that evening I learned that we had lost 2–1 at Sheffield. For the first time, I really didn't care.

We beat Stoke, who were duly relegated, then Ipswich in a re-arranged fixture on the Friday before the cup final to guarantee our survival. For the first time in at least ten years, I missed the cup final, as I had to work. Frequent phone calls home told me that United had beaten Everton, and Kevin Moran had become the first player to be sent off in an FA Cup final.

Our season finished the next Monday with a 3–0 defeat at home to Liverpool, Paul Walsh getting a hat-trick, and Frank Lampard making the last of his 551 appearances for West Ham. A few weeks later, Liverpool lost the European Cup final, 1–0, to Juventus at the Heysel Stadium in Brussels. They lost so much more than that though. They lost the credibility of English clubs in Europe who said they were on top of the hooligan element, and they lost any sympathy I might have ever found for them. For some sections of the Liverpool fans to suggest that if the Italians had stood and fought instead of running away, the tragedy might not have happened, is typical of the mindless element that was rife among football attendees at that time. I won't call them fans or supporters because they were not, they were animals.

Football was in a mess, both at West Ham and nationally. Life, which only a few weeks previously had been good, was a mess too and needed sorting. Things, as they say, could only get better.

Into the Groove. . .

Birmingham City 1 West Ham United 0 – 17.8.85

Have you ever wanted something so badly, so mind crunchingly desperately, that you would gladly sacrifice everything you owned to achieve it? How do you think you would feel if it suddenly and without warning, arrived on your plate without even having to ask?

1985 was without a doubt the highest of highs and the lowest of lows. As one purely amateur novelist remarked, it was the best of times, it was the worst of times. I experienced every emotion within a four month period at the end of the year that was too much for my seventeen year old brain to cope with, so in the end, I had no option but to write about it. Unable to find anything to blame my parents for, I now pin all the blame squarely on the beautiful shoulders of Diana Hopkins. By now we were having lunch together, I was helping her decorate her flat, I was taking photographs of her little girl, while at the same time keeping quiet about it in the office. On the opening day of the season, my boss had a barbeque at his house, and we were all invited. It was a wonderful day, warm sunshine in a big garden with plenty to eat and the company of Diana and Zoe. For once I put West Ham to the back of my mind, although Chris kindly arranged for a transistor radio to be made available which brought the bad tidings from St Andrews. Diana and I fought like children over the radio; she wanted news of the fifth Test at Edgbaston, whereas I wanted the football.

In order that suspicions weren't raised, I got a lift home and arranged to be dropped a little way from my house. I got straight onto the next bus to Bromley and went to Diana's flat. I don't know if she was consoling me over the defeat at Birmingham, or if she was in a good mood after England had taken such a big lead in the Test match, or whether she just thought it was about time something more interesting happened, I don't know.

Whatever it was we played our own little game of football on the sofa. After a little bit of warming up and a kick-in, I picked up possession in the lower half, penetrated the box with consummate ease, rounded the keeper and shot low and hard into the unguarded goal. 'One – Nil!' I didn't actually shout that, but it's an interesting thought. They say you always remember your first time. I remember it particularly well, because I won that game 3–0; it was the start of a fantastic two months, when my 'goals for' column built up nicely.

Meanwhile, it has to be said, two great ambitions could have been achieved in 1985 if West Ham hadn't got off to such a bad start. The disappointment of losing Paul Allen to Spurs was tempered by the arrival of Mark Ward, who I had heard good things about, from Oldham. Lyall also paid £350,000 for a young striker called Frank McAvennie from St Mirren. Again, we were expected to struggle, and our form in the first four games gave no reason to doubt that supposition. We had played at Crystal Palace earlier in the month, a pre-season warm-up game, and McAvennie played just behind the front two, who on that occasion were Greg Campbell and Tony Cottee. We lost the game 1–2, but I could see that McAvennie looked a useful player. My friends were not convinced, as in their minds if we lost, the team were all crap. I was developing an eye for looking further than that, and could see good things even in defeat. Just as well, really.

On the first Tuesday of the season we played QPR at Upton Park. Paul Goddard had been injured at Birmingham, so Lyall put McAvennie up front with Cottee. It was the most fortunate injury ever to occur at the club. McAvennie scored twice and Dickens once as we won 3–1, and looked terrific. Ward tried to lob the QPR keeper from the half way line and almost made it. Cottee looked sharp, Dickens and Neil Orr controlled midfield and Devonshire was back and on top form. At the back, Alvin Martin and Tony Gale having had a full season together were now beginning to gel. Ray Stewart was dependable as ever at right back and Phil Parkes was a rock in goal. The only possible weak spot was at left back, where Steve Walford played the first half of the season. You always felt that if the opposition took a run at him, they would get something. When George Parris replaced him later in the season, we had our strongest team ever.

Having waxed lyrical about the strength of the team, we then contrived to lose our next two games. Luton reared their ugly heads again the next Saturday. We had a goal disallowed for no particular reason other than the fact that we were playing Luton. We pounded and pounded at the door but the buggers wouldn't let us in. Ray Stewart, suffering from concussion, mis-timed a tackle in the penalty area and that was that. Mick Harford, one of that long line of strikers to infuriate Hammers fans by refusing to play for us, scored from the spot just after half time. West Ham lay to the Luton goal, but their goalkeeper, Andy Dibble, was having one of those days where everything he touched stuck to his hands. Perhaps I had been a little forward (no offence to Tony Cottee) in my praise for the team after the QPR game; maybe the press were right and we were going to struggle. Maybe McAvennie was a flash in the pan.

I was given no reason to change my view the following Monday, August Bank Holiday when West Ham travelled to Old Trafford. Manchester United had won three out of three and were on their way to ten straight wins. We managed to keep them out until the fifty-fifth minute when Mark Hughes scored against us yet again. Gordon Strachan added a second twenty minutes later to end the match as a contest. I listened to the game from Diana's living room, acting prim and proper while little Laura was around. We had tickets for the Test match at The Oval for the next Saturday. Her husband was having Laura for the weekend so the flat would be empty when we got back, and we could make as much noise as we liked and leave the lounge door open. It was to be the perfect day with only one exception – West Ham were playing Liverpool at Upton Park, and I was going to miss it. Then again, I did say I would have done anything for her. I didn't mean it that literally.

I Got You Babe. . .

West Ham United 2 Liverpool 2 – 31.8.85

It all began innocently enough. I bought two tickets for the Saturday of The Oval Test match before the fixture list had been published, then realised to my horror that we were at home to Liverpool. Still, it was a chance to be alone with Diana, and forget about the pressures of teenagehood for a little while. I took my transistor radio though, just to be on the safe side. Diana was taking her daughter away on holiday for a week the next day, so it was also a last chance to see her before she went away. These were the excuses I used to satisfy my brain that I was doing the right thing.

The day started well, brilliant sunshine, exquisite company and excellent cricket, England forcing Australia to follow on; a rarity in itself. At about two o'clock, the rain came, and sensing that it might take a little while to clear, I suggested to Diana that we jump on the tube and go to Upton Park to watch the game. The way the rain was coming down we could have been back in time for play to resume, and there would be an extension to seven o'clock: it would be a perfect day. Diana was not keen on the idea, feeling confident that play would resume before 3.30pm and so the idea was shelved. Did I feel any resentment? Well, maybe just a bit.

The most amazing thing to happen at The Oval, apart from England forcing the follow on, was the emergence of the peanut seller. There used to be a bloke who wandered about on the North Bank and South Bank selling bags of Percy Dalton's dry roasted peanuts. To me, he seemed to be a particularly sad character, probably mid-thirties with a pair of horn rimmed glasses, I often wondered if this was his only job, or whether he did a 9–5 as well. I never had the front to ask him. He would wander about for two hours mumbling 'Peanuts' under his breath. I often envisaged him going home and hanging his coat up, his wife saying 'Did you have a good day, dear?' and he would reply 'peanuts.' Coming back to the point, he was at The Oval muttering 'peanuts' that day, which led me to believe it was his only job. He must have wandered around there for the morning, then jumped on the train to Upton Park in the afternoon. What a sensible idea.

We sat beneath our red umbrella, sheltering from the rain, and waiting for the clouds to clear. Being the attentive boyfriend, I resisted the temptation to get the transistor radio out until half time, when I innocently said 'Shall we have some music?'

'That would be nice, shall I open the wine?' Excellent.

'Oh, hang on, just let me get the score from West Ham. . .' The news came over on the crackly old radio: 'West Ham 1 Liverpool 0' I cursed inwardly, the little sods were going to beat Liverpool, and I wasn't going to be there to see it. Why? Because I'm sitting under a brolly in Kennington watching the rain come down. Frequent switching to LBC during the afternoon allowed me to find out that we were 2–1 up with ten minutes to go, then the batteries ran out.

Play resumed again at about 5.30pm, precisely the time we would have arrived back at The Oval if we had gone to Upton Park, but am I bitter? It went on until 7pm, and we actually got excellent value, and a good day's play. David Gower's team would wrap up the match and the series 3–1 the following Monday. I left The Oval convinced that West Ham had won, that England would win, and that Diana loved me. Well, one out of three isn't bad. We went straight back to Diana's flat and got down to some serious and majorly heavy duty sex. With her going away, and my going on holiday the following week, we were going to be apart for a fortnight, and therefore reasoned that we had to cram fourteen days worth into a few hours. It wasn't a problem: I had a whole twelve months' worth built up in reserve. Parting is such sweet sorrow.

The next day, already grieving at the temporary loss of my lover and mentor, I received another kick in the gonads when I bought the paper and it told me West Ham had conceded a late equaliser and had drawn the game 2–2. McAvennie got both our goals, Johnston and Whelan scoring for Liverpool. The fact that surprised me above everything else was the attendance figure, a mere 19,762. Just two years previously, 33,000 had packed Upton Park for the visit of Liverpool – the poor start to the season had cut the faithful to the core, a fact which still grates with me today. They soon came back when we started winning.

My annoyance at conceding the equaliser was complete, and I sulked for the rest of the week. Well, until Wednesday, anyway. On Wednesday things got better. I got a letter from Diana. Not a post card, a long letter. It was the first time I had experienced the uplifting euphoria of receiving a friendly, flattering letter. She wrote 'I Miss You' across the top in kisses, and told me how bored she was without me, and that she couldn't wait to come home and see me again. To cap it all, West Ham experienced the other side of the drawing coin, coming from behind to draw against Southampton at The Dell. Cottee had been dropped for the first and only time in his Upton Park career, Greg Campbell taking his place.

West Ham conceded a goal in the fifty-first minute, and Lyall threw Cottee on in Campbell's place. Campbell never played for West Ham again. McAvennie equalised ten minutes from the end and the greatest striking partnership to grace Upton Park in recent years was forged. Following the re-introduction of Cottee, the two played every game together that season up front. Indeed, Lyall only used a total of sixteen first team players throughout the season, with Phil Parkes, Tony Gale and Mark Ward playing in every game, Ray Stewart and Alvin Martin only missed games through suspension, Cottee missed just the one start, as described, against Southampton. Frank McAvennie missed one game through international duty, and Alan Dickens missed just two games. That sort of consistency of team selection is vital for any club contemplating success, and it is a level of consistency that has never been reproduced.

The following Saturday we were due to play at Sheffield Wednesday, who, despite being in second place, had lost 1–5 at home to Everton on the night we were earning a point at Southampton. I was bundled into the family car and dragged down to Greatstone for a holiday I neither wanted nor cared about. I wanted to stay at home. I wanted to see Diana. There was no overlap period between her coming home and my departure, but there was hope, as I had to travel back up to London on the Monday to enrol at college. I convinced Mum and Dad that it would be best if I stayed over at home and came back down on the Tuesday, rather than rush straight back, so naturally I slid straight over to Diana's after enrolment. It was wonderful. She showered me with gifts and forced me to have constant and unrelenting sex with her until four in the morning, when she calculated she had better get some sleep, or she would have to do some explaining to Laura. I made a reluctant exit and travelled back down to Greatstone on the Tuesday. West Ham drew again, 2–2 at Sheffield. Surely it was only a matter of time before someone got a complete tanking. An up and down game, in that we went ahead, then went behind, then equalised. McAvennie and Cottee got one each, shooting McAvennie to the top of the strikers' charts, and giving Cottee his first goal of the season.

That holiday was the longest week of my life. On the Wednesday, the Wales v Scotland World Cup qualifier was shown live on the TV; the game at which Jock Stein suffered his fatal heart attack. England drew 1–1 at Wembley in their qualifier with Romania. The violent times continued. There were riots in Handsworth, Birmingham and in Southall, West London.

Alice's Restaurant. . .

West Ham United 4 Nottingham Forest 2 – 28.9.85

L ooking back on it now, I can't believe that I actually thought it would work. Me, a seventeen year old youth with the experience and social skills of a mollusc, and Diana a thirty-two year old temptress, of incredible proportions. The expression 'heavenly body' might have been invented with her in mind – what was she doing with me? All I had in life before I met Diana was West Ham United. It was the only thing that had remained constant throughout my entire pathetic existence: pop groups came and went; even those who changed personnel couldn't go on forever. The club was there forever, and as long as I breathe it will be all that separates me from an early entry to the funny farm. Some people take their comfort from believing that there is a supreme being; a God up in a heaven which awaits us all if we lead a good life. Some take their solace in more tangible comforts like food, drink, or, at worst, drugs.

The thing that keeps me going is the thought that one day; West Ham United will win the Premiership. It sounds daft, but then so does the idea that Jesus Christ was born to a virgin mother – and there are more people believing that than there are waiting for silverware at Upton Park.

West Ham's performances in season 1985/86 saved me from an early grave, and I will never be able to repay them for that. While I was being emotionally torn apart I took great comfort from the fact that we were shooting up the first division table and looked good for a real challenge on the title. Not one of those challenges that flounders on bone hard winter pitches, or February nights wading around in mud, but a challenge right to the last game, something we could be proud of, something we could remember forever.

At this stage of the season though, September, things were still looking highly dodgy. Despite drawing against Liverpool and having the joint top marksman in the first division, we still attended each game with a mixture of fear and resignation. It wouldn't be until March and April that we confidently expected to win games.

By the time we played Leicester City at Upton Park we could justifiably have expected three points. We had beaten Leicester on their previous two visits, and their form to date had suggested this would be no exception to the trend. Frank McAvennie, Alan Devonshire and Tony Cottee duly served up the goods in a 3–0 win. I left Upton Park with the same satisfied glow that usually follows good sex. Later that evening I left Diana's flat feeling the warm tingle that usually follows a 3–0 home win.

Mum and Dad were starting to suspect. Dad never said anything. Although he never wanted to see his son hurt, I think he was secretly saying to himself, 'Good on yer son. . .' Mum was less diplomatic in her approach, and voiced her concerns at what I was getting myself into. I told her it was nothing I couldn't handle, and besides, all we ever did was listen to music, drink a little wine and play Scrabble. After our 3–0 win at Leicester, Diana fed me, watered me, put Laura to bed, put some crazy music on the tape deck – 'Alice's Restaurant' by Arlo Guthrie and got me to lie back on the bed as she produced a cigarette she said would make me feel great. What did I need cigarettes for? Just being with her was enough. I realised then what a sheltered life I had led, and that there were more things on earth to lead a man astray than one could ever experience in one lifetime. Diana said it was my duty to try as many different things as possible while I was still young. I wasn't going to disagree with her, particularly as she had her hands in a most uncompromising position.

We beat Swansea 3–0 in the first leg of the 2nd round of the Milk Cup, thanks again to the dynamic duo, plus a penalty from Ray Stewart. We now had a regular spot on the East Terrace, as everyone was convinced this was the best place from which to view the game. A better class of spectator inhabited the East Terrace, more discerning, less interested in the singing and jumping up and down, yet not wanting to pay silly money for a seat. We placed ourselves in that category. The following Saturday, I went to the Forest game accompanied only by Natty Matty. I told him about Diana; I had largely been keeping it under my hat, but I had a good relationship with Natty and I wanted to share it with him. He told me I was mad, and that it would all end in tears. What the hell did he know about it? He was only sixteen for Christ's sake.

That sunny Saturday afternoon was the first time for a while that I had been able to totally lose myself in a game; become so involved in the ebb and flow that after ninety minutes I had to come back down to earth and remember who I was. McAvennie scored two more, Cottee got one and Dickens the other as West Ham strolled into a 4–0 lead, only to let it start to slip towards the end, and Forest managed to pull two goals back. It's hard to recall the thoughts that must have been going through my head at the time; all I can remember about that afternoon is that I was so happy I could have cried. It was glorious weather, the boys won 4–2 and Diana was waiting for me to come home.

The next Saturday we got our first away win of the season, 2–1 at Newcastle. The double act struck again. I went round to Diana's uninvited for the first time on the Sunday, to see her husband's car parked outside. Through the window I could see her favourite red jumper hanging on a coat hanger from the picture rail. It was my favourite, too, and all I could think of was the way that jumper accentuated her bust; then I thought about her husband. He'd probably come to see Laura, I guessed, but I thought about it all the way home until I'd convinced myself they were having an illicit afternoon liaison. How dare she! How dare he! Anyone would think they were married. I confronted her with it over lunch on Wednesday, and she pulled the plug out of my little bath of a world. She was going back to him, for Laura's sake. She hadn't meant to drop it on me so quickly, but I had asked. . .

To say that this was a shock is like saying Arsenal have played the offside trap a few times. It's the understatement of the century. I left her with her frothy coffee, and mine too, and went to the park to think about what she had just said. I couldn't believe it. Mum was right. My sister was right. Even Natty Matty was right. How could I have been so stupid? How could I have believed we had any sort of future together? If I'm honest I would say that I never saw us as the settling kind, but I didn't expect it to end quite so soon. I took the afternoon off sick and took a train to Swansea. It was the first time I had ever been to a match on my own before, and it was a strange experience. I'd had plenty of time to go through things in my head while I was on the train and felt totally alone. However, once I stepped off the train, and mingled with the other Hammers fans who had made the trip, I began to feel better, and felt comfortable – as though I belonged there. The fact that West Ham won the match 3–2 was immaterial. It helped me to forget, just for ninety minutes.

I had some explaining to do when I got home, Mum assumed I'd been at that wicked old woman's house, but when I told her I wouldn't be seeing Diana again, she shut up. Partly, this was due to the fact that she was finally happy – Mum had got her own way. It was also partly due to the fact that she could see that I was genuinely cut up about something for the first time in my life. I'd been too young to mourn lost grandparents. We didn't have a family dog or cat to fall ill or get squashed by a train to shed a tear for. Even John Lennon's death was a mere flesh wound compared to this. The only time I had ever appeared emotionally unstable in front of my parents was when I had to admit to being the one who had shoved the Teddy Bear comics down the toilet. She left me to grieve alone.

Usually when a couple split up, they rarely see each other again. I saw Diana every day at work, and it got harder and harder to cope with. She asked me to come round for a chat a few days after she had delivered the bombshell, and we had one for the road. Not a good idea. Although we parted on good terms, I've never fully understood what was going through her pretty little mind. I contacted Zoe and she agreed to meet me to help me out and talk to me; but not just for a while. We all needed time to sort our lives out.

Andy at college took it upon himself to help me out. While supping supremely sticky hot chocolate in the college refectory one Wednesday, talk of life, love and football made it very difficult for us to contemplate staying on the extra hour in order to attend a lecture on Public Administration. England were playing Turkey at

Wembley. 'Why don't we knock PA on the head and go to the game?' Andy said.

I did not feel inclined to disagree. 'Fuck it – let's go.' The journey from South London to North is remarkably easy, and we were at Wembley in good time for the game. England had won 8–0 against Turkey in Istanbul, and were top of their qualifying group. A win against Turkey and a draw against Northern Ireland in November would see us going to Mexico. Alvin was in the squad that night, but didn't get a game. Lineker scored a hat-trick, Bryan Robson (not 'Pop,' the crap one who played for Manchester United a few times) and Chris Waddle scored the other goals in a 5–0 win. It's perverse, but we were disappointed with that. Having won 8–0 away, we were expecting double figures. How things change. These days we are grateful for anything against the Turks, their game has improved at the same rate that ours has declined. A 5–0 victory was still not enough to raise the spirits above the horizon.

At least one thing remained. West Ham United slaughtered Aston Villa 4–1. Who got two each? You guessed it. God, I love you West Ham.

A Good Heart. . .

West Ham United 2 Watford 1 – 16.11.85

By the time we played Watford at Upton Park on the 16th November, we were in the middle of an unbeaten league run that had begun with the 2–2 draw against Liverpool on the 31st August, and wouldn't end until Boxing Day – a total of eighteen games. After the 3–2 win at Swansea, we had drawn at home to Arsenal 0–0 in an 11.30am kick off game. I always hated morning kick offs, but welcomed it in this instance as it meant I was able to see the game, whereas a 3.00pm start would have prohibited me – cousin Andy's wedding. I must have been unbearable to live with at that time. I just sulked around feeling sorry for myself. The only time my conversation perked up was if someone mentioned football. We then slammed four passed Aston Villa, and won at Portman Road through a Cottee strike, before having to make the inevitable cup exit at Old Trafford. It was a measure of the way we had progressed that we only lost 1–0, but Mark Ward had a goal disallowed. West Ham had been awarded a free kick about thirty yards from goal, when Frank McAvennie had been pulled down. Ward slammed the free kick into the net, but the ref disallowed it, as he said the free kick was indirect. I had always been led to believe that a tripping offence was punishable by a direct free kick, as did everyone else on the pitch, except the referee. We even claimed that Gary Bailey, the United 'keeper, had got a touch to it before it went into the net, thus providing the second touch, but the ref was red, and he was adamant.

The next game saw us beat the champions, Everton, at Upton Park. Trevor Steven put Everton in front mid way through the second half, but two goals from McAvennie turned the match in our favour ten minutes from the end. There was a wonderful photograph on the back page of the *News of the World* the next day, Frankie punching the air with delight as he wheeled away after scoring the winner. The photograph expressed so much emotion that I had it blown up to A2 size and put on my bedroom wall, to remind me how good life could be. Silly, really.

I missed the trip to Oxford, because an elderly relative was visiting, and Mum said it would be best if I stayed in to see her, as I might not get another chance. (That was the gist of it, anyway.) As it turned out, it was the last time I saw her. She sensed right away there was something wrong. 'What is it?' she asked me. 'It's a girl, isn't it?' I looked up, surprised at my great aunt's intuition. 'Don't worry about her,' she added. 'She's probably not worth it.' At the time, I just laughed, thinking 'But you don't know her!' But they were the truest and wisest words of advice ever offered to me. It is true to say that you never appreciate good advice until you have been through a lot of pain.

The next game was against Watford and offered me another signpost in my meandering life. The game was won by goals from Frank McAvennie and Mark Ward, the latter being a free kick which just squirmed its way under Tony Coton's body. We got an excellent view of it from the East Terrace. Worrell Stirling replied for Watford, but it was never going to be enough. There was an interesting letter in the programme from a young Nottingham Forest and Notts County supporter by the name of Christina, who was asking for pen-pals. I'd had some pen pals since the age of about eight, but they had all petered out over a period. I remember thinking at the time it was worth dropping her a line as if nothing else, it would provide me with some interesting mail.

I wrote her a letter and told her what it was like being a West Ham fan and living in London, and all the other things I thought she might be interested to hear. I got a lovely letter back from her. Like me, she was seventeen, just two days younger, in fact. She was unemployed, but used to work in the John Player cigarette factory in Nottingham before being made redundant. Her letter was bright, bubbly and without a doubt the most exciting thing that had happened for a long, long, time. That will give you an idea of just how boring life was PD

(Post Diana). Christina said she had received a number of letters, but chose mine because it was long, detailed and witty. Obviously a girl of good taste. She had sent me a photo, and was pretty, too. It was something to keep looking forward to, a mutual appreciation society, I would write saying how wonderful her last letter was, how neat her handwriting was, how exciting her life must be, how good Nottingham Forest were. She would write back and say exactly the same things, flatter my ego and make me feel wanted again.

By writing, I could be someone who I wanted to be, not the person I actually was. While I never told blatant lies in my letters, I could cover up certain things and expand on others. To use a famous phrase, I could be economical with the truth. I kept her letters in a shoe box and it was full by Christmas. We wrote profusely and always by return; a love affair by post, and one for which you never had to look your best or say you were sorry. You never had to worry about saying the wrong thing because you always had to chance to write it down and make sure it sounded right. It also meant never getting jealous or uptight. For me, it was the best way to conduct a love affair after my experience with Diana. I could cope with this. Sanity was just around the corner, but not before a quick and violent shock to the system.

Only the Good Die Young. . .

West Ham United 4 West Bromwich Albion 0 – 30.11.85

West Ham paid the price for their success, losing Frank McAvennie for the game against West Bromwich Albion due to international duty in Australia. He had already scored in the 2–0 win at Hampden Park and followed it up by helping to secure a 0–0 draw that gave Scotland victory and a place in the Mexico World Cup finals.

The game against West Brom was played on a dark, foggy November afternoon. George Parris came in for Frank and scored with the help of a deflection. Cottee, Devonshire and Neil Orr scored the other goals in a 4–0 win. It was about this time that we realised we were actually in with a shout. Unbeaten since the end of August, and six successive wins, including four away from home. This team was going places. I watched the game from the East Terrace with Barney and Natty Matty. Was I going to the game at QPR next week? You bet your life.

Kate, the bubbly secretary, phoned me at home on Sunday. I had been trying to find a decent second hand computer for her and her kids to learn programming on and thought she was probably phoning about that, but her voice was unusually cold and calm. 'Are you sitting down?' she asked. This wasn't like Kate; all sorts of thoughts ran through my head as I sat down on the stairs and propped the phone under my chin.

'You know Zoe, Diana's sister?' Yes, of course I knew Zoe: what a girl! As a younger version of Diana, she couldn't fail to be wonderful.

'Yes, of course.'

'She's dead.'

Subtlety wasn't Kate's strong point, so I should have expected her to be blunt, but not about something like this. Zoe rented a flat with a friend in Rochester. The flat had a faulty gas flue, and Zoe died in her sleep from inhaling the noxious fumes, while her friend lay in a coma, hanging between life and death for three days before they eventually turned off the machine. As Diana was Zoe's nearest relative, her parents living in Spain, the police came to see her first to break the news, and naturally, she took it very badly. Me? I took for a long walk, and went to see my sister. Her next door neighbour nipped over to the pub and bought me a large brandy. I just couldn't believe that only a few short weeks ago we had gone to see her in an amateur dramatics production of Oklahoma! Two weeks ago I had spoken with her on the phone and she was so full of life; she had so much to look forward to. Now, she was dead, and I would never see her again. It's true that in death, the living only grieve because they will never see their friend again. It is not that they feel sorrow – the dead must move on to something infinitely better than we have here; a world where there is no death, disease or 4–0 home defeats. Billy Joel was right, only the good die young. I fully expect to see my eightieth birthday.

Apart from the loss of Zoe, I was selfishly annoyed that I had been given the news by Kate, when Diana must have known how I felt about both of them. Looking back now, I know the last thing Diana would have wanted to do was phone all her friends, especially me, and tell them. I wanted to go and see her to comfort her. I went that afternoon to find that her husband had beaten me to it. It seemed he'd got his foot in the door and this was just the thing he needed to allow him to stay. A mixture of bitterness, anger, jealousy, love and hate bubbled under the surface. I rang Dobbo and we went out on the Monday night and got slaughtered. We talked football all night, the upshot of the conversation being that we were in with a good chance of winning the title this season. I told Dobbo he ought to come along more often, to witness it, and he agreed to come to Loftus Road for the game against QPR. Christina sent me a letter with a drawing on the back of the envelope, one of QPR's net with half a dozen footballs in it, and one with Sheffield Wednesday's net with a similar number lodged in the back. Unfortunately for Christina, Sheffield Wednesday won 2–1 against Forest, but she was correct about our game.

McAvennie stepped off the plane from Australia and played in the game while he must have still been jet lagged. It didn't stop him scoring the winner in a 1–0 victory. That was our fifth successive away win, a club record. Natty Matty, dressed up to the nines again, ripped his brand new leather jacket on a wire mesh fence as we celebrated the goal in the paddock at QPR. I thought he was stupid for wearing such expensive clothes to a football match, but he had the last laugh when QPR's insurance policy coughed up £200.

Now it was getting silly. West Ham were third in the table after twenty games, five points behind leaders Manchester United and three behind second placed Liverpool. On balance, at the same stage of the season in 1983–84 we were better placed, the difference this time being everyone believed we could sustain it and get a place in Europe at the very least. (If a place in Europe had been available, of course, thank you Liverpool.) There was an FA Cup campaign and easy pickings against Luton, Birmingham and Southampton to come. I couldn't help but salivate as I read the Sunday papers, particularly as we had drawn second division Charlton away in the third round of the cup, a game the BBC deemed interesting enough to show live on network television.

The day we beat Birmingham I got my first car. It was a metallic pale blue Ford Escort Mark II, the type with square headlamps. It was a T reg and in immaculate condition, or so my next door neighbour, a second hand car salesman, told me. Actually, he was right. He probably knew that selling me a duff one would not be a good move, as I was literally on his doorstep. I was still taking lessons, but my dad and brother-in-law took me out most Sunday mornings. I couldn't wait to pass my test and get rid of those horrible 'L' plates, how humiliating they were. In the meantime, I continued to get the bus and the train. The game against Birmingham should have been won by a much bigger margin than 2–0. Frank McAvennie inevitably scored, with Ray Stewart thumping in a penalty before half time to make it two. Birmingham were all over the place, and were doomed for relegation, having only just been promoted. They were up and down like a bog seat in an Indian restaurant. That being the case, it hurt very much that they had beaten us on the opening day of the season. In fact, we were starting to see that our opening four games could prove very costly indeed.

Tony Gale was beginning to look like a class defender. We already knew about Alvin, but Gale now, if anything, seemed to have a little bit more. He could pick up the ball on the edge of our own box and send onrushing attackers the wrong way with just a gentle shimmy. The whole team was functioning well, with the possible exceptions of Steve Walford, who I have already mentioned and Neil Orr, who seemed comfortable enough in midfield, but when he dropped back into defence we all held our breath. Neil was a nice bloke, the first player I ever met face to face, and he happily signed an autograph. I didn't tell him that I was always happier when Geoff Pike was in the side, but then, I've never been like that. We sold Neil on to Hibernian in 1987.

A chance for revenge against Luton Town came on December 21st. I hated Luton so much after they stole the points in August that I wasn't prepared to pay money into their coffers to go and watch the game. It would be just typical if Luton halted our run of away wins, and I didn't want to see it. As it happened, we didn't lose, but could only manage a 0-0, which effectively ended the run anyway. Luton had installed a plastic pitch, which wasn't like the one at QPR. The pitch at QPR played quite well, and didn't provide an unfair advantage for the home team. Indeed, they lost as many as they won on it, but Luton's pitch was so springy, you only had to fart and the ball went miles. Another good reason to hate Luton. It ended a run of nine straight wins, but we were still eighteen without defeat.

The run came to an end when Spurs finally managed to beat us. It was Boxing Day 1985, and we wouldn't win again on Boxing Day until 1990, our last victory having been against Swansea City in 1982. While we're on statistics like that, we wouldn't win at White Hart Lane again until 1994. Steve Perryman scored for Spurs and we lost 1-0. It hardly seemed to matter though, as we had two home games to repair the damage, against Southampton and Chelsea. It was these two games, along with the poor start, that ruined our championship hopes. Both were postponed due to bad weather, the New Year's Day fixture against Chelsea hit us particularly hard. We got to Upton Park having heard only a rumour at London Bridge, but had it confirmed half way down Green Street. We were on the best run of results for years, and if we'd had the chance to play Chelsea on New Year's Day we would have won. As it happened, we had to play them in mid April in the middle of the biggest pile up of fixtures since... er... the previous season. There wasn't to be another game at Upton Park until January 25th, and not another League fixture until February 2nd. I am convinced that if West Ham had the foresight to install undersoil heating, we would have won the Championship in 1986. Did they learn? Did they do it immediately after seeing the effect it had had on the team?

What do you think?

The Sun Always Shines on TV. . .

West Ham United 2 Manchester United 1 – 2.2.86

For the third season running, our home match against Manchester United was selected for live TV broadcast. At last our impressive form was being noticed by the national media, and after the two postponements over the holiday period, we took on Charlton Athletic at their temporary home, Selhurst Park. It was a dour game, a real struggle, but we won it a few minutes from the end, when McAvennie lobbed the keeper from the edge of the box. The ball appeared to be going in anyway, but Tony Cottee made sure from about six inches out. My boss said: 'I see that young lad who looks a bit like you scored yesterday.' Cheers Chris, I always did like you.

The pundits all said that West Ham now had a bit of steel in their side to add to the artistry. We took no notice – the pundits had been saying that every year, and still we would flounder because of a lack of strength in depth or bite in the tackle. We travelled to Anfield for the first time in years expecting to get a result. We got a result. A 3–1 defeat. It need not have been like that. We were holding out well and were only 1–0 down when Ray Stewart lost his head and got sent off. Liverpool capitalised on our misfortune and scored two quick goals before Alan Dickens pulled one back. Had 'Tonka' stayed, we might have been able to scrape a draw. McAvennie scored at Leicester, and we won there for the first time in several millennia. Despite the defeat at Anfield, the challenge was still looking good. Although we were down to fifth place, seven points behind United, we had a game in hand on them and still had to play them at Upton Park. We also had two games in hand on both Everton and Liverpool, who were only five points ahead anyway. Win both games in hand and beat United and we were laughing.

Chelsea had crept ominously into fourth place, largely on the back of a superb home record, winning eleven and losing just one of their twelve games. They were also five points ahead, but had played the same number of games and constituted a real threat.

We turned our attention to the FA Cup again, and a home tie with Ipswich Town. The match ended 0–0 on a bitterly cold afternoon. Both sides had their chances to win it, but West Ham were the more disappointed at the end. Manchester United came the following Sunday, a match we had awaited with eager anticipation. Christina had sent her best wishes for the game, and we had arranged to meet. West Ham were due to play Manchester City on the 21st February, so I invited Christina down for the weekend to take in the game. With that to look forward to, we took up our position on the East Terrace to watch one of the great games. We struggled in the first half, and looked very ragged. Devonshire went off for ten minutes to have stitches put in a head wound, and it looked as though United would trounce us. Bryan Robson burst through to lob Phil Parkes just before half time and we began to fear the worst. At least the gang with the banner managed a longer TV appearance than they had two seasons earlier. Mark Ward tried to take Kevin Moran's legs off just in front of us. Moran slid helplessly into the advertising hoarding and lay still for a couple of minutes, we thought, feigning injury. He had, in fact, dislocated a finger, and the camera was on us for a few minutes while he received attention. The usual 'Hello mums' followed.

The second half was a different story. Mark Ward hit a tremendous shot to pull us level, and a few minutes later, Tony Cottee picked up a loose ball and we were in front, a lead we held on to. That kept the championship wide open, as we were now only eight points behind but with four games in hand over United, who despite their express train start to the season, had just lost pole position to Everton. We left the game satisfied that we had done a good job of work, and that it was only a matter of time before we reached the top. The most worrying aspect, was that we were running out of time in which to cram in these four games in hand, and there was more bad weather forecast.

The next day, the draw for the fifth round of the FA Cup paired us with guess who? Manchester United. Of course, we still had to get past Ipswich, but we felt our incentive was greater than theirs. We would be at home, and with United out of the way, had a great chance of getting to Wembley. Liverpool and Everton were still in, but as long as we could avoid them, we were in with a shout. The replay against Ipswich was at Portman Road on Tuesday 4th February. The match went into extra time, and Jason Dozzell scored for Ipswich. I listened intently on the radio, sure that something would happen; someone would save our skins. It was Tony Cottee again. If 1985 had been McAvennie's year, 1986 belonged to Tony Cottee. He hit the equaliser home and looked so pleased with his effort, you would have thought he had won the cup itself. A second replay was necessary. West Ham lost the toss for venue, which I thought very unfair – why shouldn't it be played back at Upton Park, or on neutral ground? The argument is no longer valid of course, as cup tie replays are now settled on penalty kicks. The second replay was on the Thursday, and since the end of the first game, the pitch had been covered by a blanket of snow. The players all coped very well with it, and for the first time we appeared to be in control, knocking the orange ball around with ease. It was freezing out there. I had made the trip on the train and had nearly frozen my knackers off walking to the ground from Ipswich Station, which is really no distance at all. The away end was thankfully packed with nice warm bodies, which warmed up even more when Cottee slammed home the winner in the second period of extra time. We praised the lord, thankful that we did not have to add another game to the already tight schedule. Then the snow came again.

The weather ruined everything. We had to postpone our fifth round tie against Manchester United, and, to add to the two Christmas games we missed, we also had to add away fixtures at Aston Villa and Nottingham Forest, and home matches against Ipswich, Manchester City and Newcastle United. It meant life was going to be pretty hectic through March, April and May. It also meant that when Christina came down for her visit, we didn't have a game to see. Everything was off, even QPR, with their plastic pitch, couldn't provide us with a game, as they were due to play away. She came down on the Friday night, one day after I passed my driving test. It was fortunate that I had done, otherwise we would really have been kicking our heels. I took the somewhat risky move of driving to Upton Park in order that she could at least take a look around and buy something in the club shop. Driving through the Blackwall Tunnel twenty-four hours after passing your test is not my idea of heaven. The weekend wasn't a total disaster, but it wasn't far off. She went home on the Sunday, with both of us none the wiser about each other, but the letters continued to flow on a regular basis. She had been somewhat frightened, I think, by the fact that my entire family turned up for dinner on Saturday, to come and see the new exhibit. Not a pretty sight. It is often a huge disappointment to meet someone in the flesh after you have only had photographs and your own imagination to work from. In this case, Christina was more disappointed than I was, but we were both very young, and I'm sure that if we met again today we would have more to say to each other. There were long embarrassing silences which belied the fact we could often write three or four sides of A4 to each other. Weird.

The freeze-up meant that we went virtually a month without a game. The second Ipswich replay was on the 6th February. We played Manchester United at Upton Park on the 5th March. I feared that four weeks rest might have taken the edge off the players' appetite, but I was proved wrong. Frank McAvennie scored another one after Cottee had wriggled his way to the byline. We should have sewn the match up there and then, but the lay-off had obviously taken a little bit of an edge off the finishing. Frank Stapleton equalised for United, and we had to travel to Old Trafford for the fifth time in two seasons. Although United were not playing as well as they had done at the start of the season, they were still a force to be reckoned with at Old Trafford. Dobbo and Stain Tooth came round to my house to watch the game, which again had been snaffled by the live cameras. We weren't complaining in this instance. It gave us a chance to see the game we would not ordinarily have had. And what a game it was! Geoff Pike scored with a header from the edge of the box; that's how unusual a game it was – for anyone to score with a header from eighteen yards is unusual, but Pikey? We played as though our lives depended on it, and wrapped up the win in the second half with a Ray

Stewart penalty. We danced on the sofa. Three days later though, we had to play Sheffield Wednesday in the quarter final at Hillsborough. We all thought this was a bit much, coming so soon after the strength sapping fifth round replay at Old Trafford. Sheffield Wednesday scored twice in the first half and we were dead and buried. Cottee pulled one back, but it was always going to be one game too many. The weather had cost us a semi-final against Everton and possible cup final appearance against Liverpool. I'm prepared to stand by that statement, as I believe that given another few days to recover, we would have at least earned a replay at Hillsborough.

It had a detrimental effect on confidence, too. We lost at Arsenal, who weren't exactly setting the world on fire with their football in 1985–86. I seemed to be the only person inside Highbury who thought Tony Woodcock controlled the ball with his hand before shooting past Parkes for the only goal of the game. We should have won – McAvennie had enough chances – but we just couldn't find a way through. No team did the double over us that season, but the three who we only got one point from were Arsenal, Liverpool and can you guess who else, children? Yes, that's right, Luton Town. Yet another good reason to hate Luton. The following Wednesday, we played Aston Villa at Villa Park. Villa were another side who were pretty useless and who on another day we would have sent packing; indeed, they were relegated the next season, but we lost again, 2–1, and Villa even had to score our goal for us. It was not looking good, when Sheffield Wednesday came to town. Somehow, we managed to beat Wednesday 1–0 with a Frank McAvennie goal, but I was far from convinced. We seemed to have lost the goal scoring knack. We would have to improve a great deal if we were to get anything from the top of the table showdown with Chelsea at Stamford Bridge.

Living Doll. . .

Chelsea 0 West Ham United 4 – 29.3.86

I was ill again. Headaches that wouldn't go away with mere aspirin; headaches that would lay me out for days, and yet couldn't be classified as migraines. There was no sickness, just an incredible pain between my eyes. I did not connect it with the incident on Wimbledon Station; that was over a year ago, and had been more or less forgotten, but I still felt a little twinge every time someone mentioned Chelsea.

For that reason, I ignored the agony and went to Stamford Bridge to watch the game against Chelsea. Our poor run meant that we had slipped to seventh place, twelve points behind Everton, but still with four games in hand. The mathematics were staggeringly simple. If we won our games in hand, we would be at the top of the pile. Chelsea had lost some of their dominance at home, by now they had played sixteen, won twelve, drawn two and lost two, still a pretty good record. We took our position on the open terrace and immediately began to play a game of 'spot the blade of grass.' Chelsea's pitch looked like a World War One battlefield, only with more mud. When the teams came out and began to play, it looked even more like a battlefield. It was a high tension match. Chelsea were fourth, we were seventh. It was a match neither team could afford to lose. The ITV cameras were there, but not for a live transmission, a decision they no doubt regret.

The early exchanges were even; Chelsea had just won at Southampton and were putting some good results together, but the pitch at Stamford Bridge proved to be their undoing. West Ham are not noted for their ability to play on muddy surfaces, they usually like billiard table smooth early season pitches, hence the 'Christmas Decorations' label, but we adapted far better than Chelsea on the day. Alan Devonshire curled in a brilliant goal in the first half, which made my head throb. Geoff Pike nearly repeated it a few moments later, but was inches away. This was the best Hammers team. Parris in for Walford and Pike in for Orr. Good players in every position, working for each other, running for each other. Alvin Martin missed the game through suspension, and Paul 'Diego' Hilton came in and performed well. He even got a header in on goal in the first half which tested the Chelsea keeper. In the second half, Chelsea threw everything at us but the proverbial kitchen sink. Speedie got up well, but couldn't divert his temper into a goal. Kevin McAlister came on and played the game of his life, but still didn't score. Ray Stewart hit a great shot which their keeper tipped around for a corner. As he did so he fell awkwardly and hit his head on the post. I knew how he must have been feeling, and my headache grew and grew.

Then it happened. Parris and Dickens exchanged passes on the edge of the Chelsea box. George scampered through the mud on the left and crossed for Cottee to score. At 2–0 we knew we were safe, and that Chelsea's confidence would be so badly dented they wouldn't even get one, let alone the three they needed for victory. The team must have sensed this also, as they marauded forward at every opportunity. Cottee added a third, the Chelsea defenders claiming off-side with pathetic arms in the air. Cottee tried to add a fourth, but his shot was sliced and fell perfectly for McAvennie. We were in ecstasy. I can't remember an away game in which we played better, or looked more convincing, except perhaps for the 5–1 win at Bristol City in 1992. Certainly this was the best away performance I had the privilege to witness in the top flight. It put us all back on top of the world, and made us sure that we could do it.

The following Monday, we played another local derby against Spurs at Upton Park. We wanted revenge for our defeat at White Hart Lane, which had ended our unbeaten run of eighteen games. Like a player with a tweaked hamstring, it was touch and go right up until the last minute whether I would make it. I had a late fitness test and decided to go. The others had already left to make sure of a good position in the Chicken Run. By the time I arrived, the turnstiles to the Chicken Run were closed and all that remained were obstructed view seats in the East Stand. I took one, as it had to be better than nothing, and spent the entire game standing up on my seat, peering over a metal girder. How the club had the cheek to charge me £6.00 for the seat is beyond belief. I would have got a better view standing on the heaving North Bank. What I could see was good. Cottee latched on to a through ball and hit a shot through Ray Clemence. Ardiles equalised, but it was a short lived revival. McAvennie struck again to finish the scoring for the entire match. The second half should have yielded more goals. McAvennie lobbed Clemence and the ball hit the bar. Ward hit a drive which if Clemence had touched, would have taken his fingers with it. We dominated totally, a fact that a 2–1 scoreline does not reflect.

By this stage, McAvennie had scored twenty-one first division goals, and Tony Cottee eleven. Only Gary Lineker and Graeme Sharp of Everton had a more prolific strike rate. What was worrying though was the fact that only Cottee and McAvennie were scoring. Devonshire, Ward, Dickens and Pike only had a handful between them, although Ray Stewart weighed in with 10 from the penalty spot by the time the season finished. If one or both of the dynamic duo dried up, what would happen then?

With the winter backlog, West Ham were now playing at least two and sometimes three games in a week to catch up. On the 2nd April we played Nottingham Forest in a re-arranged fixture at the City Ground. Christina had been waiting for the game with eager anticipation, waiting to extract revenge for the 4–2 defeat at Upton Park in September. I was confident we would get at least a draw, but I hadn't reckoned on Johnny Metgod. Metgod struck a free kick the like of which I had never seen before, or since. Certainly Phil Parkes didn't see it, as like a V-2 rocket it flew past him and only made a noise after it had already hit the net. Cottee managed an equaliser in the second half, and the point I was expecting looked as though it was safe, but then Brian Rice popped up with a winner a few minutes from time. I was desperately disappointed. We had to win our games in hand to stand any sort of chance, and it would obviously have been a good start to win at Forest. If we couldn't win, then a draw would have been acceptable, but defeat was hard to bear. It was another case of too many games in too few days. It was also our eighth league defeat of the season, and I had read in the paper that morning that no English side had won the league title in the last twenty years with more than eight defeats. There was no margin for error. We had to go for it.

We were, at least, granted a blank Saturday, as we had been due to play Everton at Goodison Park, and they were involved in the FA Cup semi-final against Sheffield Wednesday. Somehow though, we still managed to cram nine games into the thirty day month of April.

As I stood on the East Terrace with Barney and Stain Tooth before the re-arranged game against Southampton, I remember watching our players as they were warming up. Surely they were not going to win the league? I looked at Alan Dickens in particular, and tried to place him in the same bracket as one of the Liverpool midfield players, Molby, Johnston, Wark and Whelan. It couldn't be done. I tried Everton: Reid, Bracewell, Steven and Sheedy. Dickens always looked so pale and thin, how could he be part of a midfield quartet that was going to rule the universe? It was a testament to the way that the team functioned as a unit that year, because players that were not individually as talented as their counterparts on Merseyside, kept their challenge going right to the end. Our strikers were clearly world class, the defence held out well, conceding fewer goals than all the teams above us with the exception of Manchester United, who had conceded one less. Even so, we had the best defensive record away from home in the league. That left the midfield. A touch more creativity and, to quote Kenneth Wolstenhome, we would have 'Won The League, The FA Cup, The Grand National and The Boat Race. . . '

The strikers did dry up against Southampton. Fortunately, Alvin Martin popped up from the back to score his first goal of the season, which was enough to win the game. Four days later, we played Oxford United. The strikers continued to be one step off the pace. Ray Houghton put Oxford 1–0 up and we were struggling again. It took an own goal from Oxford's John Trewick to give us the required kick up the backside. We were even gifted a doubtful penalty, and Ray Stewart unbelievably screwed it wide. There is a first time for everything; this was neither the time nor the place for Stewart to miss his first penalty in my presence. By the seventieth minute, I was biting my nails down to my armpits. Frankie came up trumps with a brilliant piece of skill to carry the ball past Alan Judge in the Oxford goal. The burden lifted, we began to play gain, and were awarded another penalty, which Stewart duly converted. It was 3–1, and again the score didn't reflect the game. Just as our 2–1 win over Tottenham was harsh, a 3–1 win over Oxford was flattering.

On the Tuesday we entertained Chelsea, in the match re-scheduled from New Year's Day. Having already won by such a big margin at Stamford Bridge we were supremely confident, but not so much that we took the game lightly. As the game kicked off, Natty Matty, Barney, Stain Tooth and I were still struggling to get into the North Bank, the gates for the East Terrace having been long closed, and all seats being sold out days before the game. We managed to force our way towards the goal, but even so, could only see three quarters of the pitch. We were directly beneath that part of the North Bank that used to jut out by the snack bar, and one guy was laying face down, his head lolling from side to side, looking as though he was about to puke. We kept one eye on the game, and one eye on him, wishing we had brought an umbrella.

It was 0–0 at half time, the whistle going just as we got to our place. In the second half, Cottee scored and we looked to be in control. Well, I'm told we looked in control, I really could see very little. I could see Chelsea attacking. Unfortunately. I very rarely like to pin blame on an individual for a defeat, but in this instance, it was obvious that one man held the key to Chelsea's revival. Tony Gale had to go off with a hamstring tweak. Neil Orr was on the bench, and I winced when I saw that he was coming on as a direct replacement. As a centre back he made an excellent window cleaner. As Colin Benson said on the match video: 'Orr slipped and allowed Spackman to pick his spot. . . ' Quite what Spackman was doing picking his spots in the middle of a football match I don't know; whatever happened, he skated past Orr and slipped in the equaliser. Chelsea suddenly smelled blood and within minutes were 2–1 up, Orr failing to clear and allowing the tiny Pat Nevin to *head* the winner.

That was it. Looking back, we never stood a chance after that night. Chelsea had even slimmer hopes than us of the title, and had already spiked Manchester United's chances by winning at Old Trafford. It was as though they were saying 'Right, if we can't win it, then you bloody well won't either!' Our only hope was that they still had to play Liverpool. If they played with the same conviction against Liverpool, we might still have a chance. That same night, Everton won 2–0 at Watford. We did exactly the same thing on the Saturday, Cottee and McAvennie back on the scoring trail just in time for the final countdown.

Spirit in the Sky. . .

West Ham United 8 Newcastle United 1 – 21.4.86

Newcastle didn't actually have a bad side. They were mid table and trundling along quite nicely when they came to Upton Park. I left work at the usual time with Sue Miller, with whom I shared an office. I remember telling her that if we won by five goals, we would go into second place, but I doubted very much whether we would. She was obviously riveted by my conversation. Sue was a good laugh. I offered her a lift home the day I passed my driving test, and when I met her in reception she was wearing a skateboard helmet and elbow pads. 'Ready when you are!' she said. Cheeky cow.

I went with Stain Tooth, and we took seats in the East Stand. The place was packed, there were people milling around in the stand who didn't have tickets but had got in somehow. They were sitting in the aisles and blocking up the exits. Fortunately, no-one wanted to leave early. Alvin Martin opened the scoring with a close range shot after just a few minutes. The Newcastle goalkeeper was suffering from an injury, and for once we showed a ruthless streak and put the pressure on him right from the start. Ray Stewart got a second with a cross cum shot that squirmed under the 'keeper. Glenn Roeder backheeled a fourth into his own goal, after Neil Orr sent a speculative shot into the top corner to put us 3–0 up. Like the Bury game a few years before, we half expected the team to sit back and consolidate. Like the Bury match, they didn't. Like the Bury match they doubled the half time score. Martin Thomas, the Newcastle goalkeeper, went off at half time, finally succumbing to his injuries. Chris Headworth had a go, and within a few minutes of the re-start was picking the ball out of the net as Alvin got his second with a header that a competent and fully fit goalkeeper would probably have saved.

Newcastle pulled one back and their fans went absolutely bonkers. They were brilliant. Even though they were on the wrong end of a pasting they kept their voices heard. Paul Goddard came on as a substitute and scored the sixth with virtually his first touch, a far post header. Frank McAvennie added a seventh with a near post header. By now, Peter Beardsley had taken over in goal. He didn't have much luck either. The Newcastle defence obliged by providing a penalty kick, which, being 7–1 up and with Alvin on a hat-trick, he took and converted. 8–1, and Alvin Martin remains to this day the only player to score a hat-trick against three different goalkeepers in the same game. (© Sad But True Facts 1994.) Another parallel can be drawn to the Bury match. On that night, Dave Swindlehurst failed to score. In the Newcastle game, Tony Cottee was totally off target. I shudder to think what the score might have been if he had been on form. He had enough shots – if he hadn't been so selfish, we might have gone into double figures again.

There was yet another comparison to be drawn to the Bury match. The game that followed promised much but delivered little. Coventry City were struggling against relegation and looked to be easy meat after the crushing of Newcastle. The win against Newcastle put another 3,000 on the gate, and Coventry put up stubborn resistance, determined not to go the same way. Mark Ward tore the Coventry full back, Greg Downs, apart and it was only a matter of time before the breakthrough came. It came in the second half, Tony Cottee swivelling to knock in a loose ball. Without having time to draw breath, we faced the eighth game of the month two days later, the match I had been due to watch with Christina, the home game against Manchester City. Stain Tooth drove in his disgusting blue Allegro Estate with go faster stripes and a wicked long aerial. We got to the ground half an hour before kick off to find all gates locked and admission by ticket only. Having come this far, we wanted to see the game, and approached two smelly touts with greasy fingers; or were they greasy touts with smelly fingers? Whoever they were, it was not something I am proud of. He sold us two seats in the West Stand Upper Tier for £13.00 each. That might not sound much, but their face value was £6.00. The game finished in another 1–0 win, a Ray Stewart penalty deciding matters.

The team were obviously very tired. They had all played on Saturday, and were all due to play again on Wednesday, when Ipswich came to Upton Park, for yet another re-arranged fixture.

We made sure we got there early enough for this one, and joined the party on the North Bank. It was the last home game of the season and we intended to make the most of it. It seemed that the effects of playing so many games was taking its toll. Despite a huge crowd being behind them, they huffed and puffed without making much progress, and Ipswich went ahead. Ipswich needed the points just as badly as we did, to avoid the drop, but eventually, the urgency of the crowd and the reluctance to let all the hard work go to waste paid off. Alan Dickens lobbed Paul Cooper from the edge of the area, then Mark Ward won a penalty when he was upended in the area. Ray Stewart must have been the calmest man in the ground when he scored. When you have scored a penalty to equalise in the last minute of a Wembley cup final, everything else must seem easy. At the final whistle, the entire contents of the terracing emptied itself onto the pitch for a huge celebration. Whatever happened at The Hawthorns and Goodison Park in the next five days, it had been a great season. No-one thought we would really do it, but hope sprang eternal. News had come through that Everton had lost at Oxford. That meant we were in second place, only one point behind Liverpool. It also meant that if Liverpool won at Chelsea on Saturday, the title was theirs. If they lost it would be a decider for the title on Bank Holiday Monday between Everton and ourselves. Manchester United, in fourth, couldn't catch us, nor could anyone below them; it was just between the three of us. Very cosy.

We made the trip to The Hawthorns knowing that it was no good hoping for the right result from Stamford Bridge if we didn't beat West Brom. They were already down, but still had their pride to play for, and despite going ahead through a goal each from Cottee and McAvennie, they pulled it back to 2–2. News came through that Chelsea were ahead. We raised our voices to urge the team on to greater glory. They responded, Ray Stewart scoring another penalty. We were elated. The news was that Chelsea were leading against Liverpool, and we had won, to set up our own cup final at Goodison Park on Monday.

Then the bombshell hit us. It wasn't 1–0 to Chelsea, it was 1–0 to Liverpool. There was no way we could win. Even if we won at Goodison we could only finish second. The feeling of anticlimax was immense, Like being mis-informed about a pools win, the disappointment was there on everybody's face, even though in their heart of hearts they will admit they never really thought it was on. The fact that a lifeline had been thrown to us and then cruelly whipped away was too much to bear. Grown men cried. We had a record breaking season, and yet nothing to show for it.

I couldn't bring myself to go to the final game against Everton. Like the team. I was knackered. Everton had all the motivation, as they still had to play for their cup final places, and won 3–1. Had we been more aware that a runners-up spot would have given us a Wembley appearance at the start of the next season in the Charity Shield, we might have played with a bit more passion, but we weren't to know that Liverpool would go on to complete the double.

When the history books are consulted in years to come, it will show Champions: Liverpool. FA Cup Winners: Liverpool. Milk Cup Winners: Oxford United. That will make the uninformed reader think that the season was a walk over for Liverpool, but that was far from the case, and I hope this account of season 1985/86 will find its way into the annals (that's annals, two n's) of history to redress the balance. Liverpool had a great side that year, but let's not forget that they didn't have one English player in their first choice side; and if anything, Everton had a more enterprising and entertaining side. They too, ended up with nothing but runners-up medals and happy memories.

After it had all blown over, there was one final game to be played. A testimonial game for Gerhard Ampofo, a youth team player whose career had been ended by a broken leg. Tottenham provided the opposition, and they were duly despatched 5–1. I know you can never read too much into testimonials and friendlies, but there is no such thing as a friendly against Spurs, and there were some nice pointers for the future in this game. Our side included Arsenal midfielders Stewart Robson and Paul Davis. I never really rated Paul Davis, but always had admired Robson. He scored a couple of goals and

I hoped that we would sign him to add that little competitive edge and creativity to the midfield. Like Clive Allen in the Pat Holland testimonial, it was a future echo, in that he did eventually join the club. Fortunately, we didn't have to wait eight years. Alvin Martin missed the testimonial game; he was with the England Squad in Mexico for the World Cup.

West Ham had just failed to win the biggest prize in English football. Could England make up for the disappointment and win the biggest prize in world football?

Handy Man. . .

Argentina 2 England 1 – 22.6.86

What better present could I request for my eighteenth birthday than a win over Argentina to put England into the semi-finals of the World Cup? Well, if I'm honest, there were a lot of better presents I could have asked for, but this is a family show. My eighteenth birthday was spent as any other self respecting moody teenager would, having my hair permed. I can't believe I did this now, but at the time it was quite trendy to look like Chris Waddle. It may have been a sub-conscious effort to try and impress Diana, but by now she was well out of reach, and by the time my eighteenth birthday party took place a week later, she brought her husband and made it perfectly clear that her body was out of bounds. Her husband reinforced the point. Shag my wife again and I'll rip your windpipe out, was the message I got from his glare, which seemed reasonable. Although he was the same height as me, he was probably twice as wide and heavy, and I wasn't going to argue.

The World Cup campaign had not been going well. For a start, playing in Mexico, most of the games started at some unearthly hour in the morning when most sensible people were fast asleep. While this would not normally bother me, I was in the middle of exams and restricted myself to the first forty-five minutes only of England's opening game against Portugal. I couldn't believe it when I heard that we had lost. England had been looking quite sexy in the warm up games and I believed there was a chance we might even win the trophy. Things got worse when we only got a 0–0 against Morocco, Bryan Robson (not 'Pop,' I mean the crap one with the perm who used to play for West Bromwich Albion) dislocated his shoulder and Ray Wilkins got sent off. At least my exams finished, which meant that the most important member of the team was now available.

I had arranged to drive 300 miles to meet my parents, who were on holiday. I had not been able to go with them from the start due to my exams. The night before I was due to leave, England played Poland in the last group match. Having lost one and drawn one, a win was vital to ensure qualification for the second phase. I was unable to get the beers in because I was going to leave very early in the morning, but I did the next best thing and dimmed the lights, mashed some tea and got out the biscuits. A brilliant first half performance saw Gary Lineker knock in a hat-trick. The whole country breathed a sigh of relief when the first one went in. I cheered alone in my front room.

I filled the car up with petrol and bombed down the M4, wondering if I would need my passport as I was going abroad, to Wales. Half way there and the needle was knocking empty. 'Strange,' I thought, 'she usually does more miles than this to a tank.' Then I realised I had left the choke in. A lot of people now learn to drive on cars with automatic chokes and have never experienced this problem of fuel mixture selection. Give me an automatic choke every time; it is four years since I drove a car with a manual choke, but I still, through force of habit, reach down with my left hand to check the choke is out when I'm driving on the motorway.

Terry Fenwick picked up a second yellow card in the Poland game, which meant that Alvin was in with a chance. He was selected for the game against Paraguay, which now took on a whole new significance. For the first time since, er. . . the last World Cup, there was a West Ham player involved in a vital game. I was nervous for him. Paraguay had looked good in the first round games, and they had a highly rated striker in Roberto Cabanas, who had been spouting off in the press that Paraguay would win easily. I always felt it was a dodgy game playing South Americans on their own patch, and my father and I stocked up more than our usual supply of beers, crisps and nuts for the game, which was watched on our portable TV with dreadful reception in the middle of nowhere, also known as Haverfordwest. At half time, we fashioned a supplementary aerial out of a coat hanger and some speaker cable and things improved.

Alvin had a steady game, but managed to get himself booked, which obviously was not good, as I had hoped that a 100% clean performance would give him the nod ahead of Fenwick, who I never really rated. I would have played Alvin ahead of him ninety-nine times out of ninety-eight. The Paraguay attack was kept very quiet, and Lineker notched a couple more, with Beardsley getting the third to give us a second successive 3–0 win.

The chance to have our first pop at Argentina since the Falklands War was not one to be missed. As it was my eighteenth birthday there was plenty of booze around in the house, although I was already high on the fumes of the home perm. We were naturally disappointed that Alvin was not in the starting eleven, and our disappointment grew as that fat git Maradona rose with Shilton to punch the ball into the net. Everyone in the front room rose as one, 'Handball!' we all shouted. Some of the players were running around and protesting, we felt sure the referee would consult the linesman and disallow the goal, but no. No-one was going to deny Maradona his tournament of glory. If he scored, it didn't matter how he scored. He could have shot Peter Shilton through the head with a Colt 45, then hit the ball in with Peter Reid's bottle of Grecian 2000 and it would still have counted. The little slag then rubbed salt into the wound by scoring a goal of such genius, we did not speak again for another twenty minutes. The only sound in the room was of beer cans opening, suppressed sobbing and the soft slashing of wrists. Later, beer cans flew around the room and we all whistled our disapproval, convinced it could be heard in Mexico.

We all agreed that if Alvin had been playing, the second goal would never have happened. Not because Alvin would have stood back à la Bobby Moore and coolly nicked the ball away on the edge of the box, but because he would have broken Maradona's legs within two yards of the centre circle. Lineker pulled one back after Barnes had come on, but it was too late, and we were out of the World Cup. As we drowned our sorrows, which were admittedly already coming up for the third time, we decided that the disappointment of England going out of the World Cup was nothing compared to West Ham's failure to win a trophy last season after playing so well. We decided not to take any chances in 1986/87 and buy season tickets for the East Terrace. Lanky's brother Chris had started to tag along regularly and was now more committed than Lanky himself, and he and I decided to go for one better – every game, home and away. The things you say when you are pissed.

Always on My Mind. . .

Manchester United 2 West Ham United 3 – 25.8.86

To say we entered season 1986/87 with high hopes would be like saying Cyril Smith needs to lose a few pounds. As long as we played like we did the previous season, we would be laughing. There were no significant additions to the squad during the close season, but that didn't bother us. Why strengthen an already strong side? We would soon learn all about that.

The season started in much the same way as it had finished. On the opening day, we beat Coventry City at Upton Park, courtesy of a Tony Gale free kick. This was Tony's first goal for the club and he was clearly delighted, as we were, of course. More than that, he seemed genuinely delighted, as though he was personally responsible for placing those three points on the board. He had an eventful game, collecting a sharp crack on the head as well and suffering concussion. The Coventry defence had obviously earmarked Tony Cottee and Frankie Mac as deserving extra special attention, which they got, and it was clear that the goal to win the game would have to come from another source. Gale's superbly flighted free kick was the first of many he curled into the top corner of the net as a West Ham player. Noting his ability from the edge of the box, it was very frustrating during his last few seasons with West Ham, to see that he was either not given the responsibility for taking these kicks, or that he did not feel he wanted to.

Monday was the August Bank Holiday. Sure enough, it rained like a tropical forest, as far as I recall, solidly, all day long. People often laugh and joke about Bank Holidays being wet, but this one was so wet it could have stood for Parliament. Dobbo, Stain Tooth and I caught the train from Euston feeling that this was probably as good a way as any of spending a wet Bank Holiday. The train journey was remarkably short, and having befriended a Hammers fan accompanied only by twelve cans of lager and a pack of cards, we got off the train at Warwick Road Station and took the long walk to the ground. I had been to Old Trafford twice before, and knew the route quite well. We were stopped by one of the West Ham stewards, who was wary of the fact that he was wearing a short sleeved shirt. The West Ham tattoos on his forearms were clearly visible to all and sundry. He asked Dobbo if he could borrow his jumper, to cover them up. It was still raining hard, and we questioned the wisdom of the guy not wearing anything more substantial in the first place, but he looked as though he might get violent. Dobbo wound him up by asking to see his ID, but lent him the jumper anyway, resigned to the fact that he would probably never see it again.

I had a can of Coke in my pocket and was told by the policeman outside the turnstile that I couldn't take it in with me. He assured me that I didn't look like the type who would throw Coke cans around, but rules were rules. I had the option of drinking it there and then, or handing it over and he would let me have it back after the game. 'Yeah, right,' I thought, 'and West Ham are going to win 3–2!' I wasn't thirsty, having had a few tinnies of lager on the train; if anything I needed the loo – taking more fluid on board would not help. Dobbo had made a sacrifice, and so should I. I handed over the Coke can, making it clear that I wanted it back after the game. I toyed with the idea of asking to see the copper's ID, but thought that might just be pushing it.

The away supporters' terrace at Old Trafford was about the size of a first class postage stamp, into which they would cram up to 3,000 supporters at a time. The atmosphere was somewhat hostile; Manchester United were looking for their first point after losing at Arsenal on the opening day. The United fans weren't to know that United would only take five points from a possible twenty-seven at the start of the season, a run which cost manager Ron Atkinson his job, and Alex Ferguson assumed control.

Items were being thrown from the upper tier – it always amuses me when I hear the term 'missile' being used to describe a coin or a stone being lobbed by someone. I always have visions of someone smuggling a small tactical nuclear weapon through the turnstiles. The rain continued to come down in stair rods, and we watched the game kick off from our position of relative comfort, leaning against the concrete wall at the back of the away enclosure. Despite being wet, it was still very warm, and being packed into a small space made things worse. The fact that West Ham took a 2–0 lead in the first half an hour also made things a bit sticky. More bits of debris rained down on us, as Frank McAvennie scored his first of the season, and Alan Devonshire also got his first.

We threw it away, of course. United levelled just after half time, and we felt that a league win at Old Trafford was probably too much to hope for. Then Frank McAvennie scored a goal which will always make me want to have his babies. With a few minutes left, he ran onto a perfectly flighted ball from Mark Ward and headed it over Chris Turner from about the same distance that Geoff Pike had scored from in the cup match the previous season. The difference was that because Frankie was bombing in on goal so fast, he appeared to be closer to the goal. By the time he had realised that the ball was in the net, he was celebrating in front of us, and we were celebrating going top of the league. Now, the rain didn't matter. The heat and humidity didn't matter, the soaking didn't matter, all that mattered was that we should hang on for the last few minutes, which we did.

The police held us back for around half an hour after the game to allow the home fans to disperse, but we didn't care. We sang and danced on the terrace throughout the thirty minute delay, so much so that by the time we reached the exit gate, I was parched and in need of liquid refreshment. I felt a tap on my shoulder, and turned round to find the policeman who had confiscated my can of Coke, offering it back to me. Dobbo stood amazed. 'It's a miracle!' he claimed. I thanked the plod and took my can. Things got better – it had been in the fridge throughout the game and was now ice cold. We shared the drink on our way back to Warwick Road station, keeping a watchful eye out for trouble as we passed the Lou Macari chip shop. 'What a fucking stupid name for a chip shop,' Stain Tooth observed. We all agreed, Dobbo adding that Lou Macari was 'a fucking stupid name full stop'. Back on the train, we peeled off wet clothing and steamed like a cattle train back to London, the unbelievable sequence of events continued when the steward presented Dobbo with his jumper, totally unharmed. The day was complete when we pulled into Euston at 9.00pm and were home by 10.30pm, able to catch the last half an hour in the pub.

Trips away like that one happen only once every two years or so. We were to find out that season, that the more you travel away, the less likely they are to occur.

True Blue. . .

West Ham United 5 Chelsea 3 – 11.10.86

Madonna got to number one again with 'True Blue'. This happened the same day we were due to play Chelsea at Upton Park, a bad omen, we thought. Was Madonna a Chelsea fan? Probably; everyone else seemed to be.

At least Diana was about to get out of my life for good. Although it hurt, it was a blessing, as having her in the same office all day every day was beginning to turn me into a lunatic. Unable to confide in anyone except friends who thought I was mad anyway, I had started drinking at lunchtime, after work and at any other opportunity that presented itself. I looked and felt awful. If West Ham had been struggling against relegation, that would have finished me off. As it was, after three games we were third, level on points at the top with Tottenham and Liverpool, in third place only on goal difference. West Ham provided the one consolation once again; the one thing in life to look forward to every week and something to be a part of. I had used my season ticket to buy an East Terrace ticket for the Littlewoods Cup game against Preston, but offered Diana the chance of one more night of sexual ecstasy before she moved to Tunbridge Wells, passing up the chance to see my beloved Hammers for her benefit. Greater love hath no man. She kept me waiting for an answer right up until the last moment, when she told me she had decided it wouldn't be such a good idea. Typical.

After winning at Old Trafford, the following Saturday Stain Tooth drove us to Oxford in his now embarrassingly adorned Austin Allegro, and after finding a convenient parking space in the middle of a roundabout, we watched a terrible game finish 0–0. To our surprise and delight, the car was still there when we arrived back, and no parking ticket. We were back home in time for tea.

The following Tuesday we played Nottingham Forest at Upto[n] Park. Despite our poor record against Forest, I was confident we would get a result, as we had been playing well, and had despatched them 4–2 the previous season. Forest came into the game with a similar record to ourselves, also on seven points from three games. Christina had written to me a few days before saying that Forest would be out for revenge and we were to look out. I dismissed this as Cloughie propaganda and watched us take a 1–0 lead through Frank McAvennie in the first half. We were on course. Things started to go horribly wrong though. Franz Carr, a tricky little winger was giving George Parris a hard time and before we had time to blink, Neil Webb and Nigel Clough had put Forest 2–1 up. This was outrageous! West Ham battled and bombed but couldn't find the required equaliser, and we suffered our first defeat of the season.

The next game was the following Saturday at home to Liverpool. After a season when we only seemed to get going after falling behind, we now found ourselves throwing things away after taking the lead ourselves. We took the lead through a Ray Stewart penalty, a shot which was so hard he broke the netting and the groundsman had to come on and repair it. Liverpool equalised just before half time, when a poor clearance came out to Ronnie Whelan to volley in. I clearly remember seeing the ball come towards him and shouting 'No! Not to him!' A split second later, the ball was in the back of the net. Liverpool took the lead when our solid defensive partnership of Alvin Martin and Tony Gale, so reliable the previous season, looked as though they had never met before and allowed Craig Johnston to score. Cottee managed to grab an equaliser when Hooper, standing in for Grobbelaar in goal, flapped at an indirect free kick given inside the area for dangerous play. Cottee blasted home the ball, a big relief for everyone, as he had gone five games without a goal.

Kenny Dalglish came on as a sub for the injured Hansen and Liverpool, having suffered the setback of an equaliser, simply raised their game and put it out of our despairing reach. Dalglish scored twice and Rush got another as we succumbed 5–2. I had never before seen us concede five at home, and have never done so in a league match since. After looking like championship material against

United, we were cruelly exposed as impostors by the mpions and FA Cup holders. It taught me to try and put rspective. OK, we had won at Old Trafford. Big deal, they g an abysmal start to the season. Had we lost, looking t, say, Christmas, it would have been a mini-disaster. After all, Charlton Athletic went there after us and won also. If Charlton could win there, then any bugger could. We got a 0–0 draw at Oxford. I mean, come on! Oxford were never going to set the world alight, were they? If we were going to think seriously about winning championships, we would have to win at places like Oxford. Forest and Liverpool exposed us for what we really were – pretenders.

One team who were setting the world alight was Wimbledon. Having won promotion in 1985/86, they lost their opening fixture at Manchester City, then beat Aston Villa, Leicester, Charlton and Watford to go top, albeit briefly. At the end of the season, and many seasons to follow, a difference in attitude, not ability, would prove to be West Ham's undoing. Wimbledon symbolised that difference in attitude. If there is anything quieter than complete silence, that is what there was in the car coming home from the Liverpool game. None of us ventured out in the evening. We were too ashamed. I was beginning to question the wisdom of my commitment to go to every game; and yet, despite such a crushing defeat, I looked forward to the game against QPR at Loftus Road, confident that we would get a result. 1986 must have been a very wet year, because as I remember, this game was played in torrential rain as well. On QPR's plastic pitch, it made life very difficult, but it didn't bother Tony Cottee, who made up for his slow start by knocking in a hat-trick. Again though, we displayed defensive frailties, allowing QPR back into the game at 3–2 to provide a nail biting finish. Again, we watched the game from the paddock at Loftus Road, and Natty Matty tried to rip his leather jacket again, as he said he could do with the compensation money. QPR had obviously wised up, and had got rid of the offending barrier.

Luton Town reared their ugly head again the following Saturday. Unlike last season, they lay down and gave us the three points, goals from George Parris and Tony Gale giving us a 2–0 win, but they still managed to upset me in two ways. Firstly, Brian Stein managed to get himself and Alvin Martin sent off for fighting, when there was really nothing to fight about. It meant losing Alvin for a couple of games, although he was subsequently injured and was out for much longer than that. Secondly, it brought into full focus the fact that Luton Town had brought in a membership scheme and had banned away supporters from their ground. They had adopted this policy following a number of problems with visiting supporters culminating in a full scale riot in an FA Cup game with Millwall. If I was going to do a complete season, this was a hurdle I was going to have to get around somehow. You may now begin to understand just why I hate Luton Town so much. It's not irrational, is it? No, I'm glad you agree.

We faced two long away trips, to Preston in the Littlewoods Cup, on another plastic pitch, and then to Sheffield Wednesday. Stain Tooth and I made both trips together, taking a half day at work to get to Preston and watch an uninspiring game finish 1–1. Mark Ward got our goal. In the end, a 1–1 draw was a good result, the plastic at Deepdale being a lot more lively than the pitch at QPR and even more than the one at Luton. The trip to Sheffield was taken by train, none of us fancied the long drive and preferred to be chauffeured, courtesy of British Rail. Although the score was identical, it was a complete reverse of the previous season's game at Hillsborough as Wednesday took the lead, then we went ahead through Alvin and Neil Orr. Wednesday grabbed a late equaliser through Gary Megson, and once again, the press went on and on about West Ham adding steel to their artistry. They had been saying this since at least 1983, and probably before, and they still say it today when we get a good result. 'The aristocrats have added strength and determination to their pretty passing movements. . . ' Utter balls. West Ham have always had players who can put themselves about a bit, and have always had artistic players. It's not very often that we have been able to find the right blend, that's all. A third away game in a row, but slightly nearer home came against Watford. We still had to walk miles to get to the ground from their special railway station, uphill and down dale. We could see the ground far in the distance, and after twenty minutes of walking through allotments and industrial estates, the floodlights still appeared tantalisingly on the horizon. Sir Ranulph Fiennes would have enjoyed that expedition. He probably wouldn't have enjoyed the game, West Ham again throwing away a 2–0 lead given to them by Alan Dickens and Frank McAvennie to draw 2–2. Kenny Jackett, at the time a Welsh international was in the side, and I remember him taking a free kick inside the centre circle, which cannoned against Alan Dickens who was all of two feet away. Not satisfied with his first attempt, Jackett picked up the ball and placed it down again. The referee, Bob Hamer, blew up to give us a free kick for hand ball. Jackett protested that Dickens wasn't ten yards away and was booked for dissent. Hamer stated afterwards that Jackett decided to take the free kick quickly – if he couldn't be bothered to wait a few seconds for the West Ham player to retreat ten yards then it was up to him. It was the best piece of refereeing I have ever seen in our favour on an opponent's ground.

Although still unbeaten away from home, we were drawing a lot of games and our home form was worrying. Having been rejected at the eleventh hour by Diana, I made my own way to Upton Park to watch the second leg of the cup tie against Preston. Although we took the lead through Tony Cottee, Preston equalised and should have gone in front. We were terrible. Hilton and Walford were playing at centre back, and the Preston forwards smelled blood. Fortunately, with the game heading for extra time, Cottee and Dickens proved their worth, Dickens getting our second, and Cottee scoring his second hat-trick of the season to wrap up a 4–1 win. It was significant that the biggest cheer of the night came when Billy Bonds came on as a late substitute. How deceptive scorelines can be. I bumped into Barney after the game, who beamed all over his face. 'Good result!' he laughed. 'Good result, shite performance.' I had never been so depressed after a win of any sort, particularly one achieved by four goals to one. Things didn't look good for the visit of Chelsea. Although they were struggling in the bottom half, we were not fooled by this. A beautifully sunny afternoon in October greeted the players as they came out onto the pitch. There was something of an intimidating atmosphere; not quite as bad as that experienced at Stamford Bridge in 1985, but pretty close. Chelsea went 1–0 up through a dubious penalty, then West Ham produced a purple patch, McAvennie equalising, and then Ray

Stewart hitting home an equally dubious penalty to give us a 2–1 half time lead. Bonds took the pitch again at half time, McAvennie having pulled a muscle, and Chelsea seized the initiative again, goals from Dixon and Bumstead putting them 3–2 ahead. I couldn't work out why Chelsea were so low in the table, they were playing some great stuff, although it pains me to say so.

Kevin McAllister handled on the line, and although Neil Orr scored, the referee insisted that a penalty kick be taken. Ray Stewart scored his second and a 3–3 draw would have been OK by me, having regard to the fact we had twice been behind. Tony Cottee wasn't having any of it though. Aware that Bobby Robson, the England manager was in the crowd, he slammed in two more goals of absolute world class. His second, our fifth, was just breathtaking. Tony Godden in the Chelsea goal had a good game, but had no answer to this shot. As we walked back, avoiding the queues at Upton Park station and going directly to Plaistow, I reflected on the last two home league games and thought how easy it would be to trade last season's results against Luton and Chelsea for this season's. Six extra points would have made us champions. I don't want to go on about it, but it's all we have had in the last ten years that has constituted any kind of success. We all hate Luton and we all hate Chelsea. And we all have good reason.

Every Loser Wins. . .

West Ham United 1 Everton 0 – 2.11.86

Barney owned a clapped out Ford Cortina Mk III, which was held together by rust and plastic padding. We all used to tease him about the quality of his motor, but he didn't care, and he always pointed out that we were quick enough to accept a lift to football in it, which was true enough. To give you an idea of the quality of car we are talking about here, when he filled in the form for his insurance, in the space marked 'Value of Vehicle,' he wrote: 'Depends how much petrol is in the tank.' Those parts of the car which still had paint were a bright yellow colour, and the stereo system was considerably more powerful than the engine.

Despite this, we entrusted him with the task of driving us to Norwich, and the car performed magnificently. Downhill on the M11, with five people on board and a following wind, it managed to reach 75mph. The excitement was such that we had to stop at a service station to recover. I had been to Norwich the year they were relegated, and was able to direct Barney to the municipal car park, a short walk from the ground. It was another warm October afternoon, and Norwich were enjoying their return to the top flight, top-of-the-league after ten games, while we shadowed them in fifth place. It was a somewhat unexpected top of the table clash, but a thoroughly absorbing and entertaining one, Norwich having the better of the first half and West Ham playing superb football in the second. The game should really have been won by West Ham, but we had to settle for another away draw, 1–1, with Goddard, in the side for the injured Frank McAvennie, scoring our goal. He missed a sitter shortly afterwards, but we had to be content with a point. I was surprised by the attitude of the Norwich fans. They pelted us with coins and other 'missiles' throughout the game. I expected better of them. Still, I made about £2.50.

Barney's car took us to Upton Park the following week for the game against Charlton. I think it was George Best who said that teams very rarely score goals straight from the kick-off because within five seconds they have given the ball away. West Ham kicked off and, within five seconds gave the ball away. Within fifteen seconds it was in the back of our net, Jim Melrose having scored. It was a blow from which the team did not recover. The humiliation was intense as Charlton carved great lumps out of our defence, Colin Walsh and Robert Lee playing out of their skins. Walsh hit a terrific shot against the bar before actually scoring to make it 2–0. Cottee managed to pull one back before half time, but the team were not playing well, and in the second half, the lack of confidence manifested itself as Goddard fell over his boot laces in front of an open goal. Charlton took full advantage and scored a third on the break.

The next game was the following Wednesday and saw us making our second trip to Watford in the same month. The ground had moved no nearer to the station in the three weeks we had been away, and we approached tentatively, aware that Watford had finished the league game the stronger team, and would be looking to finish the job that night. We were pleasantly surprised as West Ham appeared to be a different side to the one that died against Charlton; plenty of movement and bright attacking ideas. Paul Goddard curled in a superb shot in the first half, only for Kenny Jackett, the infamous free kick taker, to score from the spot to equalise. As Liverpool had done to us earlier, West Ham rolled up their sleeves and finished the game strongly, Dickens and Ward scoring to make in 3–1. David Bardsley pulled one back a few minutes from the end and, as is tradition, we bit our nails to the final whistle.

The visit of Everton had been chosen by the BBC as their live transmission for the next Sunday. We doubted their choice; why not Manchester United again? Our previous games against Everton were never anything to write home about, and this one was no exception. Considering Everton were to go on to win their second championship in three years, they gave a very under par performance, with Alan Dickens scoring the only goal a few minutes into the second half.

There were eight of us in our little group. By now, girlfriends were starting to come along, as well as part-timers who came to see what it was all about, never to be seen again as they left the ground in an advanced state of confusion. As we walked back to the cars, Barney shouted: 'Last one home buys the first round!' Barney and I had a race home which I narrowly won. While Chris, Close and Lanky all thought it was a great laugh, I told them not to expect a repeat performance. It scared the shit out of me.

The Final Countdown. . .

West Ham United 3 Southampton 1 – 6.12.86

Winter cometh, and with it, the anticipated decline of West Ham United. Despite losing three home matches, we still defied gravity and remained in with an outside chance in the title race. By the time we visited Highbury to play second placed Arsenal on November 8th we were in fourth place, just four points behind leaders Nottingham Forest. We owed our lofty perch to good away form, winning two and drawing four of the six games we had played. Now came the real test, away at Arsenal, in second place and challenging hard, and away at Wimbledon, newly promoted and a handful at home. If we could come out of those games still undefeated, we might be able to make a fresh start at home.

We played Arsenal on the Saturday morning. It was cold and windy, not the best conditions for watching football, particularly a 0–0 draw. McAvennie came back from his injury and looked sharp, we had two first half goals ruled out for off-side, the first of which I agreed with, but the second one I could not understand. In the last few minutes John Lukic made a save from McAvennie which defied all belief, and we had to settle for a point. Even if the ball had gone in, the linesman would probably have thought of something. On days like that, it's a good idea just to be grateful for what you have.

We drove to Wimbledon, parking within spitting distance of the ground, and watched Tony Cottee's goal give us a 1–0 win. This was a fantastic result for us. Not only was it eleven league and cup games unbeaten away from home, but we had played at two highly difficult clubs after disappointing home form and got four points. I was prepared to believe that another successful season may be on the cards. I should have known better.

Despite the fact that Oxford United had won the Milk Cup the previous season, drawing them at home in the latest incarnation of the trophy, the Littlewoods Cup, appeared to be a good draw, and an easy route into the quarter finals. Barney and I watched the game from the East Terrace and saw Oxford dominate the game from start to finish, but West Ham won the game with a Tony Cottee penalty after a dubious looking foul on Frank McAvennie.

It was a similar story against Aston Villa. Tony Cottee scored yet again to put us into the lead, but Villa, destined for relegation gradually edged their way back into the game, and Garry Thompson scored the equaliser late on. They were unfortunate not to get a winner, and in the end we were happy to hang on for a point. The warning signs were there for all to see, yet the slide continued unabated. We played Chelsea again at Upton Park in the Full Members Cup, a competition designed to fill the gap left by the exclusion of English clubs from Europe, but regarded by most as a complete waste of time. Chelsea thought it was wonderful, because they won it in its inaugural year the previous season. West Ham didn't bother to enter, neither did any of the 'Big Five' – Liverpool, Everton, Arsenal, Tottenham or Manchester United.

Chelsea came to Upton Park determined to get their own back for the 5–3 defeat the previous month. This, added to the fact they were holders, and our dodgy home form, all pointed to a win for Chelsea, which duly arrived. I went to this game, for the first time since we had beaten Chelsea 3–1 in 1978, with my father, who by now was a total convert to the West Ham United cause. Despite losing 1–2, he thoroughly enjoyed the game and came along again on several subsequent occasions. A certain Mr Paul Ince wore the number six shirt for the first time that night, his first team debut. Barney had seen Ince play in the reserves and raved about him, but it took a few games to convince me that he was any good. I was still unconvinced by the time we came to play Southampton at Upton Park.

The TV bods loved us. ITV wanted our game at St James' Park, Newcastle and moved it to the Sunday, November 30th. The game had everything the TV company could wish for: West Ham in the top six and unbeaten away from home, against Newcastle in the bottom six and seeking instant revenge for the 8–1 mauling they had received at Upton Park back in March. In addition, there were two young England players on show, Tony Cottee and Peter Beardsley. Paul Goddard had signed for Newcastle a few weeks earlier and played against us. It was an exciting prospect.

Confident of a result, and anxious to keep my ever present record, we took a train to Newcastle. We were 2–0 down at half time, and had Newcastle had their shooting boots on, would have extracted identical revenge for our big win. We still felt our away record would see us through. Barney remained confident, Natty Matty remained confident, and Bean Head remained confident. Unfortunately, the eleven players in claret and blue were not. They were nervous as hell, obviously suffering from stage fright, and even the arrival of Barney's hero, Paul Ince for Alan Dickens, could not turn things around. We lost the game 4–0 and with it went our unbeaten away record and a large slice of our credibility. Newcastle is a long way at the best of times. It's even further when you've just been slaughtered 4–0. We must have been the only team in history to have lost only one of nine away games, and yet still had a negative goal difference.

Southampton arrived in mid table indifference for our first game in December. After winning at Wimbledon on November 15th, and feeling confident about a challenge, the next four games, while not in the disaster category, wildly changed my views and I was just glad that we already had twenty-seven points in the bag to fall back on. We were only ten points ahead of the relegation zone, and seven behind leaders Arsenal.

West Ham opened brightly against Southampton, Devonshire scoring his second and final goal of the season with a header. Southampton equalised with a freaky Colin Clarke goal, but Paul Ince, making his full league debut, scored another header to make it 2–1. Maybe Barney was right about Ince. I was still to be won over, even though he had scored. Cottee finished the scoring in the second half with his tenth league goal, this time from the penalty spot.

Reet Petite. . .

West Ham United 4 Leicester City 1 – 1.1.87

A decision had to be made. I was doing well at college and enjoying my time there. I still found exams a bit of a bind, but realised that if I wanted to do anything in property that would earn decent money, I needed a useful qualification. That meant a degree. That meant even more studying, exams and reading of text books. Was that what I wanted? I didn't really have any choice.

Half-heartedly, I filled in my PCAS form to apply for a place at Polytechnic for the autumn. Speaking of form, West Ham's was shocking. The next four games yielded just one point. Manchester City, another side doomed to relegation after just two seasons in Division One, beat us 3–1 at Maine Road; not really a fair reflection of the game, Alvin Martin equalised for us and we looked good for a point. After having such a good away record, we now had an appalling one. After two heavy away defeats, travelling to away games became more and more of a depressing occupation. We just knew we were going to lose – any other result was a pleasant surprise. We only had two more pleasant surprises all season in the league.

We could only manage a draw at home to QPR, Cottee scored with a penalty, then Fenwick equalised in similar fashion. We walked away from the game feeling that perhaps we were a little hard done by, but Michael Robinson squandered a great chance to win the game for QPR at the end. The championship was now out of the question; it was looking good for a relegation scrap. We certainly looked like relegation material at White Hart Lane on Boxing Day.

I wanted to leave half an hour from the end, as Tottenham pulled us apart and won 4–0, Steve Hodge scoring on his debut, as players had a habit of doing. I recall very little about the game, except that the only good thing about it was that it wasn't five. John Lyall shook the team up for the next day's game at home to Wimbledon, making four changes. It appeared to have done the trick, as Cottee put us 1–0 up, but Wimbledon showed their fighting spirit (helped on by a good slice of sloppy defending) and equalised. Paul Hilton put us ahead once again, only for Wimbledon to race straight up the other end and score. It was getting silly. Before half time, Wimbledon scored a third, and held on to their lead until the end of the game, another defeat.

This was farcical. Our rapid decline was more depressing than we could have imagined. I arrived home from the Wimbledon game to a turkey tea, which I would face for the next month or so, and sulked for the rest of the day. At last the new year approached. Maybe the players would all make New Year's resolutions to do better. We faced Leicester City at Upton Park, a side who looked a good relegation bet with a dreadful away record. If we didn't win that one, we would be in real trouble.

We won. Cottee got two more, Dickens and McAvennie scoring the other two in a 4–1 win. Even so, the signs were there that we were not the team we had been a year previously. The players appeared tired, disinterested, and apathetic; the only players who were really trying were the kids who were not guaranteed a first team place, the side had rested on their laurels and had found it impossible to get up again. The pitch wasn't helping. It was already looking like a mud bath, not conducive to good football, and I wondered what would happen when the warmer spring weather came and it hardened up. I thought of all the grazes I had received playing football on concrete surfaces in the playground at school and shuddered. After the game though, the thoughts were not of disillusionment, but optimism that the new year victory heralded the start of a magnificent run of victories that would see us run away with the title. That idea was squashed within two days as we travelled to Anfield, admittedly more in hope than expectation, but played well and were unfortunate to lose by just the one goal, 1–0. Paul Ince was starting to grow on me. He replaced Alan Dickens early in the second half and played with an arrogance and swagger that belied his youthful years. Of course, this was an arrogance and swagger that would later enrage all of us, but when you have it on your side, it is a joy to behold. It was a miserable trip to Liverpool, and an even worse trip home, on a cold train which sat at Rugby Station for almost an hour for no apparent reason. The cold was biting, but it was nothing compared to Brisbane Road the following Saturday.

I have visited some of the northern most and highest football grounds in the country, but never experienced anything quite as cold as Brisbane Road on January 10th. The draw for the third round of the FA Cup paired us with our near neighbours Orient, and sparked of talk in the press of an 'East End knees up' which made me want to puke. Comparisons were also drawn to 1980, when we last played Orient in the FA Cup and went on to win the trophy. Rubbish, of course – I'd tried making comparisons like that before; they never work. Everyone felt slightly queasy when the teams marched out to the EastEnders theme tune, but the overriding priority was to keep warm. Even forcing our way into the massed ranks behind the goal we could not get enough heat together to stop us from shivering, and wished we could get out onto the pitch and run around to get the blood pumping around to the feet again. Paul Hilton scored, which warmed us up a bit, but Orient equalised from the spot a minute from the end. Fortunately, we had driven to the game in my car, not Barney's, and while my car wasn't exactly top of the range, it did have a heater that worked.

The freezing weather earned us some respite. Our home match against Manchester United was postponed, together with the Littlewoods Cup quarter-final against Spurs; a blessing in disguise, although I began to suffer withdrawal symptoms sitting at home on a Saturday with nothing to do, it being my first blank Saturday since the start of the season. It gave John Lyall time to finalise the signature of Stewart Robson from Arsenal. At last! A player I had wanted the club to sign for so long was finally going to appear in the claret and blue. I couldn't wait for the game at Coventry. Now we would show them!

The Lady in Red. . .

Coventry City 1 West Ham United 3 – 24.1.87

To the untrained eye, it would appear that West Ham had a divine right to three points when playing Coventry City at Highfield Road. Certainly we were not as pessimistic as usual as we headed up the M1 for the clash with the Sky Blues, particularly as Stewart Robson was due to make his debut. I was as confident as it was possible to be as a West Ham supporter. If supporting West Ham is a roller coaster ride, this game was a loop-the-loop with triple corkscrew. Tony Cottee, getting his millionth mention in this book, but a name of which I never tire, scored another hat-trick in a 3–1 win, and Stewart Robson bossed the midfield as though he had been playing in our side all his career. We purred all the way home, following a coach load of sixth form schoolgirls down the M6, who were making suggestive hand signals. Chris tried to write his phone number backwards on the windscreen, but the girls just laughed, and I nearly ploughed into the back of them; which under other circumstances might have been quite nice, but not in separate vehicles on the M6.

It was still bitterly cold; we finally got to play Spurs after two postponements, on January 27th. We took to the field fully expecting to extract revenge for the humiliation at White Hart Lane on Boxing Day. Instead, Spurs picked up where they had left off and cut great swathes through us, our defence had more holes than Gleneagles, and Tottenham were on sparkling form, players like Clive Allen, Osvaldo Ardiles, Glenn Hoddle, Tony Galvin and Richard Gough made us look worse than ordinary. The only surprise was that they only led 1–0 at the interval. Something was done, I'm not sure what, but Robson managed to get more of a hold in midfield and Cottee sneaked an equaliser. We could have nicked it in the second half, but it would have been the biggest injustice since 'Shaddap You Face' prevented Ultravox from getting to No. 1. A 1–1 draw was a fair result, which coming from someone as biased as me probably means Spurs should have won easily. From being their bogey team, we suddenly found it impossible to beat them.

The following Saturday we played our third round replay against Orient at Upton Park, the fourth round match had to be delayed because of the bad weather, but we at least knew that if we won we would be at home to third division Sheffield United, which was a big incentive for us; there was every chance of progressing to the fifth round. The match against Orient was played on a pitch which was half soft, half frozen. In the shadow cast by the West Stand the ground was hard, yet in the winter sunshine the east side of the pitch had softened and was even muddy in places. Footwear selection was a problem. George Parris changed his boots half way through the first half, and must have got it right, because he opened the scoring, and it looked easy. Orient fought back though, and had a goal disallowed because the referee had already blown for a free kick. As if to emphasise their sense of injustice they slammed the free kick straight into the net. Now we had a problem. Orient were on a high and we were struggling to get into the match. As if by magic, or royal command, or something, Kevin Keen rounded off a superb move to put us back into the lead, and Frankie Mac popped up at the far post to head the third. Keen then sold the most elegant dummy to the Orient keeper, Peter Wells, to let Cottee in to walk the ball into the net for 4–1. It was easy in the end, but not as easy as it should have been against lower division opposition.

Five–nil makes a game sound a bit one sided, doesn't it? Well, it was. I think we had about three shots on goal during the entire replay against Spurs at White Hart Lane. Clive Allen got a hat-trick and Claesen and Hoddle scored the other goals on a night I want to forget, but keeps coming back to haunt me whenever I eat cheese just before going to bed. To make matters worse, I got split up from the others as we got into White Hart Lane railway station and I had to ride home with a load of Spurs fans singing 'We beat you West Ham, Five–nil!' I got some funny looks, as although I wasn't wearing

West Ham colours, I was the only one on the carriage with a face like thunder, resolutely reading the programme.

Progress on the woman front was slow. I knew lots of women, I met them through work and on Saturday nights, through friends, relatives and the like, just as anyone else does, yet I did not have a steady girlfriend. Looking back, part of the reason must have been to do with the scars left by Diana, but that's an easy excuse to pull out of the hat. Another reason would most definitely be that I would not have been able to complete my season of watching every game if I had to combine the wishes and desires of a girlfriend while also 'spending the vast majority of my time and money following eleven oafs around the country who kick an inflated pig's bladder around,' (a later girlfriend's words, not mine). I had watched Barney and his girlfriend, Amanda, bickering over petty little things. Most of the time, the conversation would revolve around the amount of time an away trip might take, and I felt that women were far too time consuming to worry about a stable relationship – just yet.

At college, Andy Russell was teaching me a thing or two. He was a real character, a laugh a minute and, some would say, a bad influence on me. Had we been at school together, that may well have been the case, but at college there was more room to get away with things, and besides, deep down he was just as keen to learn as I was. We had a laugh and a joke, but always got the work done. Andy, Big Al, Brian the Luton fan and I would spend many a long lunch hour in the pub playing darts and discussing football. We kept abreast of current affairs, having both harboured secret passions to go into journalism when leaving school. Terry Waite disappeared in Beirut. A couple of years later I was passing The Oval on my way into college, where someone had daubed on the wall 'Whatever happened to Terry Waite?' It was a good question. Andy merely asked, 'What's chained to the railings of Canterbury Cathedral going rusty?'

'I don't know.'

'Terry Waite's bike.'

I would often go and stay with Andy for a weekend before exams to do revision and he would drag me protesting to a pub in Hayes called The Grapes. If we didn't pull there, we went to the night-club close by, and with his gift of the gab he always managed to ensure that we were both all right for the evening, and the following morning if need be. On one occasion, we got a taxi ride back to his house with two girls from a female taxi driver who he took a shine to. He got her home phone number as well. It was Andy's idea that we should go to Spain in the summer, just for a short break. His mate, Wreford, had an aunt who owned a villa in Benalmadina and could let us have it for a week at the end of August. I jumped at the chance, and it was booked.

August seemed miles away as we lost to Oxford United at Upton Park. All we needed was to salvage a bit of pride after the defeat at Tottenham, but instead we landed ourselves deeper in the doggy do. They scored after about three minutes and we toiled away without creating very much. It was pitiful. We had a chance to make amends two days later in the fourth round of the FA Cup against Sheffield United. I would choose this game as one of the top fifty games I have ever seen, not so much for the emphatic scoreline, but because of the quality of goals we scored that night. I had a letter published in the match programme, my first scratch at the writing itch, and a photograph was put in of the cake my sister had made for me for my eighteenth birthday, showing a man in a West Ham shirt with a little trophy to the side. I imagined it was the league championship trophy, but by February 1987 it had changed to the FA Cup. By March 1987 it was the Evening Standard five-a-side trophy. By June it was a figment of my imagination. Third division Sheffield United must have fancied their chances at Upton Park, especially as they had the incentive of a Sheffield derby in the next round, a prospect that had Roy Hattersley salivating even more than usual. John Burridge was playing for United, his ninety-first club, making his 1,000,000th appearance. At least, it seemed that way. There were three things that stood out above everything else about this game. First, McAvennie's second goal, one of the best of his career, chesting down a long ball into the box and belting it into the top corner. Secondly, Tony Gale's free kick, an action replay of his effort against Coventry on the opening day. And thirdly, a young Sheffield United player who impressed everyone on the Chicken Run that night, Peter Beagrie. West Ham won 4–0.

The ever present run was going well. There were only two more long journeys to make for league fixtures, to Nottingham, that next Saturday, and to Everton in April. I still had no idea how I was going to get in at Luton, but reckoned it would be no disgrace to miss the game if I was prevented from seeing it by law. That didn't make me feel any better about it though, and it certainly didn't improve my views on Luton Town Football Club. One long journey remained in the cup, a fifth round visit to Sheffield Wednesday. I had arranged to go to a party in Brighton that night, on the express invitation of Andy. As it was something Andy had recommended I felt sure it was worth making an effort for, and promised to attend even though I didn't anticipate getting there much before midnight.

The atmosphere at Hillsborough was tremendous, much better than for the league fixture, which seemed to be years ago, but was in fact only last September. Frankie put us in front, but they equalised in the second half and we all went home happy(ish). It would have been nice to get through first time, particularly as the draw on Monday revealed that the winners would be at home to Coventry in the next round. I could have coped with that, but would rather have played at Coventry. After all, we had a divine right to win there. As anticipated, I got down to Brighton at about midnight to join proceedings. It was a student party being held by an engineering student at Sussex University. I didn't know him from Adam, but he welcomed me in, handed me a can of beer, which was then topped up from various bottles throughout the night. It didn't take long to get into party mode, I found Andy in the kitchen with his tongue down a young lady's throat, and left him to it. A few 'shandies' later and things slowed down. The music changed from George Michael to Rachmaninoff, and a beautiful vision in red came to comfort me. We danced a tango until dawn and watched the orange sun come up over the horizon, just as a bowl of cereal came flying through the service hatch and hit the host on the back of the head. This bit wasn't imagined, and Andy and all his friends, myself included, were asked to leave. We had nowhere to go, so we retreated to our various cars to get some sleep, unable to drive in our condition. I awoke in a most uncomfortable and dishevelled state. Had I really been to Sheffield?

Was it really 1–1? Did I go to a party? My head throbbed – yes, I had. I looked in the rear view mirror. Despite my new clean cut image, I still looked a mess after a drink. The most important question was: who was the lady in red? I told my mate Chris de Burgh, and he said he might put a decent tune together about it. I'm still waiting. I walked down to the sea front to sober up and get some sea air in my lungs. I drove to Hastings and up the A21 before realising that it wasn't too clever to keep going; I decided to stop before I fell asleep at the wheel. Better still, Tunbridge Wells was on the horizon. I decided to pop in and see Diana. At nine o'clock on a Sunday morning I felt sure she would be pleased to see me

Stand by Me. . .

Charlton Athletic 2 West Ham United 1 – 7.3.87

The old trick of feeling too confident before a game came back and tripped me up when I wasn't looking. Surely getting a draw at Hillsborough meant the replay would be a formality? Wrong. I wasn't counting on our abysmal home league form transferring itself to the Cup. We lost a dreadful game 2–0.

I had still not worked out how I was going to get into Kenilworth Road to see our game against Luton. You have to understand that if there was one away game I would have liked to have missed, it would have been this one, but I had been to all thirty-nine games that preceded it and I intended to go to the fourteen that followed it. Why spoil the ship for a ha'porth of tar? I had a brainwave. It doesn't happen very often, but it happened, and fortunately, the person I needed to speak to was sitting right next to me, and I had just bought him a drink.

'Brian,' I asked slimily, 'are you going to the game on Saturday.'

'Yes, I thought I might, actually.'

'Damn.'

A spark of light illuminated his eyes, as he immediately saw my dilemma. 'Oh! Of course. How are you going to get in?'

'That depends on you, mate. . . Fancy another?'

Brian was a good mate. He agreed that it would be much more sensible to go shopping on Saturday with his wife rather than go to a boring old football match, which West Ham would probably win anyway. Although Brian was over six foot and I am only five foot, five, you couldn't tell from a passport photograph, and if I combed my hair forward and made a few other minor adjustments, I reckoned I could swing it.

I was as nervous as a man in drag at a feminist convention. I knew if I was discovered I would be lynched. Luton took their plan very seriously, so did the local police. Now that visiting fans no longer provided them with truncheon fodder, they were out to get what they could. Illegal entrants would do just as well. I took Brian's seat just behind the goal and cautiously scanned the other areas of the ground for signs of any claret and blue. It was ridiculous, of course. Even if there were any other Hammers fans in the ground at that time, they wouldn't have been showing it off. Things changed when Cottee scored. I totally forgot myself and leapt up into the air like a migrating salmon, only much less graceful. Amazingly, about a dozen other people in the stand did the same, and more in other parts of the ground. There must have been about 100 West Ham fans in the ground that day; there was even a quick burst of 'Bubbles' while we held the lead, and there was absolutely nothing the police could do. As far as they knew, we might be Luton fans who just enjoyed seeing the opposition go in front, or schizophrenic Luton fans with divided loyalties. It's stretching the imagination a little, I know, but it's possible. Luton scored twice in the second half to piss on our little firework, but it was a good job done, I had successfully bypassed the system – I have no time for clubs that ban away fans. They have just as much right to see their team play as the home fans. I have never been to Kenilworth Road since, and if I never do again, it will be too soon.

When I told Brian about the day he laughed and said it happened all the time. He even told me he'd had similar requests from Manchester United and Tottenham fans for the use of his pass, and he'd agreed to let them have it for the right price. Luton fans are so easily bought. I suppose I ought to be grateful that all it cost me was two pints of Guinness.

As we stood on the open terrace at Selhurst Park watching another pitiful display, I thought how cold I was. Then I thought how cold the English Channel was, and about the poor souls who had perished on the *Herald of Free Enterprise* outside Zeebrugge the day before and began to warm up. There was talk of Liam Brady coming to join us. We all agreed that would be something a bit special. Apparently John

Lyall had agreed a fee, it was just a matter of time. One thing did worry me though, with Stewart Robson and Liam Brady in the team, we were in danger of turning into Arsenal. It was our ex-Arsenal man who scored against Charlton, but we never looked like nicking a point, let alone three. Charlton were struggling against relegation and they were dragging us with them. By the time Brady made his debut the following Saturday, against Norwich City at Upton Park, West Ham had slipped from title contenders to fourteenth place, just eleven points above the relegation zone. We couldn't afford to keep on losing, but we did. Norwich scored in the first minute and the last minute, and all that went in between was a lot of huff and puff and not very much class or steel from the tough new academy. Liam Brady showed some promising touches, including a free kick that skimmed the crossbar, but I've always been of the opinion that a miss is as good as a mile.

Lyall was now signing players left, right and centre-back. Gary Strodder arrived from Lincoln City, a big defender with all the grace, poise and stability of Bambi on ice. He made his debut at Stamford Bridge the following Saturday on another bitterly cold afternoon. My most vivid memory of 1986–87 was that most of it was cold, wet and miserable. It got very miserable at Stamford Bridge. We lost again, but only by 1–0, which in our book was something of a moral victory. Even a draw would have brought the house down. We had a chance for revenge against Sheffield Wednesday in mid-week, but blew that too, losing 2–0 again. This was relegation form of the lowest order. When we came to play Watford at Upton Park on March 28th we had six straight defeats behind us and were without a league win since the 3–1 victory at Coventry back in January. The prospects were not good for the game against Watford. Their form wasn't too bad. In fact, it was excellent. They had beaten Arsenal twice, including an FA Cup win at Highbury, beaten champions-elect Everton and our tormentors, Sheffield Wednesday, at Hillsborough. It had been raining all day and the pitch resembled an Olympic swimming pool. We paraded yet another new signing, full back Tommy McQueen from Aberdeen. I'd never heard of him, just as I'd never heard of Strodder, but at least he was from a decent club. No disrespect to Lincoln City, but when you hear you have signed an unknown from a third or fourth division club, it doesn't exactly fill you with confidence. I was impressed by McQueen. He worked hard at left back and very rarely missed a tackle, and could cross the ball well, but when it came to shooting, he couldn't hit a cow's arse with a banjo. He was better than Steve Walford, but then, so was I.

In my view, West Ham made their most serious mistakes in signing players like McQueen and Strodder. After the most successful season in our history, we should have been spending millions on established big name players, but instead we spent five and six figure sums on donkeys. From being a potential top six side, we became perennial strugglers virtually overnight.

We showed great spirit against Watford and appeared to be holding on for a point, when with fifteen seconds to go, George Parris let fly from the edge of the box and scored a terrific goal to give us three points. The cheers that went up were cheers of relief more than anything else. The teams at the bottom were in so much trouble that with forty-one points it was unlikely that we would be caught, but we did our best to allow them to.

Nothing's Gonna Stop Us Now. . .

West Ham United 2 Manchester City 0 – 9.5.87

Home form picked up after the win over Watford and we remained undefeated in our final six home games. Away form remained poor, though. Having been unbeaten away from home until the end of November, we won only one of the last twelve games away, losing ten of them. It seemed at the end of 1986/87 that two different teams took to the field, a home team and an away team, composed of look-a-likes who were actually no more than amateur pub team players. To add insult to injury, we also failed to score in any of our final five away games. Before making my final Inter-City trip of the season to Everton, we entertained Arsenal.

Arsenal had begun their campaign of terror by winning the Littlewoods Cup. The only decent thing Arsenal have ever done in my view, is to break that annoying little record that Ian Rush had, where if he scored, Liverpool didn't lose. That really used to piss me off. Three days after they won the cup they came to Upton Park and were taught a footballing lesson. Tony Cottee scored his 100th goal for West Ham in typical fashion, swivelling on a sixpence and crashing the ball into the top of the net. Arsenal then equalised when George Parris sneezed without the referee's permission in the penalty area. Martin Hayes took the kick, and McAlister, in for the injured Parkes, saved it. The referee was clearly a logical thinker, and having seen McAlister play before, could not believe what he saw. He naturally deduced that Tom had moved before the kick was taken and ordered Hayes to try again, this time with McAlister having both arms tied behind his back. He managed to score this time, but in the second half, the ref saw sense and obviously realised he had made a mistake, as at the first opportunity, he awarded us a penalty for a similar sort of offence. I think Tony Adams farted in the six yard box, and that was enough. Cottee scored his second from the spot. Then came the legendary Liam Brady goal. It was obvious he was going to score his first league goal for us against his old club, but we couldn't have known what a special one it would be, dribbling all the way through their half to curl the ball into the bottom corner. He must have let one go as he rushed into the crowd to celebrate, because the ref hooked him. It puzzled me that the team could play so well on the Wednesday, then get torn apart on the Saturday. We were 4–0 down to Everton at half-time, wishing that there was a right of surrender. Fortunately, they felt sorry for us and didn't score any more goals. We were fully expecting to concede eight or nine; Everton were on top form on their way to another championship. On the same day, Watford were crushed 4–1 by Spurs in the cup semi final. How we laughed! Fancy conceding four goals in a cup semi final! How preposterous.

On the Wednesday we faced a revitalised Manchester United, now managed by Alex Ferguson, who had halted their slide and given them mid-table respectability. After the high octane matches against United that had gone before it was something of a surprise that we should play out a meaningless 0–0 draw. Lanky and Chris, now nicknamed 'Bean Head' for no real reason other than the fact that he didn't have a nickname, accompanied me to Leicester on Easter Saturday. Leicester had a realistic chance of avoiding relegation, and needed all the points they could get. Although there was a mathematical chance of West Ham being relegated, they were not motivated and lost a dire game 2–0.

Two days later we faced Spurs at Upton Park. We had already played them three times, scoring one goal and conceding ten. What outcome would you have predicted? This is what makes football, and West Ham in particular, such a delight to watch. Tottenham swanked and swaggered their way through the first half, obviously aware of the fact they were the superior side, but not stretching us too far. It was as though they felt they could score at any time; there was no particular hurry. It blew up in their faces, as Frankie scored just before half time, and when Tottenham needed to find an extra gear, they found their clutch wasn't working properly. They did manage to find an equaliser, Clive Allen scoring from an offside position. He scored forty-nine goals that season. Seven were scored against West Ham. The gospel according to West Ham dictated that Spurs should be made to pay for their arrogance, and justice was done when we were awarded a penalty for an innocuous looking challenge on Stewart Robson. Cottee despatched the spot kick to restore a bit of pride, and, at last a win against Tottenham.

The next Saturday the same trio who had trailed along to Leicester made the trip to Villa Park. Villa were as good as down, but wanted to put on a good show for their disenchanted fans. Stewart Robson missed a sitter in the opening minute, which if he had put away might have saved us from the humiliation of a 4–0 defeat. Newcastle came to visit and ensured there was no repeat of the previous season's debacle. Mark Ward scored a long range goal to equalise, but we should have got all the points, Cottee missing a first half penalty. We took the opportunity of a bit of sunshine to drive down to Southampton early on the Mayday Bank Holiday and take a wander around the town. Despite being sunny, it was still 1987, and therefore very cold, and we were forced to take shelter in a local pub. Shame. A meaningless game finished in a 1–0 defeat.

The end of season party took place at Upton Park against Manchester City. City needed to win to have any chance of staying up; somewhat surprising then, that we won 2–0, as we had obliged everyone else who was in need of points. Billy Bonds received the Hammer of the Year award, and Cottee and Brady scored the goals. City went down and their fans had every right to go on the rampage after the game had they chosen to do so. Instead, the West Ham fans chanted 'You'll be back!' and diffused any possibility of trouble. Scarves and hats were exchanged, and a link forged with the fans of Manchester City which remains to this day.

I didn't wait on the pitch for the players to come out. I didn't particularly think they deserved the hero worship they were receiving from the adoring crowd. For most of the season, they were totally crap. Instead, I left the party, bought a burger and walked back to the car reflecting on the season that had passed. I felt as though I had achieved a mini league championship of my own. There can't be very many people who have followed their team through every single game in all competitions through a complete season. I had been faced with difficulties and had overcome them. I felt a real sense of achievement, which compensated for the poor performances on the pitch which would have been acceptable had we not finished third the previous season. It was typical West Ham. I actually felt that I needed a break; like the players I was tired and jaded and needed some time away from the game to re-fire my enthusiasm. Having attended every game of 1986/87, I was to find that I would go to the other extreme in 1987/88. But first, I needed a holiday. . .

Y viva España. . .

West Ham United 2 Norwich City 0 – 29.8.87

Coventry beat Tottenham in the FA Cup Final, which went down well with everyone (except Spurs fans of course). It was marvellous to see unfancied Coventry beat Spurs, who had been widely tipped to win by a cricket score. Coventry were in our half of the draw. It should have been us beating Spurs at Wembley. Will we EVER play Spurs at Wembley? It is something I long to see before I die. Coventry are often described in the press as an 'unfashionable' club. The press have some wonderful euphemisms which they tend to use when they cannot bring themselves to write what they mean. Unfashionable means crap. Utility player means crap player. Mistimed tackle means crap tackle. How many times have you seen a utility player playing for an unfashionable club mistiming a tackle?

While we're on the subject of 'unfashionable' things, the new kit that West Ham revealed just prior to the start of the 1987/88 season was very 'unfashionable' but quite suitable for our team of utility players. The kit was manufactured by a company called Scoreline, and consisted of. . . well, let's just say it wasn't Adidas any more. Adidas made kit for all the big teams, Liverpool, Arsenal, Manchester United, and, until the end of 1986/87, West Ham United. What happened? What had we done to upset Adidas so badly they didn't want to make our kit anymore? Adidas still made kit for Charlton, so it couldn't have been the fact that we were useless. It was the start of the slippery slope. We paraded our new home and away strip during a testimonial game for Eddie Chapman, the club secretary, on his retirement. It was a West Ham XI versus an International XI managed by Terry Venables. Such a contrived game I have yet to see, even in World Cup matches involving South American teams. It ended

4–3 in West Ham's favour. Oh, what a surprise. The International XI included players of the calibre of Bryan Robson (not Pop, the crap one who used to play for England), Paul McGrath, Dave Beasant, Terry Fenwick and Luther Blissett. Trevor Brooking made a brief appearance, and showed everyone just how a corner should be taken. All internationals, I suppose, but it was stretching the imagination just a little bit. They wore our away kit, many of them were visibly embarrassed. Not half as embarrassed as me and Dad sitting up in the West Stand. If your team dresses like a bunch of clowns, they will start to play like a bunch of clowns, and that's exactly what happened on the opening day of the season.

I had no option but to take on Saturday work. I did a six day week at Nationwide Anglia Estate Agents in order that I could disappear off to college full time in September, keep the Saturday job and lose the five days during the week. It was unbearable. After not missing a kick of 1986/87 I was confined to barracks for the majority of 1987/88, listening to a radio or a Clubcall message. I was particularly annoyed that I had to miss our opening game against QPR because I felt sure that with a midfield of a fit again Alan Devonshire, Liam Brady, Mark Ward and Stewart Robson, and a forward line of Tony Cottee and Frank McAvennie, the league championship was as good as in the bag. The midfield was the key; creativity, experience and solidity. Just goes to show what sort of a manager I would make.

Admittedly, Devonshire didn't last more than twenty minutes of the season. That was it; out! QPR hit three goals in the first half that we had no hope of recovering from. I couldn't believe it when I heard the score on the radio. Our midfield was supposed to rip them to shreds. Yes, well.

The first division had a very uneven look about it in 1987/88. For the first time, it consisted of only twenty-one clubs, and not the usual twenty-two. This was supposed to be a gradual process, trimming it down to twenty by the play-off process. This was ingenious. The club finishing one place above the relegation zone had to play the team who finished one place outside the promotion frame in the second division to decide who stayed, who went down or who went up. It was awful for those clubs involved. In 1987 it was Charlton who ended up playing Leeds United over two legs, and Charlton won. The Football League might have been better off just handing the two managers, Lennie Lawrence and Billy Bremner a revolver, one bullet and told them to play Russian roulette. It would have been quicker, cheaper, and probably less messy. The significance of the process was that there were less games to play, less teams to potentially beat, and therefore, our chances of slipping out of the top flight were increased by almost 5%. That's a lot in West Ham's case. With the reduction in the number of fixtures that had to be played came a reduction in the number of midweek league fixtures, so whereas there had always traditionally been a game of some description on the first Tuesday or Wednesday of the season, this no longer applied. In addition, it meant that one team was left picking its collective nose on a Saturday, as there could only be ten fixtures, involving twenty teams.

After one game, I accepted that maybe the championship wasn't within our grasp, and that perhaps it would be another battle for survival. The following Saturday I had appointments out of the office all day and was able to follow progress of our 2–2 draw at Luton. At least I wasn't missing anything there – the membership policy was still in and I had left Vauxhall College and didn't see Brian the Luton fan much anymore, so I couldn't have gone if I had been free. Even so, the fact that Luton had denied us a win was another twist of the knife in a still fresh wound. Liam Brady and Ray Stewart scored our goals.

After that, it was off to sunny Spain, with Andy, Wreford and Dave. We were due to fly from Luton Airport, a thought which filled me with horror right from the start, and I should have known we would be delayed on the outward flight. We made the best of it in the departure lounge, getting all our fellow passengers up and dancing or singing along to The Beatles 1962–66. You'd be surprised what some people will do to relieve their boredom. Everything stopped at 4.40pm for the results. Wreef and Dave didn't care about football, so me and Andy crouched over the radio. West Ham 2 Norwich 0. 'Yes!!!' As the only people in the place with a radio, we were constantly being asked how various teams had got on. 'How did Liverpool get on, mate?'

'They won 4–1.'

'Man. United?'

'Won 3–1.'

'Spurs?'

'They weren't playing, you dipstick. Call yourself a fan?'

It was great in Spain. Being late August/early September the heat wasn't too intense, although I still nearly managed to lose the tops of my ears, they got so badly burned. On our first day out there, Andy came up trumps and found us four girls from Leeds who needed looking after. It was ironic, but after doing all the hard work, and setting his sights on Janine, the tall blonde one, he was the only one who didn't score because she had a boyfriend back home. Still, Dave, Wreef and I thanked Andy very much for all his hard work. The girl I got friendly with was called Janet. She was twenty-four; I was nineteen – my aptitude for older women was still prevalent. On our first night she and her friend Fliss invited me and Wreef back to their apartment to help them with their sunburn. This basically involved getting some very cold strawberry yoghurt and smearing it all over one another. West Ham were out of the window – I was busy. Although I put West Ham to the back of my mind, later in the evening I found I needed something to take my mind off proceedings. Thinking about West Ham's goals against tally for last season helped me, and Janet, immensely. At last, I had something to thank the West Ham defence for.

We found an Irish restaurant called Molly Malone's which served breakfast until two in the afternoon; convenient as we rarely got up before mid-day having been out until three or four. We would saunter down to Molly's and have a slap up breakfast, then down to the beach, a quick siesta and a shag around six, then out on the town for dinner and a boogie at ten. It was just like being a professional footballer. On the Monday afternoon, Andy and I struggled to find World Service on the radio for the football results. Portsmouth 2 West Ham United 1. Bummer. No match report, no dubious penalty decision to moan about, no reports on how many times we hit the crossbar or the post, just Portsmouth 2 West Ham United 1. Who scored our goal? How? World Service, pah!

Janet and Fliss had been to Benalmadena before and took us to a bar that specialised in exotic drinks, including tequila slammers. The thing about tequila is, like a tackle from Stewart Robson, it hits you late, and by the time it affects you it's too late to do anything about it. I had five, which was four too many. I don't remember much about what happened after that, what I do remember I'm not prepared to write down in case Spanish police get to see a copy of this. Janet told me afterwards that I went back to her apartment and burst into an uncontrollable flood of tears; totally inconsolable for half an hour, then fell sound asleep on the kitchen floor. I must have been thinking about West Ham's goal difference again.

Time came to say goodbye, which we did reluctantly. The girls had another week out there. We exchanged addresses and phone numbers, as well as body fluids, and promised to write. Yeah, right, we'd heard it all before. Andy reckoned as soon as our backs were turned they would be cavorting around and smearing strawberry yoghurt on another unsuspecting group of London boys. He would say that; he didn't pull. Silently I agreed with him though, not thinking the relationship would possibly lead anywhere and that Janet was unlikely to phone or write.

West Ham were playing Liverpool at Upton Park at the very time that we were taxing out onto the runway at Malaga and flying back to Luton. The radio wouldn't work on the plane and by the time we got to Luton the sports programmes had finished. Liverpool had a red hot side that season. They had recruited John Aldridge to replace Ian Rush, who had gone to Juventus for a giveaway fee to pacify the Italians after the Heysel disaster; an admission of guilt by Liverpool if ever I saw one. They had also splashed out on Peter Beardsley from Newcastle and John Barnes from Watford. They won their first two games without breaking stride, 2–1 at Arsenal and 4–1 at Coventry. It wasn't a question of whether they would beat us, but by how many. As I crossed the threshold at home, the conversation went something like this:

'Hello son, did you have a good time?'

'Yes thanks. How many did we lose by today?'

'We didn't. We drew 1–1.'

'Really? Who scored?'

It's Grim Up North. . .

Barnsley 0 West Ham United 0 – 22.9.87

Janet phoned almost as soon as she got back from Spain a week later. She said she hadn't enjoyed the second week as much without me. 'Flattery my dear, will get you everywhere,' I joked. She also said she had a sore throat all through the week and was going to have it checked out. It turned out to be tonsillitis, and they took her straight into hospital to whip them out. She was phoning quite a lot; Wreef had been up to see Fliss, why didn't I go up and see her? 'Me dad', as northern folk have a habit of saying, 'says West Ham are playing up t'road at Barnsley next week. Why not come and stay a few days and take in the game?' Sod it, I thought. I'll do it.

Our league form remained frustratingly indifferent. Cottee scored his fourth goal of the season, having scored two against Norwich and the equaliser against Liverpool, in a 1–1 draw at Plough Lane against Wimbledon. Then came defeat at home to Tottenham. Despite Spurs pinging goals past us the previous season like they were tiddlywinks, they hadn't managed a win at Upton Park since 1972. I always felt we led something of a charmed life at home to Spurs, an illusion which came tumbling to the ground, as I hurried off to an appointment and switched on the radio. As soon as I heard 'West Ham 0. . . ' I knew we had lost; no chance of a 0–0 draw, not against Spurs. We had played Spurs eighty times in the league up to that day, and only twice had 0–0 draws, in 1904 and 1923. At least it was only a small defeat, 1–0. Having said that, there is no such thing as a small defeat against Spurs. As any West Ham fan will tell you, it hurts just as much at 1–0 as it does at 5–0. It was a frustrating experience merely hearing results come through on the radio; it told you nothing about the game. Even talking to Barney or Bean Head in the pub in the evening failed to enlighten me, it was like something was going on behind my back, and I was missing it all.

I drove up to Leeds to see Janet as promised. She lived in a suburb of Leeds called Bramley, which appears in the *Guinness Book of Records* for having more pubs than any other town. Bramley has thirty-six pubs, and in the two days I was there, I think I had a drink in nearly all of them. It's a long drive to Leeds; had it been purely a football trip, I would have taken the train, but as I knew there was no particular hurry, and a rest could be taken at the other end, I decided to drive up. Mum and Dad were taking a short break in York and followed me up part of the way. I met Janet and Fliss in Leeds and we drove back out to Bramley together. I was thinking in terms of a sandwich and a rest, but Janet had other ideas. She booked a cab, and the three of us went in to town and we had a superb pub lunch, with too many pints of local brew. We then stopped off at a video shop on the way home, and I was allowed the luxury of a couple of hours of shut-eye, while she watched a gruesome horror film. Her dad came home. 'So you're the Cockney who's been shaggin' my daughter are you?' I thought I was in trouble, his face frowned like a traffic warden finding someone double parked on a zig-zag. Then he beamed at me. 'Yer all right, son. Just don't make too much noise tonight, eh?' I laughed nervously, then tried to explain that I wasn't really a Cockney. Janet's mother obviously thought I needed building up. She cooked the most enormous roast dinner you have ever seen, with Yorkshire pudding that on another day would have been a delight, but today was just too much to handle. I wasn't all that hungry when it was put in front of me, after a large lunch and four pints of beer, but the effort that had gone into it deserved some sort of reciprocal effort on my behalf. I felt well pleased with myself, managing to clear my plate. 'Would you like some more potatoes?'

'No! Sorry, er, no thanks, that was wonderful, thanks.' I was puzzled that Janet didn't appear to be eating. She said she'd been off food a bit since the operation, but normally they ate like this every night. I couldn't believe it. They were all skinny as the proverbial rakes. 'Now then, Robert,' Janet's mother proclaimed. 'Do you like tinned pears?'

'Pudding? Oh no, I couldn't.'

'Come on, just a little bit. There's custard, too. Janet says you like custard.' I didn't know how Janet knew I liked custard, unless I had told her in my tequila stupor. It wasn't the sort of thing one ate much of in Spain. I was served a whole tin of pears and a full half pint of custard. That was it, I couldn't move. If I did move, I would spill something. I was certainly in no condition to drive to Barnsley and stand up for two hours watching football. Maybe this was part of Janet's cunning plan, I'll never know. 'What time should we leave for Barnsley?' she asked.

I just belched, rolled my eyes and said: 'I don't really feel up to it. How about a quiet night in?'

'Fine. We can watch TV in Fliss's flat, she's away.' Janet lived with her parents in a large flat on a former council estate. Fliss lived two floors below, which was very convenient. After about an hour, I had the confidence to move about a bit. Janet suggested we go into town for a drink. I felt a bit better, and as it was far too late to go to Barnsley, in my view, the whole reason for the trip in the first place, I agreed. The Yorkshire folk were not as I expected. I expected to be given a hard time about coming from London, about supporting a pansy football team, and taking their women away from a real Yorkshireman, but they were all charming, except one of Janet's male friends, who couldn't stop going on about southern beer tasting like piss, and the drinking water being pumped full of chemicals. I knew all that anyway, I didn't need to be told by a rabid northerner. He was talking to me as though I could do something about it; as though I cared. I think he was just jealous.

Janet dragged me back to Fliss's empty flat and expected me to perform unspeakable acts of depraved debauchery, but after what I'd been through, it just wasn't on, if you get my meaning. 'Just give me the football results,' were my last words, before drifting into a semi conscious state, that almost resembled sleep.

I was awoken in the morning by a head bobbing up and down under the covers. I couldn't feel a thing and wondered if I had been paralysed from the neck down. After a time, or a couple of times anyway, the feeling came back. And how! She got up and went to the kitchen. 'No breakfast!' I yelled, and I think she got the message, bringing me a cup of tea and the morning paper. Barnsley o West Ham o. Shit. Oh well, second leg should be a doddle. Janet was looking a bit nervous. 'We shouldn't have just done what we did,' she said. 'I had to come off the pill when I had my operation. . .'

If I hadn't still been so full of her mother's cooking I would have hit the ceiling. 'What?'

I never spoke to Janet again after I got dressed and walked out of the flat. I got her mum a bunch of flowers to thank her for her hospitality and left. I felt sure that if Janet had wanted to, she could have made life very awkward for me at that point, but she let me go without another word. After the dust had settled, a couple of years later, I sent her a Christmas card, but she never returned the greeting. Wreef still went up to see Fliss occasionally, and assured me that there was no little Banksy running around in Bramley. Thank Cottee for that. West Ham didn't score, Barnsley didn't score, so why should I have been any different?

I went back to London a worried man. Not just about Janet, but the fact that West Ham had to play Arsenal at Highbury on Saturday. On top of all that, I was about to embark on my college course at South Bank Polytechnic; I was taking a degree, the one thing I had always told myself I didn't want to do. It meant working Saturdays and missing West Ham more often than not, but on balance I decided it was the right thing to do.

Throwing It All Away. . .

West Ham United 2 Barnsley 5 – 6.10.87

(after extra time)

I was beginning to hate Barnsley as much as Luton Town. That's a very strong remark for me to make; I could never hate a football club as much as I hate Luton Town, but I was starting to lean that way with Barnsley. After enticing me into the depths of Yorkshire for no apparent reason, they provided me with my first opportunity to see the boys in action on a Tuesday night, only to send me back home with my tail firmly between my legs, wishing once again that I had chosen to support someone else. Somewhere, in a parallel universe, there is another Robert Banks, who is a season ticket holder at Manchester United and is a highly successful novel writer and adored by everyone in the world, regardless of footballing, religious or racial denominations. But is he happy? You bet the hell he is. West Ham were noted for their tendency to throw away promising situations and end up with nothing. This season, more than ever, that point was rammed home.

In between being stuffed alive and almost drowned in beer in Leeds, and the defeat at the hands of Barnsley, I had started my Polytechnic course.

Around a third of the students were girls, which was a bit of a result. Some of them were real foxes, too. Karen was different to the others. She was outspoken and rebellious, very rarely conforming to the pre-conceived ideas of what an Estate Management student should be like. She was a pretty girl with a superb figure, but she always hid it under baggy jumpers and jeans, rarely wearing make-up or jewellery. She came latterly from Wrexham, but originally from

Chester, and had a lovely semi-Welsh accent, that I could listen to for hours, and often did, as we shared coffee or chocolate and cookies in the refectory.

The Saturday after the draw at Barnsley, we lost 1–0 at Highbury. Again, I followed the match on the car radio, and remember being highly disappointed, as Arsenal scored very late on when it seemed we might get a point. Kenny Sansom scored their winner, another reason to be disappointed. The following Saturday we played Derby County, newly promoted, in a first division game at Upton Park. We took the lead through a Liam Brady special, but threw it away when Phil Gee managed an equaliser in the second half. It was a frightening omen for what was about to follow.

I was excited by the prospect of the game against Barnsley. As the first leg had finished 0–0 it was a one off, nothing to pull back, nothing to defend, a good old fashioned one-off cup tie. No reason why we shouldn't win three or four nil. It looked as though that might happen, as first Stewart Robson, and then Kevin Keen from a saved Tony Cottee penalty, put West Ham 2–0 up at half time. That was it, as far as I was concerned. Goodnight Vienna. Who did we fancy in the next round? Then our refusal to hang on came back to haunt us. Barnsley were awarded a silly penalty. It was as though the ref knew the game was up and wanted Barnsley to at least have something to take back with them up to Yorkshire. At 2–1, the wheels suddenly fell off in a pretty big way. They got a free kick on the edge of the box and slammed it past McAlister before the West Ham defence had a chance to encroach. It was too late to mount an immediate response, extra time beckoned, and Barnsley were on a roll. A similar free kick put them 3–2 up and there was no way they were going to let it go. I made my way down to the front of the North Bank as the fourth, and finally and humiliatingly, the fifth goal went in. I turned to a complete stranger standing beside me and said 'Can you believe that?' He was an elderly man probably in his late seventies. He looked me straight in the eye and said 'Yes, son, I can.'

Fortunately, it was not blatantly obvious to anyone at college that I was a West Ham fan, otherwise I would have got a terrific amount of stick. Although some people wore some very dubious club shirts to college, the vast majority of students were more into rugby and hockey than football. A lot of them, it had to be said, were bloody snobs and would look down their noses with contempt when the subject arose. 'Football? Oh yes, that's what common people play isn't it?' I wanted to leap across the table and smash their faces in, but that would only have given them ammunition.

I did have one ally who suffered the same ailment as myself. Tim hailed from the West Country, but had supported the Hammers since the 1980 Cup Final victory over Arsenal. He came in with a face as long as Blackpool beach after the Barnsley game, and I immediately spotted a fellow sufferer. Ian supported QPR and could talk a good game, so the three of us would often take to the student union bar if we had a blank afternoon and practice getting pissed. By the time I left college, I had perfected it. Ian called it getting 'trousered.' I still saw Andy at college; he had opted for the part time degree, along with Brian the Luton fan and Big Al, so he was in one day a week, so we would get together and have pie and chips in the Angell Arms and keep abreast of events.

Students will always harp on about how tough it is being at college, the workload, the financial hardship and the difficult personal relationships. Admittedly, if I had moved away from home and started college straight after school, I might have been able to see their point of view, but as it was, I had learned enough in my three years at work to be able to cope with the workload, which was actually quite tough. I took on a job doing a paper round in the morning, which sounds stupid, but it paid good money; with the regular boys being so unreliable, I could often end up doing two or even three rounds in a morning and walk out on a Saturday with £40 in my pocket, no questions asked. Add to that the £35 I got for working Saturdays, and my grant money and I can safely say that I never missed a football match or a night out through lack of funds, I wasn't rolling in it, by any stretch of the imagination, but it wasn't that hard. As far as personal relationships went, I was mature enough to be able to cope with them, but I had to find one to cope with, that was the problem.

China in Your Hand. . .

West Ham United 2 Southampton 1 – 5.12.87

I'm not sure exactly when I realised that I had a real problem. I knew that my nose wasn't behaving as it should do, and that weird and wonderful things were going on in my sinuses that primarily resulted in the occasional headache, and colds that went on forever. It was as though there was something stuffed up there that simply refused to budge, a pen top or a smartie; something of that sort of size. It only bothered me occasionally, and I never worried about it, particularly as I had gone almost a year with no problems. One Sunday, I was harmlessly watching a game on the TV: Liverpool v Sheffield Wednesday, when I sneezed. That's when it all came out. Literally.

This was scary. A bogey the size and shape of a Bic biro came out of my right nostril, but remained attached firmly to the inside of my nose. This was no ordinary bogey, however, this was 'super bogey' – bogey plus, with a life all of its own. Now what did I do? Should I give it a quick yank and have done with it? No, that would hurt far too much. Should I trim it off and get down to the hospital next morning? No, this thing had blood vessels in it, what if I bled to death? There was only one option, have a good sniff and send it back up from whence it came.

Surprisingly, I couldn't feel it once it had disappeared, but I was obviously cautious, and avoided blowing my nose. Aware of the fact that I had something of alien proportions up my hooter, the doctor examined me the next day. He said I had twisted the cartilage that separated my nostrils, and that had caused polyps to form in my sinuses. That was what was giving me headaches. That was my biro shaped bogey. The chances were there was one on the other side as well, and I would probably need surgery as they were so well advanced they couldn't be removed under a local anaesthetic, and anyway, the cartilage would have to come out, which would mean going under the knife. The specialist had a look and agreed. It was reasonably urgent; he'd get me a place in hospital as soon as possible and do both operations at the same time. He asked if I had received a blow to the face at any time, that might have caused the cartilage to twist like a piece of pasta. As he asked me, I couldn't think, but a few days later, it all came flooding back and slotted into place. God I hate Chelsea. I thought of asking the surgeon to keep the polyps for me so I could send them to Ken Bates, but decided against it, as he probably receives mail like that every day. I was given a date in early December, and tried not to think about it.

After the Barnsley debacle, a draw against Charlton at Upton Park could almost be classified as a good result. Almost, but not quite. We threw away the lead once again, Paul Ince scoring, and Garth Crooks equalising. I listened to the game on and off throughout the afternoon on Clubcall, each time I dialled I urged the message to have changed for the better. It didn't.

The best result of the month was the hurricane which swept across the south of England flattening everything in sight and a few things out of sight, too. Overnight, Sevenoaks in Kent became Oneoak. All the trees in my road fell over, some crushing cars underneath. The best thing to arise out of this was the fact that there were no trains running for the rest of the day, and all the roads were blocked, so I couldn't go to college, even though I desperately wanted to. I phoned to see if I was missing anything, but they said college would be closed – a free day off.

The office was subsequently very busy with complaints the following Saturday, as all the tenants in our managed properties phoned in asking whether they were going to get a new roof or not. I'm not usually one for passing the buck, but unashamedly admit to referring all calls to the relevant department, while intermittently urging the Clubcall message to remain the same; a 2–1 win at Oxford provided a much needed confidence boost, together with a bit of credibility. OK, Oxford were to go on to be relegated, but we weren't to know that, were we? A Cottee strike, together with an own goal, gave us victory. Black Monday followed – no one knew it, but it was the start of the great depression. I wondered if I would ever live to see a Purple Tuesday or a Tangerine Friday. Why was everything always Black?

I managed another game the following Sunday; Avocado Sunday, when the live cameras were at Upton Park yet again for the visit of Manchester United. Liverpool were running away with the title, Manchester United lagged behind in fifth place, but were still favourites to beat us, a situation we always seem to prefer. Colin Gibson put United 1–0 up just before half time and everything seemed to be going to plan. I stood on my own behind the North Bank goal, Close and Stain Tooth had travelled up with me, but had season tickets for the East Terrace, so we parted at the gates. I wasn't sure whether to be jealous of them or not, judging by what I had seen of West Ham so far that season, I was better off at my desk or in the car. That didn't stop me wanting to be there, but my bank manager felt better about it. We enjoyed a little purple (or was it amethyst) patch in the second half, and got an equaliser when Mark Ward was tripped in the box and Ray Stewart scored his second goal of the season. A few minutes later, Cottee raced through, but his shot was about an inch wide of the post. There was a bloke standing to my left with his girlfriend. She complained constantly throughout the game, about having a headache, being thirsty, hungry, hot, cold, tired, bored, squashed, you name it. At first, I thought, 'What a miserable cow.' But later I realised that she was probably none of the things she was complaining about, her complaints were a systematic reaction to the fact that she simply did not want to be there. I could not accept that anyone would not want to be on the North Bank at Upton Park when there was a game on, but each to his (or her) own, I suppose. I made a silent vow never to drag anyone along to a football match, be they male or female, who really didn't want to go.

We missed Frankie Mac. At the end of September, while everyone was speculating about Tony Cottee's future, Lyall sneakily sold McAvennie to Celtic for £750,000. Not a bad return on the £350,000 invested in 1985, but he had a job to do at West Ham – he wouldn't be any use to us in Scotland. We mourned his departure as deeply as the loss of a close and loving relative. For the time being though, the side had reasonable form, and were, in fact, unbeaten in the league following Frank's departure.

After the draw with United, we won at Watford, another side destined for relegation, Cottee and Alan Dickens scoring the goals in a 2–1 win. From the relegation zone we had hauled ourselves up to fourteenth place and appeared reasonably comfortable.

Then came two setbacks. Sheffield Wednesday were even worse than us and had no right to beat us at Upton Park, but they did, 1–0. If you thought watching a game live was a frustrating experience, try not watching it – it's ten times worse. I then got my third game of the season, a Simod Cup game against Millwall at Upton Park. The Simod Cup was the new name for the Full Members Cup. Still no-one took it seriously, but it was a game against Millwall, and just like friendlies against Tottenham, everyone takes them seriously. Eamonn Dolan made his full debut in place of Tony Cottee. John Lyall deciding that Cottee needed a rest. Dickens put us 1–0 up and it didn't seem to matter, but we threw it away again, Sheringham and Cascarino scoring and turning the match in Millwall's favour. Two things remain prominent in my mind about this game. First, there was a crowd of only 11,337 in the ground that night, and yet for each fan, there were two policemen. Helicopters buzzed overhead and meatwagons waited in anticipation of arrests outside the ground. The bill for policing the game must have been three times the gate receipts. Why did we bother? Secondly, a run from inside his own half by Paul Hilton, which earned him the somewhat sarcastic nickname, 'Diego.' He ran fully sixty yards, the ball stuck firmly to his foot, sending defenders tumbling to the ground with his subtle body swerves. As he reached the edge of the area, the keeper nipped the ball off his toe. What a wet lettuce.

Hilton did manage to find the net in the next game against Everton at Goodison Park, but we were 0–3 down at the time, and it was a futile gesture.

As often happens from time to time, something happened outside the football arena which put everything into perspective. I might have been very upset about the way West Ham were playing, and under pressure to finish my Construction Technology coursework, but at least I wasn't at Kings Cross tube station the night thirty-one people died in a nightmare inferno. I sat at my drawing board in my bedroom, trying to draw a cross-section through a cavity wall, as the news broke on the radio. As each half hour passed, the death toll rose steadily, and I thought about Becky and Julia at college; they would have to go through Kings Cross. It was late, sure; they should both be home by now, but what if they had stopped off for a drink on the way home? I was very pleased to see them present and correct the next day – only a week beforehand, one of our number had been stabbed at Vauxhall Cross by a nutter with a pen-knife. She was lucky, receiving only flesh wounds, but we were all a bit edgy after that. I knew for a fact that you didn't have to be on the street for that sort of thing to happen; when I was at Vauxhall College someone was stabbed in the refectory – not a pretty sight I can tell you. The last place I would want to be stabbed is in the refectory. After Kings Cross, the only time I get uptight about someone smoking where they shouldn't be, is in a tube station. I know I wasn't there; I didn't know anyone who was there, but just like Bradford, I could so easily have been there. It was time to take stock and be grateful for small mercies, like Tony Cottee.

Cottee scored twice in the next home game, a 3–2 win over Nottingham Forest. I had only heard how good his second goal was, I didn't get to see it until the season's highlights video came out and even then I couldn't believe it. A cross came over from the right, attacking the South Bank end, and Cottee just launched his feet at it, almost parallel to the ground when he hit it on the volley, and it went straight into the top of the net. Bobby Robson watched from the stands and still failed to be impressed. What did you have to do to impress this man? (Apart from to have played for Ipswich, of course).

Our divine right to three points at Coventry came to a grinding halt with a 0–0 draw, and the evil hour approached when I faced the surgeon's knife. I had to go in on the Sunday, have the operation on the Monday, and, all being well, would be let out on the Tuesday. That being the case, I took the Saturday off work to 'prepare' by going to Upton Park to watch the game against Southampton. Keen scored a belter before the defence pressed the anticipated self-destruct button and allowed Danny Wallace in to equalise. Alan Dickens scored the winner in the second half. I had the merest hint of a cold coming, but I knew if I said anything they wouldn't let me have the operation. I wanted it dealt with and out of the way; you can imagine how I felt having all that gunge and goo in my head – I wanted it out! I had to take the last week of term off college, which was unfortunate because I missed much of the Christmas boozing, but I got a nice card from everyone in my Seminar Group. I was quite choked.

Dad took me to the hospital on the Sunday. The irresistible Liverpool were on the TV playing Chelsea, who had the audacity to take a 1–0 lead, and looked as though they might nick it. Realising that Chelsea were directly responsible for me being in the state I was in, I encouraged Liverpool to knock the wind out of Chelsea's sails, which they did, 2–1. The operation was a complete success; as I woke up post op, the guy in the next bed was having a reaction to the anaesthetic and was doing his nut. I just wanted a drink. My mouth was as dry as an Arabian pub. I asked for a drink, but the Gestapo Staff Nurse refused. She swabbed my mouth with damp cotton wool but that was like offering a starving man a Chicken McNugget. I was told I wouldn't be able to drink for seven hours. That wouldn't have been so bad if I had been able to sleep, but I had a bed that was as comfortable and cosy as a field of stinging nettles, and the guy in the next bed kept shouting death threats at everyone. To add insult to injury, the children's ward was at the end of our ward, and the little Joeys just kept on crying. Also, my dressing consisted of two sticks of cotton wool, one up each nostril, the size and shape of the average weightlifter's thumb. I had to breathe through my parched mouth and was in no condition to die, let alone sleep. Mum and Dad came to see me, Dad helpfully waved an ice cold can of fizzy Ribena in my face. I could have throttled him. As soon as I was allowed a drink I perked up. I was allowed to get up and walk about, and the next day, after watching the varsity rugby match on the TV, I was allowed home. 'Oh, and one more thing,' the ward sister said as I was leaving. 'No undue excitement, and no alcohol for a month.' Great! Christmas just around the corner, and I incur an alcohol ban. Thank you Chelsea, thank you so very much.

Happy New Year. . .

Norwich City 4 West Ham United 1 – 1.1.88

Now that I did have some time to myself, I still couldn't go to football for fear of bleeding all over everybody. It would have been no fun for anyone. I had to sit and listen from my sick bed as we drew 1–1 at Chelsea, throwing away a 1–0 lead once again, and apparently playing Chelsea off the pitch. That was some consolation for my condition, but not much. The following Saturday we beat Newcastle, including Paul Gascoigne and Mirandinha, 2–1 at Upton Park, Paul Ince scoring a goal of truly classic proportions, a dipping shot from outside the area.

By the time Boxing Day came, I had already ignored the doctor's advice and had a drink or twelve over Christmas, and hadn't keeled over and died, so I saw no reason why I shouldn't break the other rule and get a little bit excited at Upton Park. I went along to watch the home game against Wimbledon, but my doctor needn't have worried, as I hardly got excited at all, seeing us go 2–0 down in the first half, only pulling one back through a Ray Stewart penalty in the second. I was keen to get back to work as soon as possible and not dwell on my operation. I was quite candid and open with people when they asked me why I had been in hospital. I didn't want people to think I'd gone in for a circumcision or a vasectomy or anything like that. By the time I had given them a full description of the operation, and described exactly what came out, they wished they hadn't asked. I had to miss our 2–1 defeat at White Hart Lane as I was working, but had New Year's Day free and arranged to take Bean Head to Carrow Road for the game against Norwich. It was another one of those days when it never stopped raining, right from the time I left the front door to the time I got back. A miserable journey to Norwich in appalling conditions, a soaking walk from the car park to the ground, hopes raised briefly when Cottee gave us the lead in the first half only to be dashed when Norwich took the field for the second half and ripped us apart. Norwich were the only other first division side to wear the 'unfashionable' Scoreline kit, but it didn't seem to affect them in the way it affected us. Theirs looked even worse than ours because they had to wear green and yellow; difficult colours for anyone to look good in. Having said that, Norwich were below us in the league, but the following season, wearing exactly the same horrible kit, challenged for the title. Sad.

New Year's Day was on a Friday, and the next match was played on the next day, the Saturday. I wasn't too upset about missing the game against Luton Town, purely because, as you may have gathered by now, I'm not exactly fond of Luton. Another lead squandered, Ince getting the ball across the line, but hardly in the back of the net on the hour. I rang Clubcall from the office just as this was happening, but knew that because it was Luton, we would not hang on. I suppose I should have been grateful that it was only 1–1. My brain had told me it would probably be 1–3 at the very least.

It was around this time that I met Jo. Jo was the proverbial friend of a friend, who came along to one of our Thursday night drink-ups at my local pub, the Clock House in Beckenham. She was bright and lively, with long flowing brown hair, the most fantastic pair of baps you could wish for. Talk about 'hard to get' though. It took me several weeks of phone calls and gentle persuasion to get her to come out with me. When we eventually did go out we went for a Chinese meal and found that we got on like a house on fire. She had mentioned that she had trouble with her back, as the result of an accident as a young girl when she fell off a horse. This meant she still had to go to hospital occasionally to have physiotherapy. 'That's nothing,' I told her, 'next Wednesday I've got to go and have all the scabs pulled out of my nose.' I think I put her off her lychees. She was fascinated by my interest in football, and wanted to come along to a game with me. I thought about the bloke at the Manchester United game with his whingeing girlfriend, and about Jo's back, and thought that if she wanted to come, I would have to buy a seat, or preferably two.

Trouble was, I wasn't available to go for the foreseeable future. I was delighted that she took an interest though, and didn't view my obsession as an intrusion on our relationship. Not that we really had one, not until I phoned her, and her mother answered the phone and told me she was in hospital. She gave me the address and the ward, and said she was sure she'd appreciate a visit.

They say a gallstone provides the most pain a human can endure without passing out. Whoever discovered that obviously never had half a dozen scabs pulled out of their nose with long metal pliers by a junior doctor with dirty fingernails. I shudder even now at the very thought. I told Karen at college about my situation with Jo. She offered me sisterly advice; what I should take, what I should say, what I should wear, etc. I wasn't sure how much notice to take of a woman who openly stated she took no notice of romantic advances from men, and was more interested in what was on the inside, than outward superficial shows of affection. Karen was too complicated an issue for me; I listened to the problems she was having with her boyfriend, Dave, but could offer no advice to her. After all – she knew everything. I went to see Jo at the hospital and was shown to her room by the nurse. When I got in, it was clear that she had been crying. I sat on the bed and hugged her and realised I could do with some more. She had been told her back was going to cause her problems for the rest of her life, and she should accept the fact. What can you say to someone who has just been told that? It would be like being told there is no cure for being a West Ham fan. I told her just to get better and enjoy the grapes. If she behaved, I promised to take her to a game before the end of the season. Now, if that didn't speed up her recovery, I'm sorry, but I just didn't know what would.

The team turned their attention to the FA Cup. Charlton were the third round opponents for the second time in three years, this time, at Upton Park, and goals from Brady and Cottee saw them off 2–0. In 1988, the draw for the FA Cup still took place on the Monday after all the games had been played. At around lunchtime, I was at college that Monday, riding in the lift down to the library for a bit of reading in between lectures. Yes I was. As the door opened, who should be there but Brian the Luton fan. He had a grin on his face the length of the M4, and a transistor radio welded to his ear. 'Well?' I asked, 'What's so bleedin' funny?'

'QPR away!' he laughed. 'Plastic pitch. Oh well, maybe next year. See you Rob.'

I wasn't too disheartened. Despite our much publicised hatred of plastic pitches, the one at Loftus Road appeared to be causing the home team as much grief as the visitors, and in the summer that followed, they relented to the pressure and ripped it up, replacing it with a natural grass surface. In addition, we had won on our previous two visits to Loftus Road, and we had a chance for a bit of practice, as we were due to play there in the League just fourteen days before the cup meeting. Hopes were raised further when we won the league game. Alan Dickens headed the winner in a 1–0 victory. Maybe Brian the Luton fan was being a bit presumptuous. Maybe he wasn't.

In a now infamous game, a crowd of 23,651, a huge crowd for QPR spilled out onto the pitch during play causing considerable delays, over an hour in a goalless first half, so the match was still in progress when I arrived home from work at 5.30pm. David Pisanti, an Israeli international, gave QPR the lead, but Cottee equalised a couple of minutes later. Gary Bannister got a second, and a certain Martin Allen the third. Desperation set in as Lyall threw Paul Hilton up front. Surely things weren't that bad? It was very disappointing to go out at the fourth round stage, as we had made at least the fifth round in each of the previous four seasons. It also meant there would be no postponements for me to look forward to seeing on midweek dates later in the season.

The propaganda had begun. 'No Panic Buying!' was the most frequently used phrase at Upton Park since the departure of Frank McAvennie. It was clear we needed another striker, but all the good ones were too expensive or unavailable, and none of the crap ones which we could afford wanted to come and play for us. You could hardly blame them, could you?

When we played Liverpool at Anfield on February 6th, they were still unbeaten and thirteen points ahead of nearest rivals Nottingham Forest. It was built up to be the biggest slaughter on Merseyside since the 6–0 thrashing they handed us in 1984. I deliberately avoided

As one of my heroes, Alf Garnett, just before a fancy dress party. I was devastated when I discovered that Warren Mitchell was a Spurs fan.

My eldest nephew, Mark, in a totally natural and uncontrived pose. I used to put him through hell wearing that gear. It's a wonder he still supports West Ham.

Dobbo holding the banner we made for the Man United game in November 1983. It made just one appearance at Upton Park before retiring with injured pride.

West Ham remain the last team from outside the top flight to win the FA Cup. In 1975 they were the last team to win it with a team composed entirely of Englishmen. In 1980 the only non-English player was Ray Stewart. (Mirrorpix)

Phil Parkes shows why he was such a successful goalkeeper. His hands are bigger than his head. (Mirrorpix)

Three of the greatest West Ham players of the modern era: Trevor Brooking, Alvin Martin and Billy Bonds, pictured in a 2–0 win at White Hart Lane in August 1983 (*sniffs and wipes away a tear*). (Mirrorpix)

Alan Dickens was hailed as Brooking's replacement but that was an unfair burden on his shoulders. He was a good player but not in Brooking's class. (Mirrorpix)

In 1985, because of the TV blackout, no-one knew what Frank McAvennie looked like (apart from the staff at Stringfellows, of course). Here he is getting some much-needed publicity with *EastEnders* actresses Gillian Taylforth and Brian May. . . oh no, it's the other one. Sorry. Ask me and I will tell you about a dream I had about Gillian Taylforth once. I couldn't possibly divulge details here... (Mirrorpix)

Macca shows off his clapped-out old banger – and an F-reg Audi. Looks like he's just returned from rehearsals with Kajagoogoo. (Mirrorpix)

Trust me, Frank, it tastes better out of a glass.
And where the hell did you get that suit? (Mirrorpix)

A picture that epitomises the 1985/86 season. Frank and Tony celebrate again.
(Mirrorpix)

Iain Dowie in his first spell at West Ham in 1991. The ball is probably somewhere on the right.
(Mirrorpix)

Mike Small wears the popular 'Argentina' away kit at Highbury in 1991. West Ham won the game 1–0, which, considering the team also had Mitchell Thomas in it, was nothing short of a bloody miracle. (Mirrorpix)

'Bondknapp' pictured in August 1992. Billy Bonds is smiling in blissful ignorance of the fact that his best mate would nick his job two years later and then go on to manage the Totts. (Mirrorpix)

Dicksy fouls Ian Wright at Highbury and concedes the penalty that won them the game. Later after using all outfield substitutes the late Les Sealey made a cameo appearance up front. (Mirrorpix)

Julian doing what Julian does best – sending an opponent six feet in the air. (Mirrorpix)

phoning Clubcall or listening to the radio at work because I didn't want to depress myself. When I left the office at 5.00pm I switched on the car radio for the classified check. When I heard the result, Liverpool 0 West Ham 0, I was so delighted I reversed the car straight into a lamp-post.

Don't Turn Around. . .

West Ham United 0 Everton 0 – 4.4.88

Of the forty-five League and Cup matches played by West Ham United in 1987/88, no fewer than thirty-five were played on Saturdays. Early exits from both cup competitions meant that the number of midweek games available for me to watch were restricted. No league matches were scheduled for midweek, and we only played Arsenal and Nottingham Forest midweek because of their involvement in the cup, not ours. The other 'midweek' fixtures were played on public holidays over Christmas, New Year and Easter. Of the games available to me, I attended all with the exception of the midweek trip to Nottingham Forest, and the cup tie at Barnsley, which of course, I would have got to had it not been for Mrs Lister's Yorkshire pudding. I therefore had no reason to feel ashamed of my lack of attendance, particularly as I had done every game the previous season, while Barney, Natty Matty and Bean Head made feeble excuses. Home draws against Portsmouth and Oxford were Saturday games, and therefore missed. On paper, they were games we should have won, but then, on paper, we were top of the league. Away defeats at Derby (0–1) and Charlton (0–3) were also on Saturdays, a fact for which I remain eternally grateful.

The striker we had been promised finally arrived, on the day that the fumble I had been promised by Jo also arrived. Leroy Rosenior was signed from Fulham and was thought by many to be the burly hustling foil for Tony Cottee we had been crying out for. The signs were good. The day after he put pen to paper he scored the winner on his home debut against Watford. He continued in a similar vein at Old Trafford, scoring an equaliser only for United to run out 3–1 winners, and again on Easter Saturday in a 1–2 defeat at Hillsborough. If

Rosenior and Cottee could only manage to get one each in a game, we would start winning. Goals had been the problem. When we faced Everton on Easter Monday, we had scored only thirty-three goals. Liverpool had got that many in their away games alone, and both Oxford and Chelsea, who were to be relegated had scored more than we had. We needed to find a combination that clicked.

As 0–0 draws go, the one against Everton wasn't bad. Cottee and Rosenior linked up well together and caused a few headaches. Everton were reigning champions, but had hit their peak and were about to start the slippery slide back to mediocrity. Their slide took a lot longer than ours. Tony Gale made his 400th league appearance, and West Ham should have won. There you have it, the game in a nutshell.

I knew Jo wanted me, all she had to do was say the word. Trouble was, she never said the word. Two days after I had worked out a route into her drawers she dumped me. I didn't have time to be upset about it, because I was too busy working towards my first year exams at poly, and I was determined it wasn't going to be spoiled by a woman.

Just when we thought we had it sorted, with Cottee and Rosenior up front, Arsenal beat us at Upton Park. That hurt more than Jo telling me to sling my hook. It was the only midweek league match we played at Upton Park, and I was so pleased to be able to go, the feeling of depression after the defeat was truly unbearable. Tony Cottee had just hit the post with an opportunist shot, when Michael Thomas raced up the other end and scored. I almost cried. The team was right in the middle of nowhere. The management called it a period of transition, I called it a period of not really knowing what was going on. Another new signing had arrived, a young full back from Birmingham City called Julian Dicks. Julian Dicks? What the hell was going on? What were we doing signing players with names like Julian? We needed tough, rough guys out there with skill to go with it. How wrong I was. The first time I saw Julian Dicks play was in the 0–0 draw against Everton, and I fell instantly and irreversibly in love with him. Here was a man with skill and commitment in equal measure. Above all else, he was a bit of a character; not obvious at first, but over the years he would become the spirit of West Ham United.

While we appeared to be several places above the relegation scrap, there were not many points in it, and there was still a very real possibility of getting sucked in. After a 0–0 draw at Nottingham Forest, we were only two points ahead of Charlton, who occupied the play-off spot, and four ahead of Portsmouth who were in the third automatic relegation place. Another point in the home match against Coventry helped, but we needed wins to make sure of avoiding trouble. A point at Southampton would have helped even more, but in a season symbolised by the surrendering of advantages, we went 1–0 up only to lose 2–1 and found ourselves up to our necks in cack. Charlton had won, which left them in the play-off spot on goal difference only. When Chelsea came to Upton Park on May Day Bank Holiday, they were one point ahead of us. By the time we had finished with them, they were two behind us, and a victory for Charlton left Chelsea saddled with the play-off place. I rubbed my nose and chuckled heartily.

We slaughtered Chelsea. Leroy got two before half time and the game was effectively over. Paul Hilton got another from close range before Chelsea pulled one back, but Tony Cottee scored his last goal for West Ham before his transfer to Everton to make it 4–1. It was the first and only time we scored four in one game during 1987–88. If we could have picked a time to do it, that was the best moment. Other results meant that we were safe, only capable of being dragged back into trouble if we lost our last game by thirteen goals or more against Newcastle at St James' Park on the final Saturday of the season. Being West Ham, this was a distinct possibility, so John Lyall took the unprecedented precaution of naming a goalkeeper as substitute. Phil Parkes wore the No. 12 shirt, and as if to represent the season as a whole in one match, West Ham went ahead through Stewart Robson, only to lose 2–1. It was a fitting end to a crap season, which was difficult to look back on with any sense of achievement. Merely staying up was hardly an achievement when one considered we had been challenging seriously for trophies the previous two seasons, but the warning signs had been there as recently as late 1986. The downward spiral is the most difficult to break. The highlight of 1987/88 was the 4–1 win over Chelsea, which contributed enormously to their relegation. They lost in the playoffs to Middlesbrough. The only other high points were the signings of Rosenior and Dicks, and, without a shadow of a doubt, the contents of Jo's bra. On the footballing front at least, I felt sure that 1988/89 could only get better. Wrong again!

The Only Way Is Up. . .

West Ham United 1 Charlton Athletic 3 – 3.9.88

For the second year running, the unfancied underdogs won in the Cup Final. This time Wimbledon, not just unfancied but totally rejected as no-hopers, beat a Liverpool side who had swept all before them in winning the title at a canter. Surely Liverpool would win their second double in three seasons? The funny old game reared its ugly head again. Rob Fox, a new pal of mine who was a regular at my local but had a nasty tendency to support Spurs, brought some cans round and we thoroughly enjoyed the game. Liverpool had a goal disallowed and a penalty saved. Wimbledon casually strolled up the other end and Lawrie Sanchez headed a Denis Wise cross past Grobbelaar. Seeing Dave Beasant lift the cup was unbelievable, and gave us all hope. Foxy came round again later in the summer to watch England v Holland in the European Championships. England had already lost to Ireland, lost to Holland and a few days later lost to Russia. Less said about that, the better. Bobby Robson refused to learn the vital factor for the success of the England team. You must have at least three West Ham players in the side.

Pre-season optimism is a wonderful thing. I sat in the Wimpy bar in Beckenham High Street with Julie, a good friend, discussing nothing in particular, when I noticed on the back page of a fellow diner's copy of *The Sun* that West Ham had signed David Kelly from Walsall for £600,000. I had heard good things about Kelly, and at the time was quite pleased about the deal. We had finally sold Tony Cottee, stinging Everton for £2.2 million on the way. I was very sad to see Tony go, strangely, not as sad as I had been when Frankie left. That was when the partnership was broken. When Cottee left, it was something that had been expected for some time. I felt better when I heard we had signed Kelly. In addition, we had bought a new goalkeeper; a priority in my view, as both Tom McAlister and Phil Parkes were well past their sell-by dates, and I'm sure they would both have been the first to admit it. We bought Allen McKnight from Celtic for £250,000. The man was a Northern Ireland international, and therefore, I thought, of international standard. How was I to know we would have been better off signing Ronnie Corbett?

There were worrying signs right from the start. I bought four tickets for Alvin Martin's testimonial game against Tottenham on August 21st, and took Mum and Dad along with Julie, who by now had become the latest older woman in my life, being some three years my senior. Although we won the game 2–0, I was concerned that both our goals had been scored by defenders: Tony Gale and Paul Hilton. What worried me more was the way the whole defence took a sharp intake of breath whenever McKnight came out for a cross, and covered their eyes. David Kelly showed some neat touches, but fell over every time he kicked the ball further than ten yards, or if he received a pass from more than ten yards. On the way home, Dad said 'What did you think of Kelly?' I remember my reply distinctly. I said: 'I don't know. I think he looks a bit lightweight.' It was the most succinct and accurate player analysis I have ever produced. Having been quite optimistic about our chances in early August, our opening game against Southampton at The Dell became a kind of D-Day for us. A win would be wonderful, a draw would be steady, defeat would probably signal a struggle ahead for us.

I had thought the worst that could possibly happen would be a 0–1 or a 1–2 defeat. After all, Southampton weren't exactly Liverpool, were they? And surely we couldn't do worse than our opening day defeat last season against QPR, could we? I was devastated when I turned on the radio in the office to find we had lost 4–0. That was ridiculous. It was only later, when I saw the video, that I realised a local Boy Scout troop could have beaten us, we looked so inept, it was hard to stomach. The team that a few years ago had struck fear into the hearts of the opposition was now regarded an easy three points.

The trap door at the bottom of the first division gaped even wider in 1988/89. The division had been trimmed down to twenty clubs, which meant a placing of eighteenth or worse would be enough to say bye-bye. Julie knew about my obsessions, and she knew that I would want to see every available game. She was unquestioningly reasonable about it, which should have made me suspicious, but it didn't. Her father, on the other hand, was a different kettle of fish altogether. I got on quite well with him until he found out I supported West Ham, then he didn't have a good word to say about me, and gave Julie a hard time about it. Fortunately, she lived away from the parental nest, in a bedsit flat two minutes walk from my house. That was convenient, wasn't it, readers? On our first date we had been to see Crocodile Dundee II at the local flicks. As I walked he back to her flat she played hard to get, but it didn't last long. After our second date, she invited me in for coffee. After that, I would pop round for coffee as often as I possibly could, football permitting, of course. The only doubt I had about her was that her record collection contained far too many Jean-Michel Jarre albums to be healthy. As far as her dad was concerned, West Ham were a bunch of bastards, and that was that. I don't think he had ever forgiven us for beating them in the FA Cup. In 1964. Julie never said anything about her allegiances, I just assumed she would go with the flow, or that she wasn't interested.

She seemed interested enough when I mentioned I was taking a Saturday off to watch our opening home game against, by coincidence, Charlton Athletic, and asked if I should buy her a ticket too. She seemed quite happy to come along. I thought it would be a flash in the pan, and after being bored rigid for ninety minutes she would never come again. (To a football match, you dirty minded so-and-so.) We had a little accident a few weeks previously, and for the second time in the space of a year, I worried about entering the realms of fatherhood a little earlier than anticipated. Don't get me wrong, I'd love to have kids one day, I just didn't envisage my first born being conceived on the 11.53 from Chatham to Victoria. As we walked to the ground, arm in arm, she pulled me close and said: 'You'll be glad to hear you're not going to be a daddy.' The relief was tremendous. Now, I thought, I could relax, and enjoy our first home win of the season.

Charlton scored first after a defensive mix-up left McAlister stranded. It spoke volumes for McKnight's pre-season performances that McAlister was still preferred in goal. Julie smiled and squeezed my arm, in consolation. 'Never mind love; still a long time to go.'

In the second half, Stewart Robson sent a looping clearance over McAlister for our first own goal of the season to make it 2–0. Julie leapt off her chair in celebration. 'What the hell are you doing?' I asked. 'They scored, not us.'

'Oh, sorry,' she said. 'Didn't I tell you I supported Charlton?'

'No. You didn't.' What a dick-head. I should have seen it coming a mile away. With a dad slightly more partisan than Attila the Hun she could hardly fail to follow in his footsteps. It would have been cold showers every twenty minutes if she had shown tendencies any other way. Now I knew why she had been so keen to come along. I was angry. She had deliberately misled me into believing that she didn't care about football, and made me look a complete turnip.

Kevin Keen pulled one back from the penalty spot after David Kelly fell over in the penalty area, but Charlton were proving to be a bit of a tough nut to crack. Despite cup successes over them we have won only one of ten League meetings since 1986. Not good. Paul Williams, a self-confessed Hammers fan, showed his love for us by scoring Charlton's third and my misery was complete.

'The Hammer' started to turn out a run of old cobblers which was verging on the ridiculous. In the Charlton edition, the report on the Southampton match made pathetic excuses about being without Leroy Rosenior, Liam Brady and Alan Devonshire, as though they would have made a difference. It then went on to make the same statement made after each and every subsequent opening day defeat. 'Don't forget we lost the first game of the season in 1985/86 and went on to finish third. . .' Utter bollocks. What a feeble attempt to hoodwink intelligent people. The team photograph showed a first team squad that appeared to have just been drenched by the huge thundercloud over their heads. False smiles on each face. The weaknesses were there for everyone to see, we had sold our best players and bought cheap replacements. There was only one way to go, and it certainly wasn't up!

Desire. . .

Middlesbrough 1 West Ham United 0 – 8.10.88

I started my second year at polytechnic on the back of staggering success in the first year. Due to the fact I had done most of the work before during my part time course at Vauxhall, I was able to finish top, peaking with an amazing 93% in my valuations paper, which stunned me as well as my colleagues. I certainly wasn't going to complain, and gladly accepted the £20 book token reward for being a Smart Alec.

Karen hadn't done so well, and had to re-sit her Sociology paper because, in her own words, she had 'written the truth.' I told her there was no way you could get away with that. As I found in R.E. at school, it was far better to listen to what your teacher said, write what he wanted to hear and only express your thoughts when it could really hurt them – verbally, in class. She complied with the lecturer's wishes and passed the re-sit. I never really worked out why we had to do sociology anyway. Such a waste of time.

If my obsession was West Ham, Julie's obsession was Jean-Michel Jarre. Don't ask me why. It was most out of character; most of her records had a heavy metal element to them, why on earth did she want to listen to a man who made up tunes on a Rolf Harris stylophone? As she had been forced to endure a football match or two, I was dragged along to Jarre's 'Destination Docklands' concert, only I had to pay for my own ticket. Does that seem fair to you? Whatever happened to sexual equality? West Ham were playing away at Middlesbrough, and we began queuing to get a good place at around the time the match was kicking off.

West Ham were doing a very good impression of a team that wanted to play second division football. Having surprised everyone by winning at Plough Lane with a goal from Mark Ward, they allowed

Graham Taylor's Aston Villa to take a 2–0 lead at Upton Park before a fortuitous goal from Alan Devonshire and a tap in from Kelly gave us a share of the points. We then lost badly to Manchester United and Arsenal, 2–0 at Old Trafford and 4–1 at Upton Park to Arsenal. Somehow, inexplicably, between those two league games we managed to beat Sunderland at Roker Park by a thumping 3–0 in the Littlewoods Cup. Kelly got two and Rosenior the other.

I was still working Saturdays, but the office was opening on Sundays as well, and I could swing it sometimes to work Sunday rather than Saturday by swapping with the Sunday girl. It was a complex procedure and not one that my boss was particularly keen on, so it had to be kept to a minimum. I got the Saturday off to go to the Jarre concert, but didn't realise exactly what would be involved. We stood in the queue from about 3.00pm, got to our position at about 5.00pm, and the show wasn't due to begin until 8.00pm. We couldn't sit down because the ground was wet and we had no waterproofs to sit on. I was cold, tired and miserable before the concert even started. I cast my mind back again to the Manchester United game last season, and the bloke's moaning girlfriend. I sympathised more deeply than ever before, but was determined not to let Julie see I was totally pissed off. She was loving every minute of it, poor cow. The concert went on and on and on. I refused to applaud at the end as I didn't want to encourage an encore, but it came anyway and we had to queue for another hour to get a train back to Victoria. By this time I had been standing up for nine hours and gentleman or no gentleman, barged an old woman out of the way so I could sit down. All the trains to Beckenham had gone, so we had to get a train to East Croydon and ring Julie's mum to get her to come and fetch us. She was most amused. Not. To add insult to injury, West Ham had lost 1–0 at Middlesbrough, and I had to go to work the next day. Whenever I hear Jean-Michel Jarre on the radio now, I flip my lid – a natural reaction, I think.

On Monday, Karen rubbed salt into the wounds by saying she saw and heard the concert from a vantage point over a mile away, and didn't have to pay £12 for a ticket. Karen was a mucky little fox, and always told me exactly what she got up to over the weekend. I wasn't sure, but I was beginning to think she fancied me a bit. She was tarting herself up to come into college, wore more flattering clothes and stuck religiously to my side at all available times. The second biggest mistake I ever made was introducing Karen to Julie. Did I get grief!

We finished off Sunderland in the second leg of the Littlewoods Cup tie, 2–1 at Upton Park and looked a different team. However, the trend of surrendering a lead that had been started the previous season continued at Loftus Road, where the installation of a natural surface ended our three year winning run at QPR. Kelly put us ahead, but second half goals from Stein and Maddix sank us. Mark Stein used to play for Luton Town. Little git. We won at home for the first time the next Saturday. Significantly, Newcastle were to prove to be even more crap than us and finished bottom, but we weren't to know that at the time and celebrated a 2–0 win like it was a cup final victory. Alan Dickens and Ray Stewart scored the goals. Had we known we wouldn't win another home league match until April 22nd we would all have bought our Oldham street maps earlier than we did to avoid the rush. It is a sad fact, but true. Julie took me on a dirty weekend to Margate the following Friday. I had hoped that if I spent the Saturday afternoon making love to my girlfriend, and the team won, I might be able to use it as one of those superstitions which were beginning to develop all over the place. I had a lucky sweatshirt and a lucky pair of socks, both of which ended up on the scrap heap along with the lucky scarf I wore to the Charlton game. I know, as does every other mature adult who attends football, that the order in which you dress, the clothes you wear, or what you do the night before a game has absolutely no bearing on the result at all, yet we all still do it, don't we? Come on, admit it!

I spent the entire afternoon making Julie's toes curl, then realised she still had her tights on. I relaxed on the luxurious, if somewhat creaky bed, and switched the TV on with the remote control. West Ham 0 Liverpool 2 Bugger it! I quickly turned the telly off so Julie wouldn't see. She jumped back onto the bed, towelling her hair dry and said 'How did they get on?'

'Oh we won!' I lied. 'We'll have to do this every time there's an important game...' It didn't wash. She got the Sunday papers and rumbled me.

Perhaps I was wrong. Perhaps I needed an afternoon of shagging three days before an important match to make the result go the right way. If that was the case, it worked perfectly, as we smacked Derby County 5–0 at Upton Park in the third round of the Littlewoods Cup. It was totally incomprehensible. It really was as though a different side took the field for a cup match, even though the players were exactly the same dorks who got battered every Saturday. Along with the disappearance of Glen Miller, the Bermuda Triangle and Crop Circles, the difference between West Ham's form in the league and their form in the cup will remain a mystery for ever more. Alvin got two, Kevin Keen, Leroy Rosenior and Ray Stewart the others. Blinding.

I continued to abuse the telephone facilities at work, listening in to our 1–1 draw at Coventry. OK, so our divine right to a win at Coventry had gone, but we still had a divine right to come away unbeaten. Cup form then came good again in the Mickey Mouse trophy, also known as the Simod Cup. Stain Tooth and I didn't think it was Mickey Mouse as we were gifted two tickets for the West Stand outside by a guy who had two mates who couldn't make it. There should be more people like that at football. We would happily have paid face value for them, but no-one seems to accept that these days, not when a tout will give you more. We beat WBA 5–2. The WBA side had such names as Arthur Albiston, Brian Talbot, Chris Whyte, Carlton Palmer and Gary Robson, younger brother of Bryan. (That's not Pop, that's the crap one who played for England a few times.) Leroy got four, Kelly the other. We got the impression that on cup nights at Upton Park, we could beat anyone, maybe even Liverpool.

In the game against Nottingham Forest we were alternately brilliant and crap every ten minutes. Playing like that, a 3–3 draw was no surprise. Brian Moore gave it a three-changes-of-underpants type commentary and the press loved it. All the old quotes about West Ham adding steel to their artistry had changed to West Ham being too good to go down. That's all rubbish, as Nottingham Forest found for themselves a few years later. Nobody has a divine right to anything in this world, least of all a place in the top flight.

If we were too good to go down, we wouldn't have lost 4–1 at

Luton. Did I tell you that I hate Luton? Let me tell you again: I hate Luton. I hated their stupid plastic pitch, their away fans policy and, more than anything else, the fact that they would never let us beat them. I accepted that they would win, but 4–1? We were already 3–0 down by half time, and I just crossed my fingers and prayed for a crazed RAF Tornado pilot to hit Kenilworth Road with two giant Napalm bombs. We might lose the whole team, but at least the score would be erased from history.

The same day I realised I had to do something with my life. I told Julie it was over. I thought she would just accept it and put it all down to experience, but she acted like a total fool and followed me around for days. I could understand her frustration, because she wasn't sure why I had done it. I wasn't sure why I had done it. Foxy cruelly suggested that she was having a detrimental effect on West Ham's form. I told him not to be so callous, then, walking home, thought he might have a valid point. She was convinced I had someone else, but I didn't. Well, not unless you count Karen.

First Time. . .

West Ham United 4 Liverpool 1 – 30.11.88

Tony Cottee came home to Upton Park with his new friends and they duly beat us 1–0. Fortunately, he didn't score, otherwise I might have thrown a major wobbler.

After the defeat against Everton, Karen came to meet me at the office and we went on to a party being held by one of our friends at college. I was pleasantly shocked by her appearance. It was the first time I'd seen her in a dress, wearing jewellery and generally looking rather tasty. I hated the party. It was full of ya-ya's from the polytechnic and I should have known better than to go in the first place. I didn't know very much about rugby, horse riding or grouse shooting. I was driving so I couldn't drink, and by midnight I was bored shitless. I went to find Karen to see if she wanted to go home, only to find her with her tongue down the throat of some bloke with a double barrelled name, whose father owned most of Buckinghamshire. That was it, I'd had enough. I left the party, thanking the host for a wonderful evening. I turned the tape deck up loud and sang along to The Jam's 'Setting Sons,' trying to forget that West Ham were crap, and that I was crap. Could it be I was falling in love? I hadn't felt such jealousy since Steven Scott got his new bike. I felt dangerous.

West Ham had the chance to enhance their growing cup reputation at home to Liverpool four days later. We had just gone out of the Simod Cup, drawing 1–1 at Watford and losing on penalties, but that was away from home. As long as we were at home, we stood a chance. I can't believe we went to the game without tickets, but we managed to get in quite easily, only to find we had all been given seats in different blocks. Stain Tooth and I were in together, but Natty Matty and Barney were some distance away. Shortly after we had taken our seats, it became apparent that we were not among friends. The Scouse accents made us feel a little uneasy, but we were not overly worried, as we were sure that any trouble would be quickly stamped on. Paul Ince scored the two first half goals that made him a national star and it all went a bit quiet around us, We made a point of being excessively vigorous in our celebration, thoroughly enjoying our superiority. Aldridge pulled back a goal from the penalty spot just before half time, but we didn't know why. Even the Liverpool fans were a bit slow to react when the decision was given. In the second half, Steve Staunton headed one of the finest own goals in history, and Tony Gale rounded it off with one of his special free kicks. It should have been five: Alex Watson maliciously pulled Leroy down when he was clean through but got only a yellow card. Julian Dicks got a boot in the head from Nigel Spackman, but refused to go off. It was acts of courage like that which made him such an instant hero. The Liverpool fans in the West Stand were not happy Hectors. They moaned about never having seen the team play so badly, about it being the worst performance for years. I tried to put myself in their shoes; if we had won seven Championships, one FA Cup, two European Cups and four League Cups in the last ten years I would have been grateful just to have been around to see it. Greedy sods.

On the back of that win, we went to Millwall and became the first side to win there that season. Ince scored again and it seemed that maybe this would be the turning point. Tim from college wanted to go to a game, so we went to the 0–0 draw with Sheffield Wednesday, and pretty quickly wished we hadn't. The luck evaporated the moment Liam Brady's volley hit the crossbar. We were doomed. When Spurs came seven days later we were played off the park. Their attack cut through us like we weren't there, and I just prayed for a respectable scoreline. 0–2 was about the best we could have hoped for. Kelly looked totally out of his depth, Rosenior didn't get a sniff, and our midfield looked woefully out of touch. Even Mark Ward, normally Mr Commitment, looked fed up.

Karen admitted her fling with Ponsonby-Smallpiece was a one off, and she had done it to get at Dave. She was sorry to have ruined my evening or made me look like a jerk. Hey, what did I care? What right did I have to tell her what to do? This conversation took place on small pieces of paper exchanged during the final lecture of the Autumn Term of 1988. We went for a drink after college and wished each other well for Christmas. I urged her to leave Dave in the New Year. If what she told me was true, he sounded like a total pig. She could always move in with her brother, who had a flat in Lewisham. She thanked me for my advice and went on her own sweet way. She was meeting Julie without me for social evenings together. I didn't think this was healthy and told her so.

The best party of the pre-Christmas season was the office party, which I was still entitled to attend due my tenuous link at the Anerley branch. Although Diana had gone and there was no-one to polish their shoes for my benefit, we were permitted to invite a guest, preferably, in the words of the senior partner, 'of the opposite sex' from a local company, in order to promote relations with other businesses. I thought long and hard before inviting Brenda to join me. Brenda was the Saturday girl at local rivals, Dyer Son & Creasy, or Liar Son and Greasy as they were popularly known. I had a crush on her, big time. Another older woman, married; but then all the really gorgeous ones were. I used to flirt with her outrageously, and she used to encourage me. She didn't look like a Brenda, Brenda is the sort of name you would expect a forty-five year old to have. She was about twenty-eight and totally fit. She looked more like an Ingrid or an Anna, but I wasn't complaining. When I got home I heard about the Boeing 747 crash over Lockerbie, and felt immediately guilty for having had such a good time. I am cursed with a guilty conscience.

Christmas was a bore. The game at Norwich inevitably ended in defeat due to a now familiar rush of blood to Allen McKnight's head, and it was shown live on television to compound our humiliation and misery. We lost 2–1, Dale Gordon and Andy Townsend scored for Norwich, Ray Stewart got a late penalty. Big deal. We were deep in deepest smeg. From eighteen games, we had won a grand total of three, away at Millwall and Wimbledon and at home to Newcastle. Bottom place was well deserved, and we were six points away from safety without even reaching the halfway stage.

On New Year's Eve we took the twenty minute walk across the old sewage works to see a 0–0 draw at Selhurst Park against Charlton. I partied hard that night. I had good reason to want to see the back of 1988. It had been a nightmare year, not just from the footballing point of view. Surely 1989 couldn't get any worse? The start of a new year always promised much, but more often than not, the form that preceded it continued until the end of the season. That was the case in 1989, even to the extent of the cup performances being 100% better than league form. I danced the conga and saw in 1989 in the bionic grip of the arms of a pretty blonde girl called Angie. She'd gone home by the time I woke up, which admittedly was two days later. The first downer of 1989. The second was dished up by Wimbledon.

Especially for You. . .

Wimbledon came and went and took three points with them. The feeling of utter depression was tempered only by the thought that something good must come out of it. I had bought one of those horrible car stickers in the club shop; the one which said 'Don't follow me, follow West Ham United. . .' I'm sure it provided hours of amusement for the people following me. 'Ah yes!' They would say. 'There goes another total loony.' What a fruitloop.

The BBC moved us to a Sunday once again for our FA Cup match against Arsenal. Arsenal had won 4–1 at Upton Park earlier in the season, and despite our good cup form, I wasn't confident of getting a result. It appeared that we only got really good results under the floodlights in a midweek game. For midweek games the atmosphere was something really special, it must have transmitted itself to the team, made them want to please us. Saturday afternoons were bland and boring. Sunday afternoons even worse, and with the game live on TV there would be fewer people there to watch and create an atmosphere. It all pointed towards an early cup exit.

West Ham made me eat my words again. After half an hour we were 2–0 up, bottom beating top in one of those games that was just made for a *Roy of the Rovers* comic strip. Alan Dickens scored the first, and John Lukic, the Arsenal goalkeeper, revealed himself to be a closet Hammers fan as he spectacularly punched the ball into his own net from the edge of the area. Difficult to do, but superbly executed, nice one John. Paul Merson pulled one back just before half time, and all the fun went out of the game. Suddenly, we were hanging on for grim life, and Arsenal had the upper hand. It appeared we would hang on, only for Allen McKnight to make one of the blunders that put him firmly in the Upton Park hall of shame. He allowed a simple soft shot to squirm under his body into the net, and then we were really hanging on. In the end, a replay at Highbury seemed a fair result, but we had been cruising. After the game, McKnight tried to commit suicide by throwing himself in front of a bus. It went under him.

I phoned Stain Tooth after the game to see if he was going to Highbury. He was full of it. He was convinced we would win the replay. I'd never heard him so confident about anything, let alone the prospect of West Ham winning a game. It was an optimism that was so contagious, I could do no more than agree with him that we had a good chance, and we took our places at the Clock End the following Wednesday. It was one of those games which happens once a season. It doesn't matter how badly you have been playing, you always get one game like this one. A game where everything goes your way. Not just refereeing decisions, but atmosphere, team selection, and tactics. Even the dodgy looking horse burger I had bought before the game tasted reasonable. Arsenal were all over us in the first half. Brian Marwood had a goal disallowed for offside, but he clearly wasn't. McKnight was flapping about in goal like a demented parrot. Had any serious shots come in on goal we would have been buried. Ten minutes from the end, Liam Brady lifted a ball over the Arsenal defence. Adams and Lukic hesitated, and in that split second, Leroy Rosenior nipped in to head the ball into the net. That was the goal that rocketed him from 'Popular' to 'Legend' status at Upton Park. The man could do no wrong after that goal.

We sang all the way home on the tube, despite the idle threats of the gooner fans at the station. There were too many of us; they didn't try anything. The following Saturday we won 2–1 at Derby, Liam Brady scoring the goal of the season to date. That was Hors d'Oeuvres. The main course was Aston Villa in the quarter finals of the Littlewoods Cup, on a Wednesday night under the floodlights at Upton Park. A win was guaranteed.

I put 3–1 on the betting slip, but felt confident we could win by more. Villa were mid-table and not doing anything spectacular. A score of 3–1 was 25/1 with the bookmakers who had recently taken residence at Upton Park, odds which I felt were more than generous. I placed a pound with confidence. Liam Brady missed a penalty before Paul Ince put us 1–0 up. It was going to be another one of those nights, we could all sense it. Kelly scored a second late on; surely his best ever goal for the Hammers, allowing the ball to go across his chest before swinging around in the six yard box and whacking it into the top corner. A young upstart by the name of David Platt pulled one back for Villa, but it was too late, West Ham were in the semi finals of the Littlewoods Cup. If Liam Brady had tucked that penalty away, I would have been £25 better off as well, and it would have been a perfect night.

The draw for the semi-finals was a nerve racking experience, and it took place the following morning. The other three remaining teams were Nottingham Forest, Luton Town and Bristol City. Naturally we wanted to avoid Forest, who were technically the stronger side, and Luton because they were, well, Luton. Bristol City would have been a good draw for us, but we had to go and get Luton. To add insult to injury we had to play the home leg first, which meant another Sunday afternoon job. I wasn't happy about this. OK, our cup form was good, and we had proved against Arsenal that it could bridge the gap and continue even on a Sunday afternoon. But this was Luton. This was different. This was war.

After winning at Arsenal and Derby, then beating Villa in the cup, we thought we might have turned the corner. We were off the bottom of the table, albeit on goal difference from Newcastle United, so the more optimistic among us thought that now was the time to put together a decent run. Wrong again. Manchester United came to town, and despite going 1–0 up through a Liam Brady penalty, we were sent packing by goals from Gordon Strachan, Brian McClair and an Alvin Martin own goal. The match was played on a Saturday afternoon – if we could only arrange to play our league matches on a Wednesday night, we would have been fine.

At college, Karen was causing me untold hassle. Now I had seen her in all her finery I fancied her something chronic and was like a horny dog looking for a suitable leg. She had two of them and I wanted them badly. We had started to socialise outside college. I had introduced her to Julie at a party and they seemed to get along well, and they made their own arrangements to go out and about up in town. Karen was making me so jealous it hurts to admit it. I hid my feelings, knowing that it probably wouldn't last, and it didn't. I, meanwhile added to the dilemma by asking her advice on how I might win the affections of Roseanne, a mutual friend, who I didn't really fancy, but I wanted Karen to think I did in order to make her jealous. Get it? It's a tangled web we weave, is it not? This, of course backfired badly, because Karen thought I wasn't interested in her, and that I only had eyes for Roseanne, so she went off shagging everything in sight, leaving me to pick up the pieces.

She was on my mind as Stain Tooth drove me to Swindon for our fourth round FA Cup game. It was hard to believe how quickly we got there, and even harder to believe that we could park the car just outside the ground. We even found a decent chippy and were in good spirits by the time the game started. That's all I remember. I cannot recall anything at all about a dire game, which finished 0–0. Leroy scored the winner in the replay four days later before we made a return trip to Highbury.

You've Got to Hide Your Love Away. . .

West Ham United 1 Coventry City 1 – 11.3.89

I had to go to a ball. I didn't want to go to a ball, but if I wanted to keep Karen within range, I had to go to a ball. It was a college do, something I really didn't want to attend, knowing it would be full of hoorays in their dinner jackets, dicky bows and satin ball gowns. I shook the moths out of my dinner jacket and hung it on my bedroom door handle. I didn't want to go.

I arranged to meet Karen at Charing Cross Station after our game against Arsenal. The game itself had been the usual type of performance, the only surprising thing being that we didn't lose by more goals. Julian Dicks scored his first ever goal for West Ham, which makes the memory sweeter, but at the time it was just another defeat. Karen was still living with this Dave character, who by all accounts was a mean and nasty monster. I met him some time later, and a nicer guy you couldn't wish to meet. It made me wonder what picture she would paint of me to other people.

The ball was actually a charity gig, a dinner dance, which meant having to sit down and wade our way through a five course meal before attempting to achieve a double hernia on the dance floor. We sat on a table of eight, joined by John Morley, son of Eric (of Miss World fame) but no relation to Trevor. He said he had been at the game also that afternoon.

'Oh really?' I said. I knew he was an Arsenal man, so I asked him if he was on the North Bank.

'Oh no!' He said, as if to imply 'What a vulgar thought!' He looked at the meat on the end of his fork, anything rather than stare a common West Ham supporter in the eye. 'I was in a box.'

Morley had already rubbed me up the wrong way earlier in the evening, and I was beginning to wish that I could put him in a box, too. 'Well, at least we scored the best goal,' I added, thinking I would have the last word.

'Did you, old chap?' He sneered. 'Didn't see, had to leave early to get the Daimler out of the car park.' Bastard. He'd got me there.

At least Karen was behaving herself, and acting as though she wanted to be with me. She wore the most amazing low cut green velvet dress, which left very little to the imagination. She had been winding me up by getting changed in front of me earlier in the evening. By now, she knew how I felt about her; it was futile for me to make any attempt to hide it, or pretend that I needed advice on how to win over Roseanne. Looking back, I can't believe how stupid we both were.

Given the choice, I would rather not have played Luton in the semi-finals of the Littlewoods cup on a Sunday afternoon in front of live TV cameras. Stain Tooth helped me to look on the bright side. 'At least we're in the semi-finals. . .' he chirped. 'Lots of other teams would like to be in our shoes.' By the end of the day, we were both wishing we had slipped quietly out of the competition to Aston Villa in the previous round. Luton demolished us 3–0; humiliated us in front of all our friends. Mick Harford scored first after McKnight went walkabout again, Roy Wegerle slipped the second through the gaping hole under McKnight's body, and Julian Dicks committed a blatant foul in the penalty area to allow Danny Wilson to make it three from the spot. The prospect of a Wembley final to make up for the disappointment of the league form melted away within the space of about twenty minutes. There was no chance of pulling back a 3–0 score line, not at Luton on their plastic pitch. The draw had beaten us. Had we played away in the first leg, the second leg would have been under the lights on a Wednesday night without the intrusion of live TV cameras. We could have coped with that.

Instead, we travelled to Charlton for the fifth round of the FA Cup with our tails firmly between our legs. At last John Lyall saw sense and dropped McKnight, bringing back Phil Parkes, the goalkeeper that McKnight had been purchased to replace. It was the second season in a row we had played Charlton in the cup, and the third in the last four. On both previous occasions we had been successful, and the trend continued, despite Mark Ward being sent off. Stuart Slater scored the first senior goal of his career and it seemed that the disappointment of missing Wembley through the Littlewoods cup had given way to the optimism of a Wembley visit in the FA Cup. We were drawn at home in the quarter finals, which was all that could be asked, to Norwich City. It wasn't going to be an evening game, but we anticipated victory nevertheless.

It was around this time that I bought my first fanzine, *Fortunes Always Hiding*. I still have all the copies of that fanzine, up on the shelves along with the programmes. The wit and humour in those magazines was like a breath of fresh air. At last, someone had the guts to put in writing that we were crap. Not just that, they said it in an articulate and funny way, with excellent cartoons and strips as well. There were other fanzines available, such as *Never Mind the Boleyn*, *On the Terraces* and *Over Land and Sea*, but to my mind, *Fortunes...* was the best one. If you had bought all the fanzines it would have cost an arm and a leg every Saturday, so I made my choice and stuck with it.

After drawing 0–0 at home to QPR, we lost the second leg of the semi-final, as predicted. This time, it was only 2–0, but made it an aggregate 5–0 and had the statisticians reaching for their form books and calculators to find it was the heaviest margin of defeat in a League Cup semi-final since 1965. Good old West Ham, always breaking records.

I was still trying the occasional trick to try and arouse some kind of reaction from Karen. When we played Coventry City on March 11th, I told her a wicked lie. I told her I had gone to see Diana and we had spent the entire afternoon in bed, making love a total of seven times, before her husband came home and I had to slip out of the window. It's a good job Karen didn't know Diana lived in a fifth floor flat, or my story might have fallen flat a good deal earlier than it did. In fact, nothing so exciting took place. I sat in the West Stand with Stain Tooth watching us fight out a dull 1–1 draw. Coventry took the lead through a dubious penalty. Ince equalised, then the referee played about ten minutes of injury time, during which we created enough chances to have won the game handsomely, but when relegation is a certainty, that kind of thing just never happens.

When you're down, you're down.

Too Many People. . .

West Ham United 1 Southampton 2 – 15.4.89

Karen was annoying me intensely. She just would not come across. We went out more frequently than the average courting couple, and would talk long into the night about matters of global as well as personal importance. Still, it seemed, she wasn't interested in the contents of my boxer shorts. After one particularly harrowing evening she gave me a full description of her deprived childhood. This included the bit about her father walking out when she was a baby and her step father treating her like shit, having an abortion at the age of seventeen and generally having a rough time. I couldn't compete with that, and was made to feel guilty about the fact I had such nice parents and a trouble free childhood. As I was leaving, I handed her a tape I had made of two songs I had written for her. To this day they remain my two favourites. Although not necessarily the best I have written, they were certainly the most expressive, and did the trick. They were a couple of slushy numbers called 'Now that I've Hurt You' and 'I Don't Know Why I Love You.' When I got home, she rang me in a flood of tears and said: 'I didn't know you felt that way.' Lying cow. She knew damn well, she just wanted to hear me spell it out.

We drew our cup quarter-final with Norwich, 0–0. Again, it's not a game that sticks in the memory particularly well. As far as I can remember we didn't play well and were lucky to get a replay. Stain Tooth decided to go to the replay and I grabbed a lift, as he had now got rid of the embarrassing Allegro and now had an embarrassing Montego. It was less embarrassing than the Allegro, but only just. We got caught up in road works and didn't get to the ground until about five minutes into the game. We bumped into Close and one of his mates inside the ground and watched the game from the corner flag together. Rumour abounded that John Lyall was about to swoop for Frank McAvennie again in a £1.25m record signing deal. I was sceptical. John Lyall hadn't 'swooped' for ages. It turned out to be his last throw of the dice. There was an expectant buzz among the West Ham fans, chants of 'We've Got Our Frankie Back!' to the tune of 'Those Were the Days.' Appropriate, really. The mood of optimism was shattered when Malcolm Allen scored twice in the first half and we were left chasing the game. Paul Ince managed to pull one back in the second half, but as it went in I remember saying to Stain Tooth that it would probably end 3–1 to Norwich. That proved to be correct, Dale Gordon putting the tie beyond doubt and booking a semi-final date with Everton. Because of the replay with Norwich, we had to postpone our league match with Southampton. As we were due to play Nottingham Forest on Cup semi-final day, and they were involved in the other semi against Liverpool, we were able to re-arrange the fixture for a Saturday afternoon, with no extra backlog occurring. It was strange that despite being in both Cup competitions to the latter stages, we did not have to suffer the fixture pile-ups that had occurred in previous seasons. In spite of that, we were still playing crap.

A brief respite from the dross came the following Saturday as we played Aston Villa at Villa Park, and Paul Ince scored the goal of the century, running almost the full length of the pitch to fire the ball into the top corner. It was even better than Liam Brady's effort against Derby, but curiously only made second place in ITV's goal of the season competition. Had he scored the goal for Manchester United, it would no doubt have won first, second and third place. Maybe I'm just bitter and twisted. Frank McAvennie made his second West Ham debut, and things appeared to be looking up. Maybe Frank would be our saviour. Later that week, Karen and I went on our first date as an 'item'. She had finally discarded Dopey Dave and was all mine to do with as I wished. I tried to make it look as though I hadn't planned anything as I brought her home, put Rachmaninoff on the CD player and miraculously found a bottle of champagne and two glasses in the fridge. 'I always keep a couple of champagne glasses in the fridge,' I told her. 'You never know who might drop in, do you?'

I thought I was in heaven. Perhaps I was, I thought to myself as I awoke in the morning, leaving Karen to sleep off the nocturnal activity as I went and did my paper round. I had Paul McCartney's *Ram* album on my walkman, which, again, was rather appropriate. The opening track, 'Too Many People' put an extra skip in my step as I went on my round, came home, made tea and toast. I was in love, big time. I gave her a choice for the Bank Holiday Monday. Either we could go out for the day somewhere really boring, like Chessington World of Adventures, or the coast, or, we could spend a really exciting afternoon watching West Ham beat Norwich City at Upton Park. As we were still in the early stages of our physical relationship, she was as eager to please me as I was to please her, and she chose the trip to West Ham with only fifteen minutes of hesitation. Stain Tooth and Close came with us, which on reflection might not have been such a good move, but my confidence of getting a result turned out to be misplaced. Norwich beat us for the third time out of four games to leave us back on the bottom, four points behind Newcastle but with two games in hand, and ten points behind Charlton and Southampton but with four games in hand. Games in hand were all very well, but we had a total of nineteen points from twenty-five games. A dismal record by anyone's standards. Only four wins in the league all season. We would be lucky, on paper, to win one of our games in hand, let alone the four required.

The next game was away at Tottenham. Karen went back up to Wrexham to see her parents and I was left to my own devices. I remember the West Ham crowd baiting Paul Stewart, the Tottenham striker, who at the time was the most expensive player in the country never to have played for his country. I knew that chants of 'What a waste of money!' would probably be rammed back down our throats, and I was right, Stewart won a second half penalty and scored one himself to add to a first half goal from Nayim to see us off 3–0. We then faced three home games in a row in the space of a week to try and pick up some ground. Nine points would have helped out a great deal, but for a team that had won only once at home all season, three might have been the most we could have hoped for. We got one against Derby County. The team we had walloped 5–0 in the Littlewoods Cup, and beaten on their own ground in the league put up stubborn resistance and Leroy Rosenior scored our goal in a naff 1–1 draw.

Middlesbrough came down on the Tuesday night. Everything was going well, we were 1–0 up through a Kevin Keen goal, when Bernie Slaven scored twice to puncture our little escape balloon. Middlesbrough were in deep trouble too, and we expected a hard fight, but this was a cruel blow. We walked back to the tube station staring relegation squarely in the face. Our games in hand were running out. We needed to start winning, and we needed to start winning soon. Like Saturday.

Saturday saw the re-arranged game against Southampton. We desperately needed to win and therefore allowed Southampton to score straight from the kick off. After all, this is West Ham. We don't want to make things easy for ourselves, do we? Brady equalised from the penalty spot, but Paul Rideout scored a second for Southampton and it was all over. From a potential nine points we had taken one. We turned on the radio in Stain Tooth's car to find out what had been going on in the Cup semi-finals. There had been trouble at Hillsborough in the match between Liverpool and Nottingham Forest. 'Those bloody Liverpool fans been fighting again?' I asked Stain Tooth. I prayed that Christina hadn't gone, and that if she had, she was safe. The news came through that people had died. They were using the advertising hoardings as stretchers to get people out of the trouble, but in many cases it was too late. From what we could gather, a number of late arrivals at the Liverpool end had been allowed immediate access as the game was about to kick off. In their rush to get onto the terrace, they crushed and killed ninety-six Liverpool fans. People were crushed against crash barriers, against the fencing at the front, or just suffocated under the weight of bodies front and rear.

I watched it on TV that night, and once again, I'm not ashamed to say I cried out loud. As a direct result of that incident, and no other, we now have all seating stadia in the Premier League. Some say this is a good thing, others don't. Whether it was worth the sacrifice of ninety-six lives to bring it about, we can only speculate. The Taylor Report blamed the police, and everyone blindly accepts that fact. I am sure they must take a share of blame, but I have never before or since heard a Government report accepted as being 100% correct. Like Mr Clough, I have my doubts on this one.

Everton beat Norwich 1–0 in the other semi-final. The hollowest victory in the history of the game.

Revenge. . .

We should have been finished, but somehow we still had a chance of survival. The fact that Newcastle and Middlesbrough were even worse than us helped, plus the fact we had taken four points from Villa, who teetered on the brink of the relegation zone. If we were going to stay up, Villa were the realistic target we had to overhaul.

The call to arms began with a totally out of character 3–0 win over Millwall. All three goals came in the first half, and we blew them aside like a team of cardboard cut-outs. Julian Dicks scored the first of his many long range goals, Dickens and Parris getting the others. The next game was against already relegated Newcastle at St James's Park. Again, we gave them a goal start, but a miracle happened, and we turned it around through Kevin Keen and Mark Ward. Maybe there was a chance, after all. I brought myself back to reality when I saw who the next game was against – Luton Town. Our last home game of the season, and one we had to win to stand any chance of staying up. I just couldn't see Luton handing us a victory after all we had been through together.

I left Karen at my house while I went off with Stain Tooth in his now much less embarrassing Vauxhall Cavalier. As the last game of the season, we treated ourselves to seats in the lower tier of the West Stand and prepared to watch the team's escape bid undone by our Bedfordshire friends. Stain Tooth had to pinch me as I saw Alan Dickens dance through the defence and slot the winning goal into the net. We had done it. Not only had we won three league games in a row, but we had beaten Luton. Now, anything was possible. Revenge was sweet, even if it was only 1–0, the aggregate score against Luton that season made sad reading: West Ham 2 Luton Town 9.

The impossible continued at a spooky Hillsborough, as West Ham scored twice at the tarpaulin covered Leppings Lane end to secure a 2–0 win. Four wins on the trot, and looking good for survival. Only one, or rather three problems. There were three away games left. Of the three teams we would have chosen to play, they would definitely not have been Cup finalists Everton, shit-hot Nottingham Forest and title chasing Liverpool. But that's how it worked out. We had to win two out of the three to be in with a chance of survival.

Stuart Slater put us 1–0 up, but for the second time in three years we played Everton away the week before the cup final and they were all trying to claim their place in the team and pulled out all the party pieces. There was still a glimmer of hope. At 1–2 down we won a penalty. Without Ray Stewart's cool head, the responsibility went to young Kevin Keen, who hit the ball straight at Neville Southall. Everton scored again and it was looking highly dodgy. Two days later, suddenly and without warning, we won at Nottingham Forest. What the hell was going on? Leroy scored after twenty-five seconds. That just wasn't right. The opposition were supposed to score straight from the kick-off, not us. Leroy got a second and Lee Chapman pulled one back for Forest, but we held on to defer the decision to the last game.

The arithmetic was blindingly simple. If we won at Anfield in our final game, we would stay up. Aston Villa would go down with the already relegated Middlesbrough and Newcastle. I listened to the game on the radio. Liverpool needed three points for their title race against Arsenal. They also needed goals; Arsenal having a much superior goal difference to them, and they still had to visit Anfield after us to decide the championship. The odds were very heavily stacked against us, particularly when Liverpool scored. That horrible feeling crept up on me, the feeling that all the blood is sinking to your feet and your heart is pounding so heavily it almost bursts through you chest. Then Leroy equalised and there was hope once again. In the second half, Allen McKnight, playing his last league match for West Ham, conceded four. He couldn't have been blamed for any of them, Liverpool were buzzing, and our reserves were drained to the very last drop. Paul Ince was nobbled by Steve McMahon, and with him went our chances of preserving first division status. It was a significant evening, not just for West Ham, but for English football generally. Our demise meant that Aston Villa stayed up, by the skin of their teeth, and the following season, they finished second, earning Graham Taylor the England job. Had Villa gone down, the FA might well have employed someone with a decent footballing brain. Also, the fact that we lost 5–1 meant that Arsenal had to win by two goals when they visited Anfield a few days later. It was the one and only time I have ever wanted Arsenal to win. Everyone was saying that Liverpool deserved the double for their fans after the Hillsborough tragedy, but that was rubbish. They would have deserved it if they had won enough games. They hadn't. When Arsenal went 1–0 up, Liverpool sat back, content, it seemed to settle for a narrow defeat, and the championship on goal difference. Poetic justice arrived in the last minute when Michael Thomas scored a second, and Liverpool had no time to reply. Liverpool only had themselves to blame.

We faced a season in the second division. I say 'season' because I didn't meet anyone who thought we would be down there very long. John Lyall knew all about getting out of the second division, and as long as we held on to the players we had, and maybe even added a few more, there was no reason why we shouldn't bounce straight back.

In the meantime, both Karen and I had to find jobs for our year out from college. Karen had moved in with her half brother, Nick, and his French girlfriend in their big house in Nunhead. This was only slightly less inconvenient than the house she had previously lodged at in Kennington. I got a job with a West End company of Chartered Surveyors called Farrar Stead and Glyn, who were based in Sackville Street. In 1989, the commercial property market was still buoyant, and I had three companies who wanted me to work for them. Such luxury! Of the other two who wanted me, one was based in Reigate, which was a bit out of the way, and the other was the Metropolitan Police Estates Division. I couldn't bring myself to work for the police, although on reflection, it might have been a good move. I could well have my own apron by now. Karen took a job with a major national firm of surveyors placed just around the corner from my place of work. I did a very stupid thing. I asked her to marry me. She did a very stupid thing, too. She said yes.

Devil Woman. . .

West Ham United 3 Plymouth Argyle 2 – 26.8.89

At last the West Ham board showed a bit of initiative. While John Lyall was busy preparing for the new season in the second division, by polishing his fishing reels, the West Ham board sacked him. It was a difficult piece of news for everyone to believe. After all, John Lyall had been at the club for more than just a few years. John Lyall *was* West Ham United. The account of his dismissal in his book, *Just Like My Dreams*, is very moving, and one has sympathy for him in the way it was handled, but then, when you've gotta go. . .

What was even more difficult to understand was the choice of successor. Lou Macari had been successful in guiding Swindon Town out of the fourth division, and then the third, and had made them a very successful second division side. That was hardly a qualification, in my book, to make him the manager of West Ham United. Swindon were notorious for using the long ball, and we all groaned when we realised the prospect of long ball tactics at the Academy. The board were quick to make the point that Macari had only used such tactics at Swindon because of the quality of players available to him. If he'd had players who could play the ball along the floor, then he would have done. I was still to be convinced.

Paul Ince was turning into a prize twat. He had been photographed wearing a Manchester United shirt, and had made it clear that he wanted to leave the club. It just so happened that Manchester United were interested. What a coincidence. This incident angered us all so much that it rankles with us to this day, perhaps now even more so than it did at the time, seeing all the success he has had has made us very jealous. I am happy to admit that I hate the jumped up little shit, who ought to remember from time to time who gave him his success in the first place and show a little respect. Lesson over.

It seemed that Macari knew how to handle him, anyway. He played in Alan Devonshire's testimonial game at Upton Park, a 3–1 win over Crystal Palace, and in the opening game of the 1989–90 season at Stoke City. Kevin Keen scored in a 1–1 draw. That was Ince's last appearance in a West Ham shirt. Macari stated that he only wanted players to play for West Ham who really wanted to. In fact, players who would die for West Ham. This later turned out not to be true, as he repeatedly played Mark Ward despite the fact he was also desperate to get away. Still, at the time it made a refreshing change from John Lyall's 'wait and see' attitude. It seemed that at last we had a manager with balls, someone who would crawl over broken glass with his flies undone for the cause. Someone who would get results – first time.

Karen wanted results, too. My new fiancée was unimpressed with the fact that I occasionally felt the desire to go home. I couldn't understand why she didn't want to go home more often, but then, I had not experienced her family background. Whenever I was there, her stepfather was a perfect gentleman, and her mother made such a fuss it was untrue. I began to wonder if Karen had been lying to me, but the more I thought about it, the more I could see how the problems might have arisen. I managed to persuade her to come home with me on August 23rd, instead of going to see West Ham play Bradford City at Upton Park. I felt very bitter about this, as I was missing our first home match under Lou Macari just so I could do something I ought to have been able to do any time I wanted. Still, I was in love. The following Saturday. I had been allowed to borrow Stain Tooth's East Terrace season ticket, and fully intended to see the game against Plymouth Argyle. You see, the thing about Karen was, it was all or nothing. When she was in a good mood, you were made to feel like a million dollars, and she would play out any fantasy you might have had in order to please you. On one occasion, I remember her cooking me a superb dinner, then disappearing upstairs for a while, returning dressed in her old school uniform, including hockey skirt, stockings and suspenders, and demanding that I make love to her there and then on the kitchen table. On another occasion, she came to meet me in the office on a Sunday afternoon. I was alone in the office and gave her the guided tour, showing her the computer room and the downstairs kitchen area. She insisted on giving the most amazing blow job while the office door was wide open and anyone could have walked in. That was the kind of girl she was – impulsive and with a four wheel sex drive. On the down side, when she was angry, she could out-sulk anyone, and make you feel like a rapist, child molester and murderer all rolled into one. It didn't need to be anything major to flick her mental switch, either. Merely putting a beer can in the wrong bin could spell disaster. But I loved her.

That Saturday morning I was in trouble. I had asked her why she never told me when she had an orgasm, and she said it was because I was never in the room at the time. Not only that, but I had committed the cardinal sin of sticking up for one of her female friends who she was doing a character assassination on; something she enjoyed doing very much. My defending of the poor girl obviously meant that I was either having an affair with her, or had done in the past, or I fancied her something rotten. None of this was true, I just like to see justice done. I'd had enough. I walked out of the door and went to collect Stain Tooth's season ticket, losing myself in West Ham for the afternoon, and not caring what Karen was getting up to.

The game was superb. West Ham were playing very well, and Lou Macari's first signing, Martin Allen, looked a good prospect. The move down a division was bringing out the best in David Kelly. He looked twice the player in the second division than he did in the first. He had a goal disallowed before putting us into the lead. It was a very wet and warm day, the rain was driving hard into our faces on the East Terrace, but we didn't care. Shortly after the start of the second half, Martin Allen scored. Plymouth pulled one back before Kelly had another one disallowed, then Mark Ward set up Kevin Keen for a third. Although Plymouth pulled another one back, it was never going to be enough. Perhaps this second division lark wouldn't be so bad after all, I thought to myself as I left the ground. At least we will be winning more often than we lose. I didn't much care about the fact that we wouldn't be playing the likes of Liverpool, Manchester

United and Tottenham. At that time, I would rather see us beat Oldham Athletic than lose to Liverpool, and there were always cup nights to look forward to seeing the big teams again. Perhaps the only reason that I thought this was that the crowd had not been affected by the drop in status. Indeed, the average crowd had risen slightly on the previous season. Obviously income from TV and sponsorship was going to be affected, but I saw no reason why a spell in the second division should not be a good thing.

I tentatively let myself back into the house and called out to see if Karen was in. As I walked into the bedroom, she was waiting for me, in bed wearing a brand new item of sexy lingerie she had been out and bought that afternoon. 'Well,' she said, 'what do you think?'

I took off my soaking jacket and took a good look at the tempting silky underwear. 'You want my honest opinion?' I asked.

'Of course.' She nodded.

'I think Kelly should have had a hat-trick.'

That's What I Like. . .

West Ham United 5 Sunderland 0 – 18.10.89

I could see that once again it was going to prove difficult to get along to matches. For the first few months of the season, the only opportunities arose when Karen and I had a row and I had to make myself scarce. Fortunately, after the Plymouth game, it all ended in a lot of kissing and making up, but it was getting to a stage where I could see my future as a regular on the terrace at West Ham was in serious jeopardy if I went through with the marriage. Karen just didn't have a clue about football – she supported Manchester United. We were both working full time and only had weekends to spend time together. Although we had not planned to get married until 1992, it seemed that every weekend was filled with preparation; shopping for this, looking through catalogues, selecting rings, etc. After all, you can't be too careful, can you?

While West Ham were drawing 1–1 at Hull City, I had my head forcibly wedged in a jewellery catalogue, selecting an engagement ring.

'I like emeralds,' she said

'I bet you bloody do. Have you seen how much they cost? What was that? Mark Ward scored? Yes!'

'And diamonds. How about this one?'

'Come on lads, hold on 'til half time. Yes, very nice, love. What about this? This looks nice. What is it? Cubic zirconia. Sounds nice.' Not impressed. As I was only a student and working for a year, I made the token gesture of spending £75 on an engagement ring made of emeralds and diamonds that were so small you needed an electron microscope and a sunny day to see them. I fully intended to buy a more realistic one once we were both out working full time, but this was enough as a symbol, we both agreed – for the time being.

I missed the draw with Swindon because we were out doing something really pathetic, like looking at bridesmaids' dresses. If I dared to say: 'Look, the wedding is two years away – can't we do this in the summer?' I would get a hard stare and later that evening would be forced to sleep on the damp patch with no covers. Eventually, Karen relented, and realised that it was futile to make plans so far in advance, as most retailers weren't interested. Just when I thought I was saved, up popped her best friend, Ann-Marie, who announced she was getting married in July and asked Karen to be her chief bridesmaid, and me to be an usher. Naturally, this meant more weekends spent trailing around Elm Park and Basildon getting measured for morning suits, top hats and ridiculous looking cravats.

We lost our first game of the season away at Brighton. A couple of days before, spoilt brat Ince had got his own way and had become a Manchester United player, and we wished him all the best. Oh yes we did. Liam Brady missed a penalty and we went down 3–0. I think I listened to that one while travelling backwards and forwards to Nunhead shifting some of Karen's possessions in order that her former boyfriend could not lay claim to them. I'm sure he had no intention of asking for them, but it was a good way of keeping me under control. I lost my temper the morning after the Littlewoods Cup victory at Birmingham. Martin Allen and Stuart Slater had each scored in a 2–1 win, and Julian Dicks had been promoted to captain. I was in a good mood as we prepared to trail off to work from her Nunhead digs, when I spotted a pair of underpants in her top drawer that I did not recognise.

'These yours?' I innocently asked.

'Do they look like mine?' she replied romantically.

'No, but they're not mine.'

'Well, they must be.' I could see the cogs turning over in her mind. 'What are you suggesting?' she screamed.

'Nothing. I just wondered whose they were, that's all.' That was it. Enough to draw a stony silence for the next four days. I had a word with her brother and they turned out to be his. He had put them in the wrong laundry pile. Sorted. But I had offended her by implying she was having an affair with a man who wore unusual underpants.

The stony silence continued as we drove over to Ann-Marie's house in Elm Park. I explained to Phil, her fiancé, a really nice bloke and a copper, so that proves it's not true what they say. He suggested that he and I, together with his mate Barry, go to Upton Park to watch the Watford game while the girls had a good bitch. Excellent idea. Once again, and not for the last time, a West Ham victory helped me to escape, Julian Dicks scoring from the spot in a 1–0 win. Colin Foster made his debut in that game. I was amazed. Here we were a second division team, and so far Macari had bought two players, Martin Allen and Colin Foster, both from first division sides, QPR and Nottingham Forest respectively. They obviously thought West Ham were going places, even if we didn't.

When we got home, there was still an atmosphere you could cut with a truncheon. Phil and Ann-Marie made themselves scarce, and Karen spoke to me for the first time in days. She apologised for getting the hump, but that didn't mean I was forgiven. I would have to tread very carefully. Yes ma'am. The next Tuesday, I was dragged screaming and shouting to go ten pin bowling when all I wanted to do was relax in front of the radio and hear about our 1–0 win at Portsmouth. I had to settle for a quick call to Clubcall for the good news. Then followed three home matches, of which I saw exactly none. I didn't see us lose 2–3 to WBA because we had an appointment to see a mortgage advisor about the possibility of buying a flat. Quite why Karen couldn't have arranged the appointment for the morning, I don't know. Oh, wait a minute, yes I do. Eamonn Dolan scored his first competitive goal for West Ham in that match. I missed the 1–1 draw with Birmingham in the second leg of the Littlewoods Cup because I had to work late at the office and didn't get away in time. Finally, I missed the 1–0 defeat at home to Leeds because I was moving Karen out of Nunhead and into my house, with my parents.

Karen's brother had split up with his French girlfriend. He had caught her having it off with a Norwegian called Norman and he walked out. Not being a materialistic sort of bloke (i.e. mad) he let her stay at the house and found himself a small hole to live in on the other side of the river. It was called Edmonton. This left Karen in an awkward position. She had been told she was welcome to stay at the house, but was made to feel very uncomfortable. Extra lodgers arrived, and life became rather hectic. In stepped muggins, the knight in shining armour. I spent the whole day trundling backwards and forwards in my little Escort, urging the scoreline to change at Upton Park. Surely we wouldn't lose to a goal scored by Vinnie Jones? Surely? We did.

At least we had a decent kit that season. As Scoreline had finally seen sense and switched their attention to really crap teams like Blackpool and Barnsley, West Ham had a deal with Bukta, who had supplied their kit in the days before Admiral. This was a much more traditional kit, a claret body with blue sleeves. No mucking about. New sponsors, too. Avco finally got pissed off being associated with losers all the time, and we were now sponsored by BAC Windows, who, like Avco, nobody had heard of.

It wasn't looking good for the trip to Bramall Lane to play Sheffield United. They were in second place and unbeaten, while West Ham struggled along inconsistently in seventh place. I had other things on my mind that Saturday. I was desperate to ensure that we did not have to stay under the same roof as my parents for longer than was absolutely necessary. This wasn't because I didn't like my parents, but because Karen was so volatile, she was like a time bomb waiting to go off. I went out looking for a flat to rent. As luck would have it, I had been talking to my former colleague, Sue Miller, who had a flat in Beckenham, which had just become vacant. She agreed to let me and Karen rent it for six months if we both liked it. We took a look and both fell in love with it. It was huge. It was a split level maisonette, with two bedrooms and a bathroom upstairs, and a big lounge and kitchen downstairs. We struck a deal and agreed to take possession on November 4th. The day was complete when I heard we had won 2–0 at Sheffield United. Some days were good. Very, very good.

Tim, my friend from college was experiencing similar trouble to myself. He had been unable to get to a game all season and was pining for the North Bank. However, his girlfriend wouldn't let him out of her sight. We discussed the matter over lunch and decided that it was time we put our collective feet down, as it were, and told them that we were going to watch West Ham play Sunderland whether they liked it or not. To our dismay, they readily agreed. It was another one of those Upton Park nights when everything went right. Martin Allen hit a goal from about twenty yards. Stuart Slater scored a brilliant goal. Parkes hit a long clearance, which Dolan headed on, and Slater controlled the ball on his chest and slammed the ball into the back of the net. It hadn't touched the ground. Kevin Keen scored another from an impossible angle, virtually on the touchline, and Sunderland, who were three places above us in the league, were blown away in the first half. Dolan added two more in the second half, followed by his now fabled 'Irish Jig' and 'Douglas Bader' celebrations. Dolan was often compared to Douglas Bader. Not very mobile on the ground, but fucking brilliant in the air. We'd had a few jars before the game, and I was still a bit tipsy when I rolled in at 11pm, expecting a right rollicking, but I was welcomed into bed and made a total fuss of. The bed sheets bobbed for a few hours, and I began to feel that life was worth living. Karen wasn't such a bad old stick, after all.

Where the Heart Is. . .

West Ham United 0 Newcastle United 0 – 11.11.89

Life could not have been much better. Following the 5–0 tanking of Sunderland, Karen and I went away for a mucky weekend in Hastings, the only downer being the fact that West Ham had twice thrown away a lead to draw 2–2 at Port Vale. I had the flat sorted out, and Saturdays were now spent buying things for the flat rather than the wedding. It was a cross I was reasonably happy to bear, because it stopped Karen having a go at me. At last, I had done something right in her books.

In the week, West Ham got a highly creditable 0–0 draw at Aston Villa in the third round of the Littlewoods Cup. Villa were buzzing at the time and were to go on to finish second. Only a couple of weeks later, they beat Everton 6–2 on live TV, David Platt scoring four and earning himself a regular spot in the England team. On Saturday, while trailing around Allders department store, the lads were beating Oxford United 3–2, and during the first few days of November, drew 1–1 at Bournemouth, and lost 1–0 at Wolves. The defeat at Wolves was the first in seven games, a run which had pushed us up into the play-off frame. It seemed the play-offs would be the best bet, as Sheffield United and Leeds United appeared to have the top two automatic places sorted for themselves. The game against Wolves also heralded the moving into the flat at Littlestone Close. I was excited and nervous, too. I was moving away from home for the first time. Naturally, Karen didn't understand, as she had been living away from home since the age of seventeen, but then, I didn't expect her to understand. My brother-in-law, a serious body builder, helped us to lug all our worldly goods up six flights of stairs, and I made several trips back and forth in the van I had hired for the weekend.

We were due up in Wrexham the following weekend, so I arranged for both Karen and myself to have tickets for the replay against Aston Villa, to make up for the fact I would have to miss the home game with Newcastle. That way, I reckoned, there would be no objection. As long as she felt she was the centre of attention, I could have taken her anywhere. Even to football. In fact, she quite enjoyed coming along to football and embarrassing me in front of my mates by telling them all what we got up to when the curtains were drawn. In many ways, it gave me a bit of a kick too, but I never did work out exactly why she felt she had to do it. She was developing a big crush on Julian Dicks. I couldn't work out whether she was doing it to wind me up, or whether it was real. After all, as far as I was concerned, he looked like a dog's bum with a hat on, but there's no accounting for taste. We watched the game from the lower tier of the West Stand with Stain Tooth and Close. The object of Karen's desire scored a cracking goal, which was enough to see us through.

Karen had developed a worrying tendency to cross examine me about my own desires and wishes in the female direction. What sort of girl did I like? What particularly attracted me to a woman? Did I ever fantasise about women at work? As I had always eulogised about Diana, and how hard it was to work with her after our affair, I think she thought I had a thing about women in the office. She kept on and on and on at me until I finally admitted there was a really cute little secretary at work called Jackie, who I thought was really horny and needed a good seeing too. I thought this would satisfy her perverse curiosity, but instead I had to endure another twenty questions about Jackie, followed by that now familiar deafening silence. It wouldn't have been so bad, but Karen had arranged to meet me at my office at mid-day on the Friday so we could drive straight up to Wrexham. When she arrived, Jackie was sitting on my desk with a hand on my shoulder, laughing at one of my jokes and showing a not insurmountable amount of stocking top. There was absolutely nothing in it, but the silence lasted all the way up to Wrexham and all the way through tea with her mother. I wanted to sort it out, but waited until I had heard the disappointing news from Upton Park, that we had managed only a 0–0 draw with Newcastle. We needed to be beating teams like Newcastle, also in the play-off zone, if we were going to achieve anything. I thrashed out another compromise with she who must be obeyed. We agreed that Karen wouldn't ask me any more searching questions, and I wouldn't give her leading answers that I knew would wind her up. It worked for about three weeks and when it started again, didn't stop until Jackie left to become an au pair in Italy. I actually liked Jackie very much. She used to wiggle around the office like she had a wasp in her knickers. If I had my time again I wouldn't have minded giving Karen something to really get worried about. But hindsight is a wonderful thing. Karen's parents, at least, seemed to like me. Her step father had been built up as some huge ogre who I would have to mind, or face problems for the rest of eternity, but he was a pussy cat. Once I got him onto the subject of football, he was a delight. He was a real Manchester United supporter, who actually came from Manchester. He was pleased that Lou Macari had made it as a manager, and hoped that he did well. What a nice guy. Her mother was a strict disciplinarian, who wouldn't allow us to so much as kiss under her roof, so I had to sleep on the sofa while Karen had a double bed all to herself. It grates to this day that not once did Karen sneak down in the middle of the night for a bit of forbidden nookie. Perhaps she was thinking exactly the same thing. At least I could have made the excuse I was looking for the bathroom.

Meanwhile, back on the pitch, Slater was emerging as a real star. He scored another goal against Middlesbrough, and Julian Dicks added a penalty as we won 2–0. The Littlewoods Cup came around again. In the fourth round we beat Wimbledon 1–0 at Upton Park with a Martin Allen volley. Justin Fashanu joined us on trial and was involved in the build up to the goal. Shortly afterwards it was revealed that he was gay, and suddenly he wasn't really wanted any more. Gosh, we football supporters are so prejudiced, aren't we? The match was won with ten men, Julian Dicks having been sent off for the first time as a West Ham player, but certainly not the last. The press concentrated so much on the brawl that preceded the sending off they almost forgot that we had beaten another first division side, and were now in the quarter finals, with another home draw against first division opposition, Derby County.

On November 25th, for no apparent reason, the season went pear shaped. We were playing Blackburn Rovers at Ewood Park. Blackburn had a decent side, but were only mid-table and should not have been able to go 4–1 up by half time. Despite a spirited fight back, West Ham lost 5–4 and won only one of the next thirteen games. From fifth place and confident of a play-off place, the whole season disintegrated like a sugar cube in a cup of coffee. We beat Plymouth again, in the ZDS Cup, another incarnation of the Full Members/ Simod Cup, but even that took extra time. 5–2 was a flattering scoreline by all accounts. A winter of discontent beckoned.

Fade to Grey. . .

Torquay United 1 West Ham United 0 – 6.1.90

After a promising start, things rapidly ran downhill. It was rather like my relationship with Karen. After beating Plymouth in the cup we could only manage a 0–0 draw at home to relegation fodder, Stoke City. We then managed to lose away at Bradford, 1–2 and at home to Oldham Athletic. The game against Oldham was one of those games where we appeared to be a team of boys playing against giants. Every time the ball was played into the Oldham half it came back with interest. Oldham dominated from start to finish and scored through Milligan and a Foster own goal. Tim and I watched on, unimpressed, from a sparsely populated West Stand. A few days later we threw away another promising situation, after leading 3–2 at Chelsea in the ZDS Cup, they scored two late goals to go through 4–3. Their team included our former midfield 'dynamo' Alan Dickens, who had run off when the prospect of second division football beckoned. How much good did it do him? He was last spotted playing for non-league Brentford. So much for career advancement.

Macari's reluctance to play Allen McKnight resulted in him bringing in Perry Suckling on loan from Crystal Palace. Suckling was like McKnight in many ways, he was similar in appearance, and, as we feared, in capability. The man who once picked the ball out of the net nine times at Anfield was at it again against Oldham. After a Christmas which was spent quietly at home with family and Karen, we lost at Ipswich on Boxing Day; almost unheard of – losing to Ipswich! Things were bad. Four days later we lost again at Filbert Street to a Leicester City side that included Gary McAllister. It was no disgrace to lose to a cracking goal from Ally Mauchlin. The team showed two new faces. Mark Ward had his wish granted and moved back up north to Manchester City. In a straight swap deal, we gained Trevor Morley and Ian Bishop. Both played against Leicester, but showed no hint of the good form that would follow. The next day, a further signing: Jimmy Quinn from Bradford City. The arrival of Quinn was excellent news in my view. I had seen him play for a lot of teams, including Swindon, Bradford and Blackburn Rovers and he always got goals. He was a Northern Ireland international, but I didn't read too much into that. After all, so was Allen McKnight. On New Year's Day I was granted leave from the pre-marital nest to watch the game against Barnsley. All three new boys played in an unrecognisable line-up. The goal scorers were familiar, however. Martin Allen got the first, Kevin Keen added two and Julian Dicks a penalty. What was also very familiar was the way we gave away two late goals as we took our foot off the accelerator towards the end. 4–2 was a decent scoreline, though, and went some way towards paying Barnsley back for the Littlewoods Cup defeat in 1987.

There then followed a completely inexplicable result. We lost in the third round of the FA Cup at Torquay. I mean, Torquay! Hardly a hot-bed of football, is it? It's not as though they were sleeping giants from the past, like Bolton or Preston. Torquay! As far as I was concerned they had nothing but a nice beach. I was driving Karen home from Ann-Marie's when I heard the news. I was grateful for two things. Firstly that we were not a first division side, and therefore did not attract banner back page headlines. Also, for the fact that I hadn't gone. I'm not sure I could have dealt with that. It was this period of instability that contributed to our failure to win promotion. As we stuttered, Leeds, Sheffield United, Newcastle, Swindon, Sunderland and Blackburn all put together steady little runs to put them in the frame. We could only look up and watch.

At least we managed a point in the next game; another trip to Devon to play Plymouth Argyle. The game ended 1–1 and Jimmy Quinn scored his first goal for West Ham. The good news was that Quinn, Bishop and Morley looked like useful players, the bad news was that they were all cup tied and couldn't take part in our Littlewoods Cup campaign. Derby County arrived at Upton Park amid accusations that Lou Macari was something less than whiter than white. It had been alleged by several newspapers that in his Swindon days, he had bet on Swindon losing a cup tie at Newcastle to cover expenses for the trip.

Swindon duly lost, and Macari collected an undisclosed figure. There were other irregularities surrounding his time at Swindon which defied explanation. He was a man under pressure. Julian Dicks relieved some of the pressure with a spectacular goal, beating Peter Shilton from about twenty-five yards out. Tony Gale had a nightmare though, and underhit a backpass, which Dean Saunders latched on to and slid past Phil Parkes. A replay at the Baseball Ground was not the result anyone, except perhaps Derby fans, really wanted. To add insult to injury, Macari changed the team for the visit of Hull City, bringing back the cup tied players, only for City to win 2–1. Trevor Morley scored his first for West Ham, netting Stain Tooth a return of about £10, but even so, things were looking bad, even by our own poor standards.

The replay at the Baseball Ground finished in a 0–0 draw even after extra time. Kelly had the ball in the net, but it was ruled out for offside.

The second replay took place a week later at Upton Park, Slater and Keen scored to put us into the semi-final for the second season running. Surely we wouldn't throw it away two seasons running? Would we? The draw was made and we were paired with Oldham – the team who had made us look fifth rate before Christmas and who had a plastic pitch that made Luton's look like a ploughed field. The groundsman used to come out at half time and polish it. This was a severe blow. At least the away leg came first, so if we could keep the score down, we stood a chance at home under the lights. One more triumph came for Macari, a 3–1 win over Brighton at Upton Park, cup-tied Jimmy Quinn scoring twice and Julian Dicks the other.

Macari was now under intense pressure with the rumours surrounding his activity at Swindon. The first leg of the semi-final against Oldham turned out to be his last game in charge. It was played on a cold and wet St Valentine's night, and Karen wasn't impressed at the fact, as we stood on the open terrace and proceeded to get drenched and frozen, while Oldham banged in six goals. It's easy to look for excuses: plastic pitch, injuries, unsettling position of the manager, etc., After all is said and done, though, the eleven players who took the pitch were all professionals who had a job to do. To lose by six goals was unforgivable, and merely gave the Oldham Commercial Department an extra fortnight to prepare their Wembley memorabilia.

As we drove home down a wet and windy M6 motorway, we were passed by a lunatic in a black XR3i. Three miles on, we passed him. A dead lunatic. Possibly, we thought, a deliberate attempt to end it all by a disenchanted West Ham supporter. The scoreline was enough to finally push Macari over the edge and he resigned a few days later. The club were left managerless, floating in mid-table obscurity and as good as out of the Littlewoods Cup.

Billy, Don't Be a Hero. . .

Sunderland 4 West Ham United 3 – 24.3.90

Stranded in twelfth place, West Ham travelled to Swindon and came away with a 2–2 draw. For some reason the game was played on a Sunday, but I cannot remember why I didn't go. I can have a good stab at a guess though. The game was significant in that we finally found a decent goalkeeper to replace the ageing Parkes. Macari's parting gift to West Ham was the towering Czech international goalkeeper Ludek Miklosko. He was the last player Macari signed, from Banik Ostrava for what now seems like a bargain £300,000. Ronnie Boyce took charge of the first team while the board considered the task of appointing Macari's successor. The press put some strange names into the frame, but we all knew who we wanted.

Billy Bonds was appointed successor to Lou Macari on February 23rd. I learned the news from an Evening Standard news vendor on Shaftesbury Avenue, the only time I have ever bought a newspaper on the strength of a headline. 'Billy Bonds Takes Over' read the main headline. 'West Ham turn to the old guard' ran the sub headline. I was delighted. Bonds had been a fine leader as a captain, and I saw no reason why he shouldn't do the same as a manager. He had only achieved mediocre results in his spell as youth team manager, but it seemed to every supporter that Bonds was the man we needed to lift morale for a final assault on the play-offs.

His first match in charge was against fellow play-off contenders Blackburn Rovers at Upton Park. West Ham played with an attitude and commitment seldom seen before or since, but inexplicably only had one goal to show for it at half time. The post and crossbar had both been bruised, and the Blackburn goalkeeper must have thought he was in for a Jane Fonda type workout. Jimmy Quinn scored a brilliantly executed header, but we could well have been five or six goals up by half time, a reverse of the game at Ewood Park. We paid for the missed chances, Bonds learned his first hard lesson as a manager. Blackburn equalised and the day ended as a bit of an anti-climax. However, we came away from that game knowing that if we displayed the same passion and commitment for the rest of the season, we had a good chance of a play-off place, and a good chance of reaching respectability in the second leg of the cup semi-final against Oldham. Bonds got his first victory as manager at Middlesbrough the next Saturday, a 1–0 win, Martin Allen scoring the winner. The following Wednesday we had a chance to get back at Oldham. No one had any doubt that we would win, but whether we could win by a seven goal margin was another matter. The bookmakers were quoting odds of 80/1 for a 7–0 victory. I took a piece of that action, knowing that Oldham would probably sit back on their six goal lead. If we played like we did against Blackburn, we had a chance. Unfortunately, we were without our cup-tied trio, so the team was different, but we were still three up inside an hour. When Julian Dicks hit the crossbar with a rasping drive, there was an audible intake of breath from the away supporters' section. Apparently, it came to light after the game that the Commercial Manager at Oldham was shitting himself at that point, as he had already spent a vast amount of money on Wembley hats, scarves, flags and other rip-off-the-fans-and-get-rich-quick memorabilia. Had the fourth one gone in we would have been within spitting distance of taking the tie to extra time. The lads put up a tremendous show. Alvin Martin, Julian Dicks and David Kelly scored the goals in a match which ended 3–0, 3–6 on aggregate. Despite conceding six, we had managed to avoid losing by a heavier margin than the previous season against Luton. I haven't mentioned Luton for a little while, have I? You'll remember Luton, that little Bedford-shire club, who I hate more than anything else in the world — even more than lumpy custard.

Karen was beginning to annoy me intensely. She had been a constant thorn in my side while I was trying to win her affection. Now that I had it, she was pushing the thorn like a barbed hook. She was now as regular a fixture on the North Bank as I was, which was a source of constant amusement to my friends, and embarrassment to me. When Portsmouth came to Upton Park, I had good cause to thank the Lord for Jimmy Quinn, a man who will always be a hero of mine. No sooner had we taken our regular spot behind the goal but slightly above and to the left, Quinn began his usual warm-up routine with Miklosko. Occasionally, a wayward ball would find its way into the crowd. Karen was giving me some severe grief about something, I can't remember what, but Quinn let fly from about twelve yards and the ball hit her squarely on the jaw, the smile falling from her face so fast you could almost hear it hit the floor. I caught her before she collapsed in a heap on the terrace, but was shaking with suppressed laughter as the St John Ambulance man gave me a hand to get her to the first aid room. She recovered in time to watch the game, insisting that she was all right and didn't want to go home, but she was blissfully quiet for the rest of the afternoon. Later, she demanded that I defend her honour by writing to Quinn and demanding an apology. I sent him a letter, but it didn't demand an apology. It thanked him most sincerely for shutting her up for the afternoon. He wrote back and apologised anyway, and sent a signed photograph. What a nice guy. The game against Portsmouth ended in a 2–1 win, Martin Allen and Julian Dicks scoring again. Another win, away at Watford meant that West Ham were in with a chance of the play-offs again, particularly as we still had to play main competitors, Leeds, Sheffield United, Newcastle, Sunderland and Oldham. Problem was, all but one of those games were away from home.

The next game was the away fixture at Elland Road. Confident, but without key player Julian Dicks through suspension, West Ham put up a brave show until the latter stages of the first half, when Lee Chapman scored twice. The match was beamed back to Upton Park on big screen TV. It was called big screen TV, anyway. It was actually a bank of TV sets about five by five, which built up to present the full picture. The quality of the picture was awful, as was the quality of the performance. No sooner did Trevor Morley pull one back, then Leeds raced up the other end and went 3–1 up. Most people left at that point, but I had learned my lesson the hard way, and was rewarded with a goal for West Ham which was initially credited to Colin Foster, but later analysis showed it was an own goal. A 2–3 defeat wasn't too bad against the league leaders, and second placed Sheffield United made the trip to Upton Park four days later. If we could edge a result against them we were in with a real chance.

Ludek Miklosko, or Ludo as he immediately became known, was proving to be one of our most influential attackers as well as a world class goalkeeper. He could launch long punts up field for Morley and Quinn to feed off. It was ironic that this tactic should come into play after the departure of Macari: it was something we would have expected from him, not from Bonds. It was used to full effect against Sheffield United, as Morley collected a long clearance to put us 1–0 up. In the second half, United sat back and invited us on to them. West Ham accepted the invitation and scored four more goals, Quinn getting a hat-trick and Martin Allen the other. If we could beat the second placed team 5–0, surely we had a chance? Think again. Sunderland were our nearest rivals in the promotion race, and a result at Roker Park was crucial. We took the lead twice, only to lose 4–3. There were many parts of the season which could be highlighted as being costly in terms of a play-off place. Certainly failing to win a game in December was one, but losing to the team that eventually pipped us by two points must be regarded as significant. A draw would have been enough. At least the strike force continued to flourish, Quinn bagged another two and Morley the other in the defeat. We were now in tenth place, seven points off the last play-off spot. We only held one game in hand over Swindon, having played the same number as all our other rivals. Taking that fact into account, it is a miracle we came as close as we did.

It was around this time that I met Stuart the QPR fan. Stuart the QPR fan loves QPR as much as I love West Ham, but he doesn't give anyone a hard time about it. Nowadays, it would be fair to say that he goes to more games than I do, home and away. He has had a season ticket at Loftus Road for as long as he has been able to sit upright, encouraged, obviously, by his father. What I liked about Stuart the QPR fan when I first met him was that he could talk about football in general terms, not just about QPR or West Ham; he has a general love of the game and doesn't think the football world starts and finishes in Shepherd's Bush. For that reason, I enjoy watching football with Stuart the QPR fan, especially at Loftus Road. It's great every now and then to sit as a neutral in among totally committed and partisan fans, just to hear the ridiculous comments that are made. They will claim that black is white if they think it will earn their team an advantage, when anyone with half a brain can see that it was a goal kick, not a corner. It makes you realise that you do exactly the same thing every week, and scares you just a bit.

I bumped into Stuart, and his fiancée, Vicky at a party. People often meet members of the opposite sex at parties, but I met a firm male buddy in Stuart the QPR fan at this one. We have remained good friends despite West Ham and QPR being in the same division and playing each other subsequently, and despite him getting married and moving away from the locality. As he left the party, he wished us good luck for the game against Port Vale. It was another one of those occasions when we could have used just a bit more luck.

Touch Too Much. . .

West Ham United 4 Wolverhampton Wanderers 0 – 5.5.90

David Kelly was sold to Leicester City, and nobody cried. Perhaps the only concern was that we had given him so much stick during his eighteen months at the club that he might return to haunt us.

Meanwhile, Frank McAvennie was set to make a return against Port Vale after breaking his leg in the opening game of the season at Stoke. Let me re-phrase that. After he had his leg broken by Chris Kamara on the opening day of the season at Stoke. Port Vale should have been a push-over. Julian Dicks missed a penalty in the first half, but we didn't worry too much about it once Trevor Morley put us 1–0 up. Somehow, Vale managed an equaliser, but Tony Gale scored a rare headed goal to put us back in front. It should have been curtains when we won another penalty. Dicks didn't fancy it, so handed the responsibility to Quinn, who also missed. When Vale equalised again, even the emergence of Frank McAvennie couldn't raise us the extra notch required. A 2–2 draw against Vale was two points dropped, not one gained, and was unforgivable, particularly when there were two chances to put the game well out of Vale's reach, but they were both blasted into the crowd. The West Ham fans deserved better than that.

It got better. The next two games were both away from home but yielded maximum points. At WBA, Ian Bishop scored his first goal for West Ham, Quinn and Keen getting the others in a 3–1 win, and at Oxford, goals from Quinn and Morley completed the double over Oxford. It was Grand National day and I managed to lose a tenner. It was good to have West Ham as back-up. We had closed the gap on sixth place to just four points, lying in eighth with Wolves one point ahead of us. Oldham and Ipswich had games in hand on us and could have overhauled us, but failed to do so. It was a straight fight between the top eight. Two would lose out.

Tim came to the game against Bournemouth with me. Bishop scored again in a 4–1 win over his former club, managed by former Hammer Harry Redknapp. He obviously wanted West Ham to win promotion as his team laid down and died at Upton Park. The bloke behind us on the North Bank had a fiver each on 4–2 and 5–1. He was urging anyone to score, he didn't care who, but he lost his money. Life's a bitch. We drew away at Barnsley, 1–1 with a Trevor Morley goal, then beat Ipswich at Upton Park 2–0, Kevin Keen making his 100th League appearance and scoring one of the goals. It was all going well, when we had to make the traumatic journey back to Boundary Park. It was the sort of scenario that football commentators loved. I could just see the headlines the next day, and the copy underneath being something like: 'West Ham returned to the scene of their St Valentine's Day massacre and extracted sweet revenge with a battling display to earn three points for their promotion campaign.' Nothing of the sort happened, and we were tanked 3–0.

I was beginning to think it might be time for Karen and I to go our separate ways. Although I loved her very much, I could not foresee a time when I might live happily ever after with her. We had to find a new flat, so I decided to get the move out of the way and give it one more chance. These things had to be worked at after all. As we took a 1–0 lead at Newcastle, we were looking at potential new homes. We looked at some in Charlton, which were OK, but I didn't really want to live in Charlton. As we went 1–2 down at Newcastle, we viewed another flat in Beckenham, and put down the deposit money straight away. Another problem sorted. The flat was dealt with, promotion wasn't. Defeat at Newcastle made life very awkward. It meant that if Sunderland got a point at Port Vale, we couldn't catch sixth place. Sunderland won, and Port Vale had done a Chelsea on us.

It meant that the last two home games, against Leicester and Wolves, which had both been made all-ticket in anticipation of a grandstand finale, would be something of an anti-climax, but we found something in both matches to retain the interest. The game against Leicester saw the return of David Kelly. We just waited for him to score the winning goal against us, but surprisingly, he played for Leicester exactly the same way he had done for us; falling over at every opportunity and being generally ineffective. Leroy Rosenior was back from injury and scored a great headed goal. Kevin Keen knocked in a penalty re-bound and Trevor Morley scored a third in a 3–1 win. That just left Wolves.

The final Saturday of the season had a carnival atmosphere about it. It was a bright sunny day, and although we knew we couldn't get promotion, we also knew that we couldn't get relegated. Wolves, too were out of the fight and we looked forward to a feast of football. The more optimistic among us were looking forward to next season. If we showed the same commitment under Billy Bonds then surely promotion was a formality. Liam Brady had decided to retire and this was to be his last competitive game. The Hammer of the Year trophy went to Julian Dicks, with Trevor Morley and Stuart Slater runners up. The game lived up to all our expectations.

Although there wasn't the commitment that the team had shown against Blackburn, I would go as far as to say that the first forty-five minutes against Wolves that afternoon was the best display of attacking football I have ever seen from a West Ham side. The movement off the ball was fantastic. The passing was crisp and accurate. The only department slightly lacking was finishing. Had that been on song we could have been in double figures by half time. As it was we had to settle for two almost identical goals, both diving headers from Trevor Morley and Kevin Keen. In the second half, Stewart Robson, playing his last full game for West Ham, strode through the Wolves half and unleashed an unstoppable shot. Cue Liam Brady. The script could have been written just for him as with a couple of minutes remaining, he danced through the Wolves defence and curled the ball into the top corner. The crowd flooded onto the pitch to greet their hero in the now traditional end of season celebration.

I remained on the terrace on the North Bank. Not through some snobbish reluctance to mix with the euphoric mass, but I was day dreaming. I had a vision of the crowd invading the pitch at the end of 1990/91 to greet a Second Division Championship and a glorious return to Division One. I had vision of great new players arriving at the club, together with the emergence of youthful talent and the useful experience of the older players. Then I woke up.

Another summer. For the first time since 1958 England would be in the World Cup Finals without a West Ham player in the squad. Failure was guaranteed. More importantly, Karen and I had to move to the new flat in Lennard Road and sort out our own situation. I didn't want to split up, but the lows were getting lower, the silences quieter and the gaps between wonderful sex longer. Having installed ourselves into the new flat, I went to Phil's stag night; the only man in the pub who wasn't a policeman, and yet the only one who was able to win their silly games, drinking or otherwise. Karen went to Ann-Marie's hen night and we met afterwards on Charing Cross Station. She assured me she hadn't had too much to drink as she threw up all over me on the train. It was the last train home and it was packed. I was wearing my best suit and was not amused. I was embarrassed publicly, then embarrassed privately as I took my suit to the dry cleaners the next day. Karen then compounded the felony by removing her dress to find she had a gashed knee and promptly fainted. I had to get her down to casualty in a taxi, praying she wouldn't puke again, then negotiate the triage system to get her patched up and ready for the wedding in two days time. They were getting to know us quite well at Bromley casualty. We were even on first name terms. I'd never been there before I met Karen. Now, after close encounters with a corned beef tin, a set of step ladders and a pair of pinking shears, we were season ticket holders. When I finally got her home, we had both sobered up and she was feeling randy. I wasn't interested. It was the last but one straw that broke this camel's back. The last one came just before the start of the new season. I was livid. I didn't want the lads to get upset at such a crucial stage. It could affect confidence if the boys knew I was unsettled.

It's All Over Now. . .

Tottenham Hotspur 4 West Ham United 1 – 17.8.90

Ray Clemence Testimonial

West Ham scored eighty league goals in 1989/90. That was pretty good going and a good sign of things to come. In all competitions, the total was ninety-nine. Defensive frailties had proved to be the undoing and were the biggest concern about a return to the top flight.

The weekend before the start of the season saw two testimonial games take place. An unusual fact in itself, made even more strange by the fact that they were both for goalkeepers. On Friday, West Ham played Spurs at White Hart Lane in a benefit match for Ray Clemence. On the Sunday, Ipswich Town visited Upton Park in a testimonial game for Phil Parkes. I travelled to the Tottenham game alone, straight from the office, meeting a fellow lone traveller on the tube and we watched the game together. Nothing unusual about the game – Spurs had a good side with Gascoigne and Lineker at their peak after the World Cup. One would have expected them to win, especially as it was a benefit game for a Tottenham player.

On the Saturday night I had been due to go to a party – on my own. Karen had finished her year at work. Unable to stand her a minute longer than was absolutely necessary they had released her dead on twelve months. I, on the other hand, being sweet and lovable (and the author of this book, therefore able to create whatever impression I like) was allowed to stay on until I went back to college. I got on well with everyone at Farrars and was grateful for the chance to keep working. What pissed me off was coming home at seven in the evening and finding Karen had been lounging around watching TV all day, while the flat looked like a small nuclear weapon had gone off in the lounge. I encouraged her to get a part time job, and she got one behind the bar of a local pub, which meant working unsociable hours. It did, at least, give me the chance to do a bit of socialising alone. I had fully intended to go to the party, but after taking Karen to work on the Saturday night I looked at my surroundings; the pile of ironing in the corner and the dirty dishes in the sink, and decided to blitz the flat instead. With the flat spick and span, I finally retired to bed. Exciting, this little story, isn't it? I awoke at six o'clock on Sunday morning to find the other side of the bed empty. I took a quick look around the flat to see if Karen had crashed out on the sofa so as not to disturb me, but knew she was not that considerate. She was nowhere to be seen. It was a measure of my resignation that I ignored her absence and went straight back to sleep. I woke again at eight and phoned the pub. I spoke to an extremely irate manager, who said she had slept over at the pub because she had finished very late and was very tired. I demanded to speak to her. She trudged from her bed, blissfully unaware of the fact that I didn't really give a toss, but I was going to make the bitch stew for this.

'Where the hell have you been?' I demanded.

'Oh, I was so tired. . .'

'Too tired to call me to let me know you weren't coming home?'

'I'm sorry.'

'I should fucking well think so.' I slammed the phone down very convincingly. I decided to leave the flat immediately in case she had any ideas about coming straight over to explain. I went over to Ann-Marie's house, which took an hour and a half, during which time, Karen had already rung her.

'Karen just phoned,' Ann-Marie said. 'She wanted to know if you were here and if you were angry.'

'What did you tell her?'

'I told her I'd be bloody angry if I was Rob.'

'Nice one, A-M. Put the kettle on!'

I told A-M all about what had been going on, and despite being her best friend, she advised me to walk away. I wasn't sure. In a perfect world, Karen would walk away from me. I didn't want to have to go back to my parents with my tail between my legs. But then, this isn't a perfect world. In a perfect world, West Ham would do better than a 1–1 draw against Ipswich in a testimonial game.

The match was like a West Ham old boys re-union. Billy played for our side, and the visiting team included Alan Devonshire, who had moved on to Watford, Geoff Pike who was at Notts County, Bobby Barnes from Northampton Town and Paul Goddard who was trying to resurrect his career at Millwall. Jimmy Quinn inevitably scored for us, and I went home to face Karen. She was hiding under a quilt on the sofa. I ripped it off and asked for an explanation.

'Do you want to try again?' she asked.

'No,' I said, staring out of the window. 'I've had enough.'

Karen had nowhere to go. Her brother only had a tiny flat and she couldn't go back to her parents because she needed to be in the area to go back to college. The flat at Lennard Road was a contractual obligation: we had to keep it until November, so I agreed she could stay at the flat, while I packed a few things and went back to Mum and Dad. A very difficult and, in hindsight, brave thing to do.

My first phone call on Monday morning was to a good pal of mine, Kevin. Kevin had been going out with one of Karen's friends and we had become close mates. He had just graduated from Southampton University and was working as a solicitor in Bromley. He was an idealist; and a confirmed right winger. He was a Young Conservative and proud of it. He had ambition, too. He still has. Watch this space. This guy wants to be Prime Minister and he seriously believes he will make it. Both myself and Michael Heseltine have our doubts however. Kevin invited me to a reception held by the President of the Board of Trade. Kevin's MP introduced us to Heseltine, saying that Kevin had a burning desire to be a politician.

'Is that right?' Heseltine asked. 'You'd like to be Prime Minister?'

Kev put on his best *Yes Minister* voice and replied mockingly: 'Well, if my country saw fit to call upon my talents, I would seriously consider it.'

Heseltine just looked at him and said: 'You might as well not bother, then.' I laughed. Heseltine has his own reasons for doubting that Kevin will be Prime Minister, I have my own – who ever heard of a Prime Minister called Kevin? He had a sympathetic ear in those days. He had listened when we had been to the theatre as a foursome with his girlfriend a few weeks earlier and was half expecting the news. He was upset when I told him we had finished. He said he liked Karen. I said I would like Karen if I didn't have to live with her. He just laughed and bought me another pint.

It was during these troubled times that I realised how many good friends I had. I was very lucky. My parents supported me through thick and thin. I still haven't found anything to blame them for. My bed was waiting for me when I turned up that Sunday evening, and both Mum and Dad revealed that they didn't like Karen in the first place. I had thought as much, but it's not the sort of thing you tell your son, is it? My sisters were both delighted that I had got shot of her. They were always suspicious of her motives. I was just blinded by her body. On several occasions I went back to the flat to pick up clothes and possessions and on two occasions we ended up back in bed. In the end it made me hate her for being a tart, but if the truth be known I was the biggest slag of them all. Since I met Karen, I've never had a pure thought in my head, and I doubt I ever will again.

At work things continued to rumble along. They all knew Karen quite well because she used to come into the office to meet me after work, and to check I wasn't feeling Jackie up behind the filing cabinet. They were all shocked, too. 'We thought you were perfect for one another,' they all said. Just goes to show how wrong you can be.

On the opening day of the season I was still up to my neck in books, records, tapes, football programmes and financial settlements. The fact we had drawn 0–0 at Middlesbrough was incidental. Close used to work around the corner from me, and he came around to the office to meet me before the game against Portsmouth. My colleague, Rod MacLeod, a professional Scotsman and brilliant wit, remarked the next morning that he didn't think much of my new girlfriend. The first home game of the season was a disappointing 1–1 draw with Portsmouth. We needed to win every home game – a draw was not acceptable. At least Frank McAvennie showed that he might be back on form and scored his first goal in his second spell at the club. The following Saturday, we played Watford at Upton Park. It was an action replay of the previous season's game, winning 1–0 through a Julian Dicks penalty, but the performance was far from convincing. Close and I were going to more and more games together. Most of the others had dropped out: Bean Head came along occasionally, and Stain Tooth was still a regular, but the original gang was depleted. Close couldn't be bothered to go to Leicester. After the performance we had witnessed against Watford, we felt the only logical result was a defeat. Instead, we watched the video highlights of season 1989/90 at his flat, and wondered if we would make it this season. We flipped over channels for the football results. We had won 2–1. Maybe we would.

Here I Go Again. . .

Newcastle United 1 West Ham United 1 – 22.9.90

I wasn't looking forward to going back to college. I would have to make sure I got my side of the story in before madam did. Rule number one in broken relationships – always get your revenge in first.

I splashed out on a season ticket for the West Stand, determined to get a good view of our promotion campaign. This meant watching the game away from the others. It was a weird situation. Stain Tooth had an East Terrace season ticket, and Close stood on the North Bank, so we would travel to the game together, then each go off in different directions to watch it, and meet up again afterwards. It made for interesting conversations on the way home, because each of us had seen the game from a different angle.

September 15th 1990 was the 50th Anniversary of the Battle of Britain. This was a subject which had always fascinated me; indeed, my first ambition in life was to be a Spitfire pilot, and I was most upset when I realised Spitfires were no longer in service with the RAF and that the Second World War would not start up again just for my benefit. I went with Dad up to Trafalgar Square to watch the very impressive RAF fly past. As the aircraft flew overhead, everyone started clapping. This has always bothered me. Why do people clap when they know they can't be heard. I had experienced it at the live screening of the Leeds game at Upton Park. The crowd were singing and chanting as though the team would reap some kind of benefit. It's like people clapping after seeing a film at the cinema. 'Well done, projectionist – jolly good show!'

After the flypast, we had a spot of lunch and wandered across to Upton Park for the game against Wolves. We saw another mildly disappointing performance. I hated to say it, but Frank McAvennie was just not hitting it off with Trevor Morley up front. Morley was the one of the two who was looking sharper, and I called for Jimmy 'The Tree' Quinn to be re-instated. Alvin Martin scored our goal against Wolves. West Ham fans will never learn – they baited Steve Bull for fully seventy-five minutes before he buried the equaliser past Ludo. Another home draw was not what the doctor ordered.

Bonds finally saw sense in the next game, at home to John Lyall's Ipswich. It appeared to be one of those games where the old master would come back and teach the young whippersnapper a lesson, like Darth Vader and Luke Skywalker locked in mortal combat with their light sabres – well, a bit like that. Ipswich took the lead and held it well into the second half, when Bishop squeezed in an equaliser. It looked like another draw, but Bonds threw Quinn on and he immediately produced the winner. Morley scored a third and we were away.

Kevin had taken it upon himself to cheer me up after my break up with Karen. He couldn't grasp the concept that I was actually quite pleased to be out of it, but he was determined to get me fixed up again without delay. The following Saturday I was suffering badly with a cold. I had a sore throat, a runny nose and was feeling awful, when Kevin rang and asked if I would make up a four to go to a night club. West Ham had drawn at Newcastle. I was in a reasonable mood, but was hardly fit to go out clubbing. I tried to make an excuse, but he was having none of it. He came over and persuaded me that I would feel much better for it. His new girlfriend, Liz, was bringing one of her friends and she was really pretty, and I would soon forget all about my sore throat. I already knew Liz, but I had never met Jenny before. She was, as Kevin had said, a pretty girl: about my height with short black hair. I wasn't interested, however. For a start, she was younger than me. Even Karen had been six months older. The prospect of going out with a younger woman just did not appeal. She didn't seem all that interested either, but made an effort to please Liz, and I did so to keep Kevin happy. I danced a slow dance with Jenny and we all said goodbye. I thought no more about it. Every time Kevin phoned, he would ask me if I had spoken to Jenny. 'Why should I have done that?' I would ask him.

'I thought you liked her,' he said.

'I do, but then I like your gran, too. That doesn't mean I want to go out with her on a regular basis.'

'She'd say yes if you asked her.'

'Who? Your gran?'

'No, Jenny, stupid.' I wasn't convinced at first, but the more I thought about it, the more attractive the idea became. Considering Kevin thought she'd be such a pushover I found her a tough nut to crack, and it was eight months before I persuaded her it was a good idea to be alone with me.

Although West Ham were still unbeaten, the performances left a lot to be desired. A 3–0 win over Stoke City in the latest version of the League Cup, the Rumbelows Cup helped, then a confidence boosting 1–1 draw at Hillsborough against a Sheffield Wednesday side who could have buried us alive in the first half had it not been for some poor finishing and some inspired goalkeeping. I listened to the game on the car radio driving home from my grandmother's house in Hailsham. When we went 1–0 down, I knew we would come back. It's a rare feeling as a West Ham supporter. Another patchy performance saw us win 2–0 against Oxford. As Stuart Slater said in the post match interview: 'When we finally put it together someone is in for a right pasting.' That someone turned out to be Hull City the following Saturday. It was a horrible October day. There was rubbish floating around on the pitch even before the teams came out. To add to it, the wind was swirling and there was a hint of rain. It was very unpleasant. Jimmy Quinn opened the scoring, but Hull equalised, and we feared a repeat of the previous season's debacle. However, straight from, the kick off, Steve Potts surged forward and hit a shot the Hull keeper could only let slip through his legs. Potts had scored at last! Not the best goal in the world, but a goal none the less. He was no longer the girly goal scoring virgin. In the second half West Ham stopped messing about and made up for lost time. Morley won a penalty which Dicks converted. Parris scored a fourth, Quinn got the fifth and Morley the sixth before Dicks rounded it off with a superb solo goal to make it 7–1 at full time. It was the biggest win since the 8–1 win over Newcastle and we all celebrated accordingly. After all, it's not every day any team scores seven. Let alone West Ham United.

Double Dutch. . .

West Ham United 1 Blackburn Rovers 0 – 24.10.90

After spanking Hull City, we faced three away games in a row. At Stoke, we completed the second round Rumbelows Cup win with a 2–1 victory. Martin Allen scored his first two of the season. Frank McAvennie was struggling to get into the side. At Bristol City, he came off the bench to score an equaliser in a 1–1 draw. A week later he went one better and came off the bench to score the winner at Swindon. The season had progressed well after the dodgy start, fourteen games unbeaten and third place behind Oldham Athletic and Sheffield Wednesday. With three going up automatically and one more via the play-offs, it was our best chance of getting back into the first division.

Just as my season ticket came through, I discovered I had to go away on a trip with college. It was supposed to be a five day excursion to a European capital city, but turned into a full scale piss-up, with only token resistance put up by our lecturers and organisers. We had a choice of Madrid, Paris or Amsterdam. I fancied Madrid, but saw that Karen had already put her name down, so I went for Amsterdam as I had already been to Paris. The drinking started on the seven hour ferry crossing to the Hook of Holland and stopped on the crossing back to Felixstowe. Someone bought a bottle of peach schnapps and was sharing it around. I developed a bit of a taste for it and five or six of us went to the duty free shop to buy our own bottles.

I tried to phone home to find out how we had got on against Blackburn Rovers. I discovered that you can't ring 0898 numbers from overseas, and tried Mum and Dad but couldn't get through. The next morning I rang Close at work. He had borrowed my season ticket, so the least he could do was spare me a few minutes to tell me the score.

'Where are you ringing from?' he asked.

'Amsterdam,' I said. He was so shocked it took him a few minutes to tell me we had won 1–0 with a goal from Ian Bishop. That was all I had wanted to know. Anything else was just costing me money.

We came home knowing we would have to justify the trip by producing some sort of project and/or presentation, which we did as a group just before Christmas. The way we put across the presentation you could have believed we had actually done some work while we were there. In the meantime, I finally managed to use my season ticket for the home game against Charlton. Martin Allen got another brace in a 2–1 win and the run continued. The same gang who had made the trip to Oxford in 1986 retraced their footsteps in 1990 for the Rumbelows Cup tie. We even found the same parking spot in the middle of a roundabout. We arrived at the ground just as Trevor Morley put us in front; but the writing was on the wall right from the moment Oxford equalised and missed a penalty. We thought we would be lucky to get a replay. That proved to be the case. Oxford scored right at the end to give them a win they deserved. That was the end of the sixteen match unbeaten run, but the league run continued. Me and Close drove up to Notts County, again missing the kick-off as we still had to park in the cattle market after being held up in road works. County's ground, Meadow Lane, was a shambles. The toilets were a slit in the ground with a wall to piss against. The catering facilities offered such delights as hot meat pies that burned your lips on the outside while being full of ice on the inside. It was basically a tip. At least Morley's goal in the second half lit up an otherwise miserable day. Julian Dicks had succumbed to an injury that would rule him out for over a year. In his place, West Ham signed Chris Hughton on loan from Tottenham, and he proved to be an adequate replacement, but he was never going to be another Dicksy. After driving home from Nottingham, resisting the temptation to pop in and see Christina, I dropped Close off, got changed and went to a party in Orpington. Who should be there but Jenny, looking pretty as a picture. She didn't want anything to do with me, though. Kevin had split up with Liz and broken her heart in the process. Jenny assumed that as a friend of Kevin I must be tarred with the same brush. Silly cow.

A week later we played Millwall at The Den. There were fights going off all over the place; in the car park, at the station and in the ground. The match seemed to be the last thing on everybody's mind. When it finally got under way, Frank McAvennie scored our goal in a 1–1 draw which secured second spot behind a rampant Oldham Athletic. After the game, we tried to get out of the queue and take a train to Beckenham, but the police wouldn't let us. We had to take a train to Whitechapel with the other sheep. Bloody marvellous. That put an extra hour on my journey time home, and meant that I was walking down my road at exactly the same time as Karen, who was walking to her Saturday night bar job. 'I see you can still afford to go to football, then?' she said bitterly, in reference to my reluctance to give her a share of the deposit money for the flat. The fact that I had paid for her to stay at the flat for three months – around £900 – did not seem to enter the equation.

On the Monday night, West Ham played Tottenham in a testimonial game for Billy Bonds. Guess what? We won 4–3 and Bill scored the winner from the penalty spot. Who says these games are contrived? Me, that's who.

A New Flame...

Barnsley 1 West Ham United 0 – 22.12.90

West Ham came from behind to beat Brighton 2–1 at Upton Park, and news filtered through that Oldham had lost for the first time that season to Port Vale. A perfect day. The euphoria experienced in winning a game is multiplied exponentially when coming from behind. It hits the roof when your nearest rivals lose as well. The unbeaten league run was now seventeen as we travelled to Plymouth and became the first team to win there that season. The score was 1–0, Frank McAvennie scoring. Oldham lost again and we went to the top of the table. We could do no wrong. Reputations were laid waste, and but for a slight aberration at Oxford, we had forgotten what it was like to lose. A nineteenth game unbeaten came at home to WBA, 3–1. Frankie's goal, the third, was an exquisite lob from about forty yards. It was a pity that we had been knocked out of the Rumbelows Cup because it would have been nice to test our all-conquering team against some first division opposition. In retrospect, perhaps it is better that we did not play higher placed opposition sooner, otherwise the fatal flaws in the team might have been exposed earlier than they were. We made it twenty at Portsmouth, Trevor Morley scoring the winner, and twenty-one against Middlesbrough, albeit in a disappointing 0–0 draw.

Now then, I haven't mentioned Luton Town for a while, have I? Our brief outing in the ZDS took place at my favourite club, and Bonds showed how important he felt the competition was by making five changes to the side, including Allen McKnight in goal. If Bonds hadn't wanted to take part in the competition, it would have been a lot less painful all round if he had just withdrawn. The combination of playing Luton away on their plastic pitch, with McKnight in goal was potentially disastrous. It proved to be in practice. Luton won 5–1 and our goal was a dodgy penalty which was only scored on the rebound. Another good reason to hate Luton. Although not a vital competition, the damaging effect was that confidence was knocked for the trip to Barnsley, another of our favourite sides, and they ended our record twenty-one match unbeaten league run. Removed from the top of the table, it was not the best preparation for our Boxing Day clash with nearest rivals Oldham.

Meanwhile I badgered away at Jenny. I was going to get her if it was the last thing I did. Whenever I knew she was going to a party I phoned to offer her a lift. What a creep. On Christmas Eve I took her a huge bouquet of flowers as a Christmas present, making out that I did the same for all my female friends. Yeah, right – students can all afford to do that, can't they? She got me a present, too. A drinks holder for the car. Hmmm. Somehow, I detected a 'reserve' present feeling about it. I didn't worry. I knew I had no serious competitors for her affection and I knew if I remained patient I would succeed.

On Boxing Day we beat Oldham 2–0 and everything seemed to be back on course. Oldham were surprisingly easy meat. I felt sure we would have to fight every inch of the way, but goals from Morley and Slater saw us through and we could even afford a missed penalty from Jimmy Quinn. Lack of success from the spot highlighted the fact that we were missing Julian Dicks in more ways than one. It should have been just as easy to get past Port Vale, but by the end of the game we were grateful for a point in a 0–0 draw. Darren Beckford had a wonderful chance to inflict our first home defeat but hit the side netting. The game was played on a pitch that was ankle deep in water in places, more suitable for water polo than football. That evening, a mutual friend of Kevin and I, Brett, unexpectedly turned up at a party. He was sorry to hear that Karen and I had split up. I was surprised he remembered her. 'Of course I remember her,' he said. 'She was that loud bird with the big tits.' I had to agree that his description was painfully accurate. On New Year's Eve I dashed between two parties seeing in the new year with a former school friend who was combining a new year's party with a housewarming. It was a real trip down memory lane for me, the majority of the guests being former pupils at Balgowan, my primary school. I perfected my get-pissed-quick technique of pouring a good measure of whiskey into a can of Guinness. The heathen didn't have any Irish Whisky, but Scotch seemed to do the trick. It was so nice to see so many old friends, even if they were all drunk and more successful than me.

The new year started well, Jimmy Quinn scoring the winner at Bristol Rovers. The FA Cup campaign began in rather odd fashion. We had drawn fourth division Aldershot away, but they decided to switch the tie to Upton Park to maximise the potential income. That meant that for the first time certainly in my memory, West Ham played a competitive fixture at Upton Park wearing their away strip. Did I say competitive? I do beg your pardon, I meant crap. It was hard to see any cup success coming from a performance like that. OK, technically we were away from home, but let's face it, we were at home against a team that the next season would go out of the league. The former QPR keeper, Peter Hucker, kept goal for Aldershot and played reasonably well, but he could have got away with an off day, we were that poor. As Bonds admitted afterwards, we could have played until midnight and still not scored. Our FA Cup dreams were shattered when the draw was made for the fourth round. Luton away. Goodnight, and thank you. The new police directives meant that we had to wait ten days for the replay, and in between, Morley scored another goal at Watford to set us off on another little run. The replay against Aldershot finally exposed the difference between the two sides. We were 4–1 up at half time through Morley, Slater, Parris and Bishop. Ludo made an uncharacteristic error in allowing Aldershot to pull one back, but if he was going to make an error, this was the night to do it. Morley and Quinn added a couple more towards the end and we ran out 6–1 winners. The following Saturday we beat Leicester at Upton Park to complete the second 'double' of the season. George Parris scored the only goal. It was worrying that we were not scoring more goals. I know football fans are never happy, and we were top of the league, but Oldham were winning matches by threes and fours whereas we were scraping through. If the defence decided to have an off period, we were in trouble.

We expected defeat at Luton. We had the chance to watch it on those marvellous 'Big Screens' at Upton Park, as Luton had allocated us only half a dozen tickets. Hopes were raised as we appeared to be playing quite well and scored just before half time through George Parris again – his third goal in a row. Kingsley Black equalised in the second half, but a 1–1 draw was a much better result than we could have wished for. It gave us a chance to test our unbeaten home record against them in a replay.

It's a Thin Line between
Love and Hate. . .

West Ham United 5 Luton Town 0 – 31.1.91

The whole point of buying a season ticket, as far as I was concerned, was that I would never have to miss a game at Upton Park through arriving late, or being unable to get a ticket via normal channels. I knew that the replay against Luton would not be covered by my season ticket – it only covered two cup ties, and they had been taken account of by the two games against Aldershot. Tim had said he wanted to go to the replay, so not to bother booking a ticket for my usual seat, I could watch it with him on the North Bank and save myself a few bob in the process. I reluctantly agreed, feeling that we would have to get there very early to ensure a good position. It was the day before the game that Tim hit me with the suggestion that he bring his girlfriend, Nicky as well. It didn't bother me, but we had to pick her up from Guys Hospital, where she worked. This made the journey to Upton Park by car very awkward. We got to the Rotherhithe Tunnel bang on schedule, but then hit a traffic jam which saw us locked bumper to bumper all the way to Upton Park. We raced around to the main gates to find they had been locked, and it was ticket holders only. I looked at Tim and Nicky and raised my hands as if to strangle them both, but realised it was futile to lose my temper. To make matters worse, the programmes had all sold out, so I had nothing to read while I listened to the game at home on the radio. To this day, it remains the only home programme missing from my collection. It's almost symbolic – the missing Luton programme – testimony to my undying hatred for the club. The fact that we won 5–0 did not pacify me. In fact it made matters worse. If we had lost I could have been philosophical about it and said: 'Well, I didn't miss anything then. . .' But we beat Luton, and we beat them 5– 0 and I wasn't there to see it. It was criminal. I listened to the demolition job via sketchy reports on the radio. As Morley stroked in the fifth I felt like crying. Watching the highlights on the TV later that night did not help. What did help was a cushy fifth round draw at home to Crewe Alexandra.

Into February, and a rare league defeat. This time it was Wolverhampton Wanderers who beat us 2–1 at Molineux. It was a day for unexpected results. Chelsea unexpectedly beat Arsenal for their one and only league defeat of the season, and I unexpectedly went to watch Welling United against Aylesbury Town in an FA Trophy game. I can't remember the score, it was that boring, but I had gone along to keep Kevin company and try to take my mind off the game against Wolves. It didn't work, because the bloke standing next to us had a radio and kept shouting the scores out. It was a bitterly cold day, a prelude to the bad weather that forced postponements in our matches at home to Newcastle and away to Ipswich. It meant the next game was the fifth round tie against Crewe. Kevin came along, under protest, claiming to be a Liverpool supporter even though he knew nothing about football. He knew less than the average club chairman. Actually, the more I think about it, the more it makes sense. As always happens when bringing guests along, West Ham played like a bunch of tarts and only just scraped a 1–0 win with Jimmy Quinn coming off the bench to notch the winner. Crewe played well and deserved more, but I wasn't complaining. We had made the quarter finals. Wembley wasn't such a distant dream after all; a home draw and we were virtually guaranteed a semi-final place. The draw was indeed at home, to Liverpool or Everton. It took them three goes to settle their fifth round match, a draw at Anfield followed by that classic 4–4 draw at Goodison, when Tony Cottee came on as a substitute and scored twice for Everton. After that game, Kenny Dalglish resigned and Everton won the second replay 1–0.

Meanwhile, we picked up our league trail with a 3–1 win over Millwall at Upton Park. We were still top, but Oldham always remained in striking distance. The biggest the gap had ever been was four points; hardly enough to spark off premature championship celebrations, but we had to be happy with the fact we were top. Millwall proved the point that the more you taunt a player, the more likely he is to score. Their fans sang to Ian Bishop 'Where's your caravan?' as he trotted across to the South Bank to take a corner. He floated the corner over and Frank scored the opener. Beautiful.

Another disappointing result followed, a 0–0 draw at WBA. As front runners we should have been winning at venues like the Hawthorns, where West Bromwich Albion had managed only five wins all season. That disappointment was nothing compared to the shock of hearing the news that Trevor Morley had been injured in a domestic argument. We never did get to the bottom of that story. Whatever the truth, it robbed us of our top scorer for the game against Plymouth, and our lack of cutting edge cost us dear, as we let in two goals at home for the first time in a 2–2 draw. Parris had a chance to win the game from the spot near the end, but it would have been rough justice on Plymouth. It was not good preparation for the visit of Everton in the cup quarter final.

This time, I took no chances. Despite Tim's protests, I applied for my usual seat in the West Stand and watched the game from there while he sat at home, unable to get a North Bank ticket. Sorry Tim. It was one of those great nights at Upton Park. There was a buzz in the air before the game and the team played with 120% commitment. Colin Foster scored a goal of such quality it had to be a fluke. I'm sorry Colin, but can you put your hand on your heart and honestly say that you meant to pivot like a wild dervish and send an unstoppable volley into the top corner of the net? If it was a fluke, the team deserved it. Stuart Slater doubled his transfer value with a display which combined skill and aggression. He chased back, tackled, ran at the Everton defence and shot accurately in such a way that he reminded me of Bryan Robson at his peak, (Not 'Pop', the crap one who played for England a few times and was always injured). Slater deservedly scored the second goal, before West Ham let in the traditional goal at the end just to make the last few minutes that bit more exciting. After all, it would be no fun to be 2–0 up with a minute to go, would it? We already knew it would be Nottingham Forest in the semi-final because our quarter final was played on the Monday following Forest's win over Norwich in their quarter final. The other semi was to be between Tottenham and Arsenal, for the first time ever, at Wembley Stadium.

The win over Everton went to the player's heads. Admittedly, it was a bit unfair to be expected to pick up the pace for a league match against Oxford just two days later, and they lost 2–1. Even worse followed the next Saturday when the home record went. To be fair to Sheffield Wednesday, they played us off the park. We had a spell in the second half when we looked dangerous and pulled the score level, but there was never really any doubt who was going to win the game. Paul Williams, the West Ham fan who had destroyed us when playing for Charlton two seasons previously, repeated the dose. Another player who had caused us headaches in the past was Franz Carr. I had always been impressed by his pace and crossing ability when playing for Nottingham Forest and was delighted when he came on loan. However, he played like a complete gimp and the less I say about it the better.

Bristol City came and provided us with three points we needed to get the confidence flowing again, but at a cost. Tony Gale's free kick was enough to win the game, but Frankie was sent off and was thereby ruled out of the cup semi-final. On the Saturday, while the boys ground out a 0–0 draw at Hull, Tim and I queued at Upton Park for our semi-final tickets. We got there at nine and left at four. I had grown a beard by the time I got my ticket. We bought train tickets at the same time and circled the date in our diaries. We were excited. Although we had seen semi-finals before, they had been home and away affairs. This was a major showpiece one-off on a neutral ground, Villa Park.

Thoughts of the semi-final had to go to the back of the mind for the time being. Not only did we have a hectic league programme over Easter and the two weeks leading up to the semi, but I faced my finals in June and had to set about some serious revision. On Good Friday we played Oldham at Boundary Park and earned a creditable 1–1 draw. Ludo played a blinder and saved our skins in the first half. In the second half, Ritchie handled on the line (should have been sent off!) and Bishop scored the penalty. At last we had found a decent replacement for Dicks from the spot, we thought. The hero worship was obviously too much for Bish and he immediately rushed up to the other penalty box and whipped Gunnar Halle in the face with his hair. Ritchie equalised and a draw seemed a good result as we had won the series against Oldham, a win and a draw.

On Easter Monday, I just happened to turn up at the pub in Sevenoaks where Jenny was having a drink with Liz. I didn't quite resort to begging, but it would have been quite amusing to have stood back and watched myself try to persuade her to go out with me. Every time I failed, I asked myself why I did it. I didn't need it. Ten minutes later, I had convinced myself once again that I did. I had to rush to get my seat against Barnsley. By half time I wished I hadn't bothered. 2–0 down, I was beginning to think that Barnsley were just one of those teams that we were destined to lose to at vital times. If West Ham, as a club ever died, their tombstone would read: 'If it hadn't been for Luton, Barnsley, Chelsea and Notts County. . .' Bonds must have thrown a few cups around in the dressing room at half time because the boys came out and turned it around 3–2. I was amazed. We had a new signing, Iain Dowie, who had won the Football League Mr Ugly competition six seasons running, and only scored goals because opposition defenders couldn't bear to be photographed with him. I remember watching him in our 5–0 win over Luton and thinking: 'Yup, that Iain Dowie looks totally crap.' Sure enough, within a few weeks he was a West Ham player. He did nothing for the whole game against Barnsley except score our equaliser. I hate players who do that. I couldn't work out why Bonds had bought him. If it was cover for the cup semi it wasn't such a hot idea because Dowie was cup tied. Morley was on the way back and Quinn was still the apple of my eye. Why complicate matters? The game against Barnsley was the last home game before the Cup semi and we gave the team an appropriate send off. There were still two games to be played though. At Port Vale, we won 1–0 through a fine Ian Bishop goal. The stadium at Vale Park ran Meadow Lane a close second for quality, but at least the pies were hot all the way through. Our preparation was naturally completed by a defeat, 1–0 at Brighton. That was the first and last time I have ever watched a game progress on Ceefax. It makes phoning Clubcall seem like actually being there.

Despite the fact we were without Trevor Morley, Frank McAvennie and Iain Dowie for the semi-final, I remained quietly confident of a result. After all, it was our third semi-final in succession. It had to be third time lucky.

I Don't Want to Talk about It. . .

Nottingham Forest 4 West Ham United 0 – 14.4.91

F.A. Cup Semi-Final

Well, I don't want to talk about it if that's OK. I'd much rather talk about something else. Ah yes, the wonderful Helen. Remember her, from chapter one? Alarming as it may seem, she arrived back on the scene as a friend of Liz and Jenny. I can visualise you all now saying: 'Hang on a minute, Banksy. That's just a little bit too convenient for us to believe.' Well, they say truth is stranger than fiction and that's what happened so there. She had got rid of the pig tails and the holier-than-thou attitude, but she still walked around with her nose in the air. It was such a nice nose that I let her off. At first I didn't twig who she was, but it came flooding back to me in a dream. She looked just like Darryl Hannah, and for all I knew she probably tasted like her as well. Kevin was smitten. He wouldn't admit it, but he fancied her something rotten, and I couldn't blame him. For my part, there was still the matter of the awkward Jenny to negotiate. Kevin and I made a pact to help each other in our quest for personal satisfaction.

I still don't want to talk about the semi-final, or Keith Hackett. After all, there may be children reading. We just lost and that was that. Trevor Morley came back from his stabbing to score the winner at Ipswich and set us up with the chance to clinch promotion the following Saturday at home to Swindon. Swindon were a bit of a giggle. They had won the play-off final at Wembley against Sunderland, then Lou Macari's misdemeanours cost them their place in the first division. Instead of playing the likes of Liverpool and Arsenal every week, they struggled to avoid relegation to the third division under new manager Glenn Hoddle. You had to laugh. I had thought it was a bit strong that having relegated Swindon, they automatically gave Sunderland a place in the first division as play-off runners up. It would have been much fairer to start the play-offs again, with the team in seventh place taking part. Guess who finished seventh? Well, it would have been fairer, wouldn't it? Swindon obligingly laid down and died, allowing us to win 2–0. All we needed was the right result from Barnsley. If they had failed to win, we were up. There was a hushed silence around the ground, when the announcer stated that Barnsley had drawn 1–1, and West Ham were a first division side once again. I don't recall being too elated about it. I remember feeling that it wasn't worth anything unless we won the title. Bonds made his first big managerial mistake. He was quoted in the press as saying that the championship meant nothing, it was promotion that was the main thing. He was right, of course, in the financial sense, but he was being too honest. We wanted to hear him say that he wouldn't be happy until we had beaten Oldham into submission and finished top of the pile. Admittedly, it looked as though that would happen anyway, but the damage had already been done. The attitude appeared to be reflected in the players' performance against Newcastle United the following Wednesday. The main job had been done, they didn't want to over-exert themselves. We managed a 1–1 draw but deserved to lose in an appalling display of lethargy. I couldn't go to Blackburn Rovers, but did the next best thing and went to Ipswich to cheer them on in their game against Oldham. It was reminiscent of the game in which Oldham had beaten us 2–0 the previous season. Ipswich were like little boys against a very strong Oldham team, who won 2–1. West Ham blew it at Blackburn, another team struggling against relegation. It seemed that now we were up, there was a combination of lack of effort on our part, together with an extra determination from the opposition to beat us. We lost 3–1 at Blackburn, all the goals coming in the first half. We were still top after that game, but I was so depressed as I drove back from Ipswich that you would have thought they had taken promotion away from us. The trend was not healthy. I had bought tickets for the Bank Holiday game at

Charlton, but had what I perceived to be a better offer. A mate of mine, Ken, was desperately trying to get into Liz's knickers and had invited her to join him for a weekend on his parents' narrow boat on the Grand Union Canal. To make it look kosher, he invited me and Jenny to join him. It was a great weekend, all four of us had a cracking time, and Dad enjoyed himself with my ticket at Charlton as we drew 1–1, opening the gap to two points as Oldham lost. The narrow boat weekend finally cracked the toughest nut I had ever come across. Jenny finally agreed to go out with me, but I had to fork out a substantial amount of dosh to secure the deal, buying two tickets to see Paul Simon at Wembley Arena. Was it all worth it? I asked myself, as I wrote out the cheque. I decided that it was; after all, when you have worked as hard as I had for this, it had to be worthwhile. I was achieving my own first division status.

The following Wednesday, we tentatively beat Bristol Rovers, 1–0 with a Stuart Slater goal. It left the Championship down to the final game. We were top, ahead of Oldham by two points. Sheffield Wednesday in third couldn't catch either of us; it was a straight fight. Our last game was against Notts County at Upton Park. Having already beaten them at Meadow Lane, we were confident of getting the right result, especially as Oldham had an equally tough game, against Sheffield Wednesday at Boundary Park. It was knife edge stuff. As long as we won, we were OK. A draw wouldn't be enough if Oldham won, their goal difference knocked ours into a cocked hat. If we lost, we just had to pray that Wednesday would do us a favour. At half time, it still looked good. We were 2–0 down, but then, so were Oldham. If it finished like that, we were home and dry; dust down the trophy cabinet, Mavis. Parris scored in the second half, but County were jostling for a good play-off position and were not going to give up. Even as the final whistle went, we were Champions. Elton Welsby said so on the TV. The fans rushed onto the pitch to celebrate. The latest score from Oldham was a 2–2 draw and heading for injury time. We were Champions by a point. Hold it!

Oldham scored in the last minute and we lost the Championship. To say we finished second sounds good, but when you consider the whole season was really a two horse race, it was as good as finishing second in a boxing match. One fan summed it up as he left the ground and shouted through the dressing room window 'You fucked up West Ham!' It was a huge disappointment, so near and yet so far. So typically West Ham. I really don't want to talk about it.

The One and Only. . .

West Ham United 3 Aston Villa 1 – 28.8.91

During the half time interval at the Notts County game, the new West Ham kit for season 1991/92 was paraded around the pitch. We all stood stunned and amazed, mouths open and looking at each other. Surely this was some kind of bizarre joke? Surely they didn't expect the players to wear that, did they? It was worse even than the old Scoreline kit we had suffered between 1987–89. It was an insult to the players who had to wear the claret and blue. The home strip was a kind of Picasso design – no-one understood it. It was a claret shirt with blue and white stripes over the shoulders and around the bottom of the sleeves. The away kit was better. A slightly modified Argentina shirt. For the first time, there was a third choice kit to waste your money on, all white with claret and blue trim. Revolting. I knew from that moment we would struggle. People would be rolling about in the aisles the moment we took to the pitch, let alone when we started playing.

I scraped through my degree examinations despite the distractions of Jenny, who had now passed her driving test and was doing a passable impression of a limpet. Having struggled so hard to win her over, I now found that I couldn't shake her off. I wasn't used to it and I felt claustrophobic. We did, however, spend a very pleasant weekend in the Lake District over the weekend of my twenty-third birthday, and on returning home decided I had better buckle down and find a job. The job market for surveyors was not the same in 1991 as it had been in 1989 when three companies were falling over themselves for my signature. Now, I couldn't even get an interview. Things were tough. Although it wasn't exactly what I had in mind, I replied to an advert in the local paper for a Residential

Sales Negotiator with a local firm of estate agents, Jordans, and to my surprise, was called in for an interview. The company had recently been bought out by a local entrepreneur; a Mike Baldwin type character called Mike Larkman. I sat in his office for four hours while he 'interviewed' me. I think I spoke once – to ask for coffee with no sugar. His secretary was something else; a real fox. She was another Karen, and for ease of reference, dear reader, I will call her Karen II because I know how confused you all get from time to time. I was bloody confused, I can tell you. After clapping eyes on Karen II, I was determined to get the job. As it turned out, Mike was determined to give me the job, and moved heaven and earth to make the position sound as attractive as possible. I had another year to go before I qualified as a Chartered Surveyor, and strictly speaking, Jordans was not the right kind of company for me to gain experience to qualify. He therefore arranged for me to spend two days a week at his consultant building surveyors, Carroll & Roth in Crystal Palace. By doing that, I was able to gain the necessary experience to qualify as a Chartered Surveyor in the Autumn of 1992, and would then be able to add an extra dimension to Jordans' business. Mike had it all worked out. The job seemed brilliant. There wasn't a great deal to do; the odd valuation, a bit of sales work and general paper shuffling, plus I got to sit opposite Karen II, which was an added bonus. I was to receive a VW Golf 16 valve automatic with car phone, which immediately made me wet my pants. I had never had a company car before and the prospect of driving around in this monster was too much to handle. A real pose-mobile. A fanny magnet. The company was small, not what I was used to. There was just the one office, Mike was Managing Director, Karen II was his secretary and Elaine did the accounts. Mike's brother, Phil acted as company secretary and would come into the office and make us all fall about laughing. He wasn't particularly funny, but he had an interesting line in training shoes. His feet were so big he always looked as though he was wearing a couple of canoes on his feet.

Meanwhile I had trouble suppressing the canoe in my pocket as Karen II placed my coffee on the desk and wiggled out of the office. 'Blimey!' I thought.

I started at Jordans on July 1st. A week later, my exam results came through. I had to rely on Tim to go and fetch them for me and read them out to me over the telephone. I knew I had done enough to pass, but the grade was all important. I got a lower second; a 2–2, or a 'Desmond' as we called them. Only two people got 'Geoff's' (Firsts), the majority, including Tim, got upper seconds. Bastard. At least I didn't get a 'Douglas'. That was it. College was out of the way, and I could add the letters BSc (Hons) after my name. Big deal. Although it stands for Bachelor of Science with Honours, a lot of bitter and twisted people, mainly those who don't have them, say it stands for Big Silly C**t.

The only drawback with the job at Jordans was that I had to work six days a week. As I had to do two days at Carroll & Roth, I would otherwise only be available in the office at Jordans three days a week. I therefore had to work Saturdays to justify my position within the company, and to give Mike time off. Now I could see why he was so keen for me to have the job. He saw the word 'Mug' stamped across my forehead. I had been due to pick up the Golf on my first day, but Karen II broke the bad news to me. Mike had left the car in the car park overnight while it was serviced and someone had smashed it up. This was bad news, not just because I wasn't going to be able to pose for a while, but because I had already sold my Escort, and was therefore without a car. I had to go to appointments on my push-bike, which was very embarrassing and a constant source of amusement to Phil. Mike said the car was a write-off and he was going to buy me a new one. 'Great!' I thought, 'a brand new VW Golf 16 valve with sun roof and CD player. Wicked!' Wrong! I got a brand new VW Polo with an engine the size of a matchbox. At least it had a phone in it, so that had a bit of pose value. After a while, I grew to love that little car and wasn't in the least disappointed that I hadn't got the Golf. It was 100% reliable and never let me down.

Working Saturdays was a bore. There was very rarely anything much to do. We had a Saturday girl, Ruth, who used to come in and write letters or make phone calls all day. I'm not complaining about that. I could have got her doing some really pointless work, but as long as she was there in case a punter came in, I didn't care. In the end, I spent most Saturdays writing letters and on the phone, too.

West Ham played in the Makita tournament at Highbury the weekend before the season started, and got thumped 6–1 by Sampdoria. Arsenal beat Panathinaikos of Greece in their game, so we had to play the Greeks in the 3rd/4th play off on the Sunday. We drew 1–1 but lost on penalties. It was a sign of things to come. On the opening day we played the lovely Luton at Upton Park and drew 0–0. I resisted the temptation to take a radio into the office, knowing that it would bring about the same result we got against QPR a few seasons previously. I was very upset that we hadn't beaten Luton. After all, they were the team we had beaten 5–0 a few short months before. We had not made many changes to our team. Two new signings played that day, Mitchell Thomas, from Spurs and Mike Small, signed from Brighton. After the signings of Breacker and Dowie the year before, it seemed that West Ham were assembling a team of former Luton Players. My stomach couldn't take it. In mid week, we drew 1–1 at Sheffield United, Mike Small putting us ahead, only for throw away mode to come back into play. We had gone longer than anticipated without defeat, but still only had two points when we played Wimbledon at Selhurst Park. They had moved out of Plough Lane because it had quite rightly been condemned. I was confident of a result, as we were unbeaten on Wimbledon's patch, but we still only had two points at the end of this game. We lost 2–0 despite John Fashanu being sent off.

I had phoned Close and Stain Tooth to see if they were going to the Villa match, but got pretty short shrift from both of them. They now viewed me as the part-timer; someone who couldn't be bothered to go on Saturdays, whereas they went to more or less every game. I wasn't going to rise to it. I went on my own. It was a funny feeling, standing on the North Bank. I was hardly alone; there were 23,644 people in the ground, but I felt as though I was alone. Someone tapped me on the shoulder and asked why Dowie wasn't playing. I told him he had been sold to Southampton that day, and we got chatting. You're never on your own very long at Upton Park. Villa looked strong and I feared the worst, especially when Tony Daley put them 1–0 up in the second half. A rousing display saw us turn it around. Mike Small scored his first goal at Upton Park, and Leroy Rosenior the second before Kenny Brown belted in a swirling shot towards the end. I couldn't wait to get back to the car, and was relieved to find it still in one piece. I rang Jenny from the car and went home a happy man. Perhaps things weren't going to be so bad after all. Perhaps I had been a little pessimistic. One defeat in four games wasn't too bad. Perhaps we would stay up.

Breaking Up Is Hard to Do. . .

West Ham United 4 Bradford City 0 – 9.10.91

Notts County were slowly working their way into my all time hated top ten. Having been instrumental in robbing us of the title by winning at Upton Park in May, they won the play-offs and did it again in August. This time it was 2–0 and the feeling of deflation was just as great. After playing so well against Villa, I had expected better. We managed a 0–0 draw at QPR which meant Stuart the QPR fan and I could remain friends, then drew again against Chelsea at Upton Park, once again throwing away a good lead. Then we lost 1–2 at Norwich. I had to content myself with listening to games on the car radio or on Clubcall again, work was an all consuming thing, and even the majority of mid-week games had to be missed due to work commitments. During the whole of 1991/92 I attended Upton Park on only three occasions. Kevin had got it together with the wonderful Helen and I was jealous as hell. They were renting a house in Sevenoaks together with Ken (of narrow boat fame) and another friend, Claire. I had been invited to join the merry band, but I didn't see that it would be very useful, as at the time I lived two minutes away from the office. What was the point in moving miles away just for the sake of it? I had been living away from home in recent memory, and was enjoying being waited on again; having my shirts ironed and dinner prepared and edible.

I was desperate to get shot of Jenny, but couldn't pluck up the courage to do it. She was more clingy than ever. After we won 3–2 at Crystal Palace, she phoned me up and said, 'I see we won at Crystal Palace then.'

I was outraged. 'We?' I said. 'What do you mean, we?' She had always claimed to be a Liverpool fan, if anything, and now she was trying to encroach on my territory. The following Saturday, after a particularly depressing 1–2 home defeat at the hands of Manchester City, we had dinner with Kevin, the wonderful Helen, Stuart the QPR fan and Vicky. On the way home, I ended it. It was surprisingly easy to do; Neil Sedaka was wrong. Breaking up was a piece of piss compared to getting together in the first place.

We drew away at Bradford in the first leg of the Rumbelows Cup, 1–1, Mike Small getting another goal. Then we drew 2–2 at Nottingham Forest, a bit of a moral victory after the cup semi-final, Mike Small got both goals. He was proving to be a bit of a find, but outside the penalty area, both he and the other new signing, Mitchell Thomas, played like complete dorks. After losing at home again, to Coventry City, we were five off the bottom of the table, only three points away from bottom placed Sheffield United and a long, long way from leaders Manchester United.

One of my three games was against Bradford, in the second leg of the Rumbelows Cup tie. After winning 4–0 I considered myself to be something of a lucky talisman, as in a season laced with defeats, I somehow had a personal 100% record.

Winning against Bradford was the start of a seven match unbeaten run, which was much needed. We drew at Oldham, despite their team not playing the game. They had installed a natural surface after plastic pitches had been banned in the top two divisions, but to compensate for this, they broke the unwritten law. When the ball is kicked out to allow a player to receive attention, it should generally be given back to the team who conceded possession. Oldham took the throw and scored. We still managed to get a 2–2 draw, Frankie coming on to score the equaliser. That was a sight for sore eyes, or rather, a sound for sore ears. We beat Cambridge in the ZDS Cup, 2–1, then one of the biggest prizes of all, a 2–1 win over Tottenham. Mitchell Thomas and Mike Small scored after Gary Lineker had put Spurs ahead. As an added bonus, Gordon Durie was sent off after a waist high tackle on Slater.

Then came two remarkable away wins. In the Rumbelows Cup, we beat Sheffield United at Bramall Lane 2–0 and won at Highbury, beating Arsenal 1–0. It was the high point of the season. The win lifted us to fourteenth place and we were all in danger of getting nose bleeds. Arsenal had just signed Ian Wright from Palace and were in fifth place, reigning Champions. For us to beat them at Highbury was unthinkable, and all the more enjoyable for that. I was working on the computer, listening to the commentary when Mike Small slammed in the winner. I leapt out of my chair, punching the air with delight. Ruth hadn't realised I was listening to the radio and rushed over to see if I was all right. I wore my West Ham tie to work at Carroll and Roth the next Monday. John Parker, one of the partners, suffered from being an Arsenal fan, and I grasped the opportunity to rub it in. It doesn't happen very often, so when it does, you have to make the most of it. I now suffered from the delusion that we could beat anyone, and our next two games, home to Liverpool and away at Manchester United, did not constitute a problem in my eyes. The game against Liverpool was live on the TV but I had to work again. It was a 0–0 draw, but the commentators enthused over the game. Kevin Keegan said it was the best 0–0 draw he'd ever seen. Yes, well. The following Saturday the bubble burst at Old Trafford. Manchester United retained top spot by beating us 2–1, although Frank McAvennie scored a brilliant goal, lobbing Schmeichel from the edge of the box.

I was still not too depressed. After all, Manchester United were Manchester United, and we beat Brighton in the ZDS before Sheffield Wednesday came down and brought a few home truths with them. We lost again, 2–1, and Martin Allen broke Carlton Palmer's leg with a crazy tackle. Despite the general doom and gloom that surrounded the game, lots of better things were happening in the world in general. Terry Waite was allowed out to fetch his bike and there was much rejoicing in Blackheath. John McCarthy was released, too, and arrived home after years of imprisonment, only to find that his campaigning girlfriend had gone all coy on him. The England rugby team got to the final of the World Cup, but lost to Australia. But then, who gives a toss about rugby?

Back in the real world, we went out of the Rumbelows Cup at Norwich, 2–1. Everton slaughtered us 4–0 at Goodison Park, Tony Cottee apparently taking great delight in scoring.

To cap it all, the West Ham board announced details of the Bond

Scheme. This was supposed to be the thing that saved the club from financial ruin, by asking the supporters to pay through the nose for the privilege of watching West Ham. Basically, the idea was to give the club a minimum stake of £500, for which you would receive *the right* to buy a season ticket in future, once the ground had been re-built in accordance with the Taylor Report. The average fan found this rather a difficult concept to cope with. 'Excuse us,' we said. 'Are you trying to say that if we want to be guaranteed a season ticket in future, we have to pay you a monkey NOW?'

'That's right!' said the board, still with a grin on their faces.

'Bollocks!' said the ordinary fans.

The last game before Christmas was an awful 1–1 draw with Sheffield United at Upton Park, but we had Dicksy back, which made us feel better. Meanwhile Karen II continued to cause a commotion in my trousers. She happened to mention that she didn't have a tape recorder, so I bought her one for Christmas. Things were so simple then. I haven't a clue where I got the money from; it was probably all the money I saved by not going to West Ham. Karen II was divorced and lived in a rented flat on the other side of Beckenham. She was older than me, but then, I guess you could have worked that one out for yourselves. She wasn't that much older though, only five years or so – hardly Britt Ekland. I took her present round there shortly before Christmas, thinking it unfair to arouse suspicions in the office. I thought she would be pleased to see me, but I couldn't help but get the impression she couldn't wait for me to leave. Having said that, she kept plying me with coffee and made no attempt to change out of her dressing gown. She let her little boy, Andrew, stay up until about 11pm. I had been hoping she would put him to bed so I could let her open her present then screw her senseless on the carpet in front of the Christmas tree. But there you go – you can't have everyone. I left the present and waited for the reaction after Christmas. She came into the office while I was working the Saturday after Christmas and said she couldn't accept the gift.

'Why not?' I asked.

'It's too much,' she said.

'Don't be daft,' I said, mentally urging her to hand it over so I could get my money back, assuming that a shag was out of the question. She smiled at me and I melted again. What a dipstick.

Like me, West Ham couldn't stop losing. They lost 1–3 at Aston Villa, 0–3 at Notts County and 1–3 at home to Leeds. It was the start of the slippery slope to oblivion. There was no way back. Only the Cup could save us.

You're an Embarrassment. . .

Farnborough Town 1 West Ham United 1 – 4.1.92

As a top flight side, the worst thing that can happen, after relegation or a trip to Luton, is to be drawn away to a non-league side. This happened for the first time in my football-watching career in 1992, when West Ham drew Farnborough Town away. For the second season running, the tie was switched to Upton Park, and for the second season running, the result was a rather embarrassing draw. The thing about playing a non-league side is that it is the biggest hiding to nothing imaginable. It's like putting £100 each way on the 99/100 favourite. OK, so there is a 98% chance of progressing to the next round, but what happens if you don't? You could never show your face in public again, could you? I mean, on non-match days, how many Coventry City supporters do you see? On this occasion, I was again absent and beginning to earn my reputation as a part-timer. Unfortunately I had a choice of drawing dole or working Saturdays. Julian put us ahead from the spot, only for Dean Coney, the former Fulham and QPR striker, to equalise in similar fashion. I tried not to think about it, and looked forward to the replay, which promised to provide a similar result to the Aldershot game a season previously. It didn't. It was the third and last game I managed to attend in 1991/92, and when I look back on it, I can understand why. It was a truly awful performance. We faced the ignominy of being taken to extra time by a non-league side before Trevor Morley scrambled the ball over the line and ended the contest. In between the two cup ties, we had drawn 1–1 with Wimbledon. The search for our first league win since November continued in vain.

Jill found it all most amusing. Jill was my latest pen-friend, and lived in Longmont, Colorado, U.S.A. After I had split up with Jenny

I found myself idly flicking through the pages of *Loot*, the free ads paper, and stumbled across the international pen-friends section. Jill's ad said that she was twenty-three and looking to correspond with an English guy for fun, friendship and maybe more. It sounded interesting, so I scribbled a quick note and sent it off, not expecting to hear back. I figured if I found something half as good as I'd had with Christina it would keep my spirits up. Christina didn't write as often as she had done, I would be lucky to get one letter every three of four months. Jill wrote back immediately, with a photograph and a lengthy explanation of her situation. She was the biggest Anglophile in America. She loved everything about England, its history, its culture, its Englishness. I was at the stage where I would have fallen in love with my goldfish if it had looked at me for more than ten seconds, and I fell for Jill through our correspondence. We would write literally, by return of post, at least one letter a fortnight, which for international Air Mail, wasn't bad going. After a while we began to send gifts, sweets, tapes of our favourite music, cards, photographs, etc. She wanted to meet me. What could I do? She didn't know much about 'soccer' but I kept her up to date with what was happening at West Ham, anyway. She insisted on calling us West Hamm with two m's. I sent her my old 1989–90 shirt so that West Ham could be seen in America. It all got very deep and serious. I arranged to fly out and meet her at the end of February. It was something that had to be done. I treasured her letters; she could be so flattering and had me twisted totally round her little finger. I almost totally forgot about my lusting for Karen II and the wonderful Helen. Here was somebody who openly admitted to being in love with me even though we had never met. Karen I had forced me to throw away all the letters I'd been keeping from Christina and Diana, even that one from Diana where she wrote 'I Miss You' in kisses. What a bitch. All together now: Booooo! Jill's letters therefore meant a great deal to me and I couldn't wait to meet her. I have kept them to this day, and every time I need an ego boost, I read through them again.

I took great personal satisfaction from the fact that we beat Luton 1–0 at Kenilworth Road and dragged them kicking and screaming with us into the relegation mire. Mike Small's goal that day meant more than anything else. A win over Luton was, in my book, worth any two over Arsenal you may care to mention. But then, I do have an irrational hatred of Luton. Meanwhile, another reminder of Karen I stared me in the face. We had drawn Wrexham in the fourth round of the cup. Again we only drew in the first match at Upton Park, and I didn't fancy the trip to Karen I's home town, as they had already knocked out Arsenal in the third round. I deliberately avoided commentary on the game and watched the edited highlights on *Sportsnight*, delighted to see that a Colin Foster goal was enough to see us through to the fifth round.

In between the two Wrexham ties, we beat Oldham 1–0 at Upton Park. The grudge was starting to wear off. It was apparent that Oldham were just as bad, if not worse, than us. At Sunderland in the fifth round of the cup, West Ham did the hard bit and got a 1–1 draw, bringing the tie back to Upton Park for a replay and almost certain victory. Sunderland were generally easy meat at home. The last Saturday before I left for the States, we played Sheffield Wednesday at Hillsborough. Mike Small put us ahead, a lead we held until the last few minutes, when sickeningly, we conceded two late goals to give it all away once again. It did nothing for the confidence as we faced Sunderland at Upton Park. I knew I should have gone, and I felt very guilty about it afterwards. I could have gone, but I was due to fly out two days later and hadn't done any packing. It sounded like a cracking game though. Ray Atteveld was in the side, one of those names that will go so far down in Upton Park history that everyone will say 'Ray who?' He was on loan from Everton, remember? Or was it Bristol City? No matter, he was crap and contributed to the two goals flying past former Tottenham goalkeeper Tony Parks, in goal for the injured Ludo. Martin Allen took the game by the scruff of the neck and single-handedly pulled it back to 2–2. The impetus should have been with us, but somehow Sunderland scored a third and went on to reach the final, losing 2–0 to Liverpool in May. I am sure that the reason we lost, is that in the Sunderland programme, on the statistics page, there was an entry for the 9th March that read 'Chelsea Away FAC6 (provisional)'. Talk about presumptuous. If I had been a Sunderland fan reading that I would have gone potty. As it was, I tried hard to put West Ham to the back of my mind and concentrated on my two week holiday. I was nervous and excited all at the same time. It was as though I was going to see West Ham in a Cup Final. It was something I desperately wanted, but I was scared stiff of being embarrassed. As it turned out, my biggest problem in the States would be trying to find out the football scores without being told how the Broncos got on.

American Pie. . .

Liverpool 1 West Ham United 0 – 11.3.92

The first leg of my journey took me to the twin cities of Minneapolis/ St Paul. I had a five hour wait at Minneapolis; my first taste of American culture. I don't know why, but I expected everything to be so much different, and I was a little disappointed to find out it was just like England. Maybe it would be more accurate to say England is just like the USA. Perhaps I was anticipating an experience like one of those dreams, where everything is familiar, but different in such a subtle way that it is unnerving.

I passed the time swilling beer in the airport lounge, exchanging stories with some Australian tourists en-route to Atlanta.

Arriving at Denver, I finally met Jill as she waited in the lounge with her nine year old brother, Scott. It was a very difficult moment for us both. I wasn't sure whether to sweep her off her feet, hug her or shake hands. In the end, a nervous peck on the cheek sufficed as an introduction and I was quickly inundated with a barrage of questions from little Scotty, who was to become my close buddy over the next couple of weeks.

Jill's parents, Jim and Deb, were the kindest most understanding hosts I could have wished for. They turfed poor Scotty out of his bed, despite my protests and insisted that I take his room, while the poor child languished on the sofa.

I was desperate to find out how West Ham had got on against Everton, but felt it was rude to ask to use the phone so early in my visit. I tried to get hold of an English newspaper, but we weren't in New York or Los Angeles – English newspapers took a week to get out there. I kept waking in the night; the change of altitude gave me a nose bleed. Longmont is well over a mile above sea level. I was treated to my first American breakfast of hazelnut coffee and doughnuts. Doughnuts for breakfast sounds disgusting, and believe me, it is.

That afternoon, we took in a 'movie' at the local cinema. We saw *Wayne's World*, which had just been released. Some of the catchphrases from the film stuck throughout the holiday, and on returning to England, Kevin thought I had flipped, until he saw the film for himself. That evening, I met Jill's grandpa, Hank. He was still bitter about Pearl Harbour, but took a great interest in what was going on in my life.

Having spent a few days with Jill, I realised that romance wasn't in the air. It wasn't that I didn't want romance to be in the air; it just wasn't there, and we both agreed, which was rather fortunate. Deb had the Monday off and offered to take me into town. I asked her to drop me on the other side of town and said I would walk back. She couldn't believe it. 'Walk?! Are you crazy?!' She couldn't understand the concept that I actually wanted to walk somewhere.

I decided it was time to see more of America. I went to the travel agents opposite the record shop where Jill worked and discussed the matter with Beth. The help and advice I was given were second to none. She arranged a flight for me to Anaheim, California which would fly over the Grand Canyon. The trip would last three days and would include visits to Disneyworld, Los Angeles and San Francisco. Jill couldn't join me, so when Beth found out I would be travelling alone, she phoned her friend, Karen (Karen III) who agreed on the spot to drop everything and look after me for three days in Los Angeles. I was told Los Angeles can be a dangerous place for a young foreigner on their own. Karen III did her utmost to ensure I had a good time, and did, indeed, drop everything. I found the American people, particularly in LA, to be the friendliest and most considerate anywhere in the world. Maybe I was just lucky.

I was still concerned about the result against Everton, and by now we had played Southampton and Liverpool away as well. Despite being in L.A. I still couldn't get an English paper. I had to call Dad when I got back to Longmont. I was devastated. We'd lost all three games! Everton, 2–0, and the two away games, both 1–0. I reasoned that losing 1–0 at Liverpool was almost as good as a draw, but now it was looking severely bad. The day before I left for home we had a photograph session, with Jill, Scotty and I all wearing various West Ham shirts. Scotty had his eye on my England shirt, which eventually found its way onto his back. I had taught Scott the basics of cricket, which I explained to him was a proper version of baseball. It took several days for him to get used to the idea of a vertical bat. He already played soccer at school, but I was resigned to the fact that when he grew up, he would be forced to play either of those shite sports, basketball or American football. No-one that I spoke to realised that the 1994 World Cup was being held in America. The heathens really didn't deserve it.

On my last day I gave a talk at Scotty's school about what life was like in England and faced the usual and now expected barrage of questions. I loved every minute of it. Being 'out in the sticks' and an Englishman was something of a rarity, and far from being treated as a freak of nature, I was given the red carpet treatment wherever I went. It took all day to do my gift shopping as each shop keeper stopped me to ask if I was English, and if I knew Mrs Robertson who lived in London. They were shocked when I told them there were five million people in London, and the chances were slim. Deb made a fuss of me on the last day and baked me some walnut and chocolate chip cookies for the flight home. She also let me have her little swear box, which I had taken a shine to. You press a little button and it says 'Fuck You!' with feeling.

I got home early Saturday morning and was raring to go. I was itching to go to Upton Park for the game against Arsenal, but by 10 o'clock I was zonked out in bed and couldn't be woken. By the time I did wake it was seven in the evening and we had lost 2–0. Dad broke the news very matter-of-factly as he brought me a cup of tea. He could at least have told me to sit down first. I decided it wasn't a good idea to go on holiday while the season was still going. I wasn't the superstitious type, you understand, except for my lucky boots, lucky sweatshirt and lucky turnstile, but it seemed when I had to communicate from abroad and rely on second hand information, we invariably lost. I decided never to do it again – until next season.

Don't Look Down. . .

West Ham United 0 Crystal Palace 2 – 20.4.92

Bottom. A paltry twenty-seven points from thirty-one games, we were seven points adrift of safety and a place in the new Premier League. We added another point against QPR in a 2–2 draw. Somewhat stupidly, I had arranged to have dinner at Stuart the QPR fan's house that evening and was dreading another defeat. Fortunately, a draw saved any possible blushes, but the difference between the two sides was highlighted by the quality of the goals scored. Our two, from Small and Breacker were scrambled efforts, only just over the line, in off the post and rebounds. Rangers' goals were superbly executed, both by Bradley Allen. The following week we gained an unexpected point from a 0–0 draw at Leeds. Any thoughts of this being a morale boost were quickly dispelled as we lost the next game 0–3 at Tottenham, who had an abysmal home record, but still managed to beat us, then we lost 2–1 at Chelsea. Clive Allen had just joined us from Chelsea and scored on his debut against his old club, to no avail. At least I managed a win on the Grand National, and had the pleasure of the company of Karen II for a whole Saturday. It was a pity Ruth, the Saturday girl, had left. Karen II used to have great fun on Monday mornings playing jig-saws with the ripped up letters Ruth had written and thrown away. We used to look forward to the juicy details of Ruth's discarded letters.

My eldest sister, Lynn had been busy. Virtually overnight she produced three children. Triplets didn't run in the family, but they do now; and very fast too. Two girls and a boy, Catherine, Emily and Andrew. Three more little Hammers. Meanwhile I had to interview likely candidates for the Saturday assistant's job at work. If you have ever been nervous going for a job interview, take a step back and ask yourself how your interviewer feels. He is probably just as nervous, if not more than you are. Whereas my boss, Mike liked to take a few hours over an interview, having a good old gas, my interviews rarely lasted more than twenty minutes; the most important questions being:

1) Can you type?
2) Can you spell?
3) Can you cope with extreme boredom?

I gave the job to a young fox by the name of Jane, and I stand by my decision to this day; my mind was not in any way deflected by the fact that she looked good enough to eat. I reasoned I was having to sacrifice my Saturdays, so I might as well have something to look at as well as talk to. On her first day, Karen II came in to show her the ropes. I went out for an hour on an appointment and by the time I came back, Jane was completely conversant with my life history. Women! Such gossips. (Totally sexist statement, but totally true. I would only qualify the statement by saying that men are just as bad, if not a little worse.) Jane only lasted a few weeks; she had a full time job and her boss had asked her to do Saturdays. That was the reason she gave. I was pretty sure it was because she was bored out of her rather expansive mind. It was the second most mind-numbingly boring job in the world, second only to being visiting goalkeeper at Upton Park. I rang Fleur, the girl who came second in the interview stakes, and fortunately she agreed to step into the breach. As a student, Fleur was much more reliable and was even able to come in during the week on occasions. I should have worked that one out and given her the job in the first place, I suppose. We live and learn.

Our freak result of the season was a 4–0 home win over Norwich. It had to be a freak, there was no other explanation for it. It was totally against form and out of character. Matthew Rush scored two identical goals and Dicks and Bishop added the others. Norwich must have been gutted, losing by four to the bottom side. They must have learned something from the experience though, as the following season they led the Premier League for much of the time, eventually finishing third and bagging a UEFA Cup place. I'm not bitter, but what about the UEFA place we earned in 1986. Eh? Eh? Manchester United won the Rumbelows Cup, beating Nottingham Forest in the final and making it their third trophy in successive seasons. The big one was still frustratingly out of reach. My heart bled for them. The way the press went on about it, you would think they had some sort of divine right to a league championship every two or three years. What about poor old Preston North End, or Huddersfield? When was the last time they won the league?

Just to prove that the result against Norwich was a fluke, we lost in mid-week to Southampton, and then away at Manchester City. The game was almost up. Defeat against Crystal Palace on Bank Holiday Monday would be the end of it. I could have gone to the game. I should have gone to the game, but I was so tired of losing all the time. That hadn't bothered me in 1988/89, but this year, as I had been to so few games anyway, and having already been branded a part timer, I felt that my urge to attend games was wearing off. I was slowly winning the battle towards becoming a normal and rational human being again. I couldn't have stood it, watching my beloved West Ham consigned to the second, or rather, first division again. In fact it wasn't quite over. We still had three games to play and if we won all of them and Coventry lost all of theirs we were in with a chance. We had to be realistic about it though. We had won only seven games all season, what were the chances of winning the last three? In fact, we won two of them. Unfortunately the one we lost was against Coventry at Highfield Road, shattering our divine right to collect points at Coventry. Just before that, we had at least not gone out without a fight, and contributed towards Manchester United's failure to win the prize they desired most. Had United won, they would almost certainly have pipped Leeds to the title, and they played as though they meant to do so. The press were always dragging that old red herring across the path, about United clinching the title in 1967 by winning 6–1 at Upton Park. I doubt if they will be so quick to recall that they lost it in 1992 by losing 1–0 at Upton Park. Kenny Brown scored an unbelievable second half goal, which the cruel bastards in the press said was a fluke, but I was prepared to believe it was fully intended. Either way, 24,197 fans went absolutely bonkers, and at last we had something to savour from the season.

The season came to a grateful end against Nottingham Forest at Upton Park. It had often been pointed out to me that Frank McAvennie often got two goals in a game, but had never scored a hat-trick. It was his last appearance for West Ham, and, as if by magic, the Forest defence parted like the red sea to allow Frankie to sign off with a hat-trick. I was so pleased for him, I had to have my grin surgically removed.

Despite taking part in a season that had included wins over Manchester United, Tottenham, Arsenal, Nottingham Forest and, most significantly, Luton, we had absolutely nothing to show for it. Funny game, football. Can't you hear me laughing?

I arranged for Jill to come over and work for my sister, helping her to look after the triplets as a sort of unofficial au pair/nanny. She came over in early June on a three month visa and although we all took a lot of trouble to make her happy, she never settled and was back home again within a month. I'm afraid to say I rather lost patience with her. We had all bent over backwards to help her achieve her ambitions, but she threw it all back in our faces. Less than a year after we had first written to one another, it had all turned sour. That little chapter in life was over. My professional qualification exam was due in October. I decided to forget about women for a few months and work hard to achieve professional status. A lot of faith had been shown in me by Mike and by Brian, the senior partner at Carroll and Roth, and I was determined to re-pay them for it.

What's Another Year?

Portsmouth 0 West Ham United 1 – 27.9.92

England paid the price once again for failing to include any West Ham players in the squad for the European Championships. The Turnip Taylor plotted his own downfall, pathetic 0–0 draws against Denmark and France followed, capped by a bloody awful 1–2 defeat at the hands of Sweden. The only consolation, and a pretty hollow one at that, was that we had drawn with the eventual winners of the competition, and the Germans didn't win.

The evil hour when I would have to sit my professional exam approached. I had been given a date of Tuesday 29th September, and the days leading up to it just melted away, as I panicked, realising I didn't know the difference between an equated yield and an all risk yield. Elementary stuff, wouldn't you say? I was still working Saturdays, which helped, as I was able to study during quiet periods in the office, but deep down inside I knew I wasn't ready. The exam took the form of an interview, with a panel of three experts, lasting approximately an hour, followed by a short written paper. I couldn't wait to do it – and get it out of the way.

Kevin and the wonderful Helen bought a house together. I resigned myself to the thought that it must be serious, and that the wonderful Helen was strictly off limits. Besides, she never seemed interested in me; we exchanged pleasantries, but we never really spoke in depth. That changed after they bought the house. Kevin is to DIY what King Herod was to babysitting. Helen's father did most of the work, with various brothers and other relatives chipping in, but when I had a few spare moments I would go over and help him hang a few rolls of wallpaper, or paint a ceiling or two. I did this thinking that I might be able to store up some credit, and that when I eventually got my own place, he might come over and help me. Kevin displayed his political powers, persuading all manner of people to come over and help and then proceeded to wander about, watching everybody. He called it supervision. I called it being a lazy bastard.

With the creation of the new Premier League, West Ham had the dubious distinction of being the first club to be relegated from the old First Division to the new First Division. I was philosophical about it. At least it put an extra year of wear on my 'Div 1 – Here We Come!' T-shirt. Also, with Sky TV taking exclusive rights to live Premiership games, and the BBC mopping up with *Match of the Day* and the FA Cup, it meant that ITV had Sunday afternoons free to show First Division games. Over the next nine months, West Ham were on TV more often than a bowl of fruit.

During our opening game of 1992/93, I was pulling up floorboards in Kevin's lounge and trying to support the staircase. Kevin watched, while the wonderful Helen made tea and peanut butter sandwiches with one hand, and painted radiators with the other. West Ham won at Barnsley, 1–0. At last, I thought, the Barnsley ghost had been laid to rest. Clive Allen scored the goal that gave us our first win on the opening day for six years.

It was difficult to get too excited though. The next Saturday, we lost at home to Charlton Athletic, who had moved into Upton Park as tenants while their old home, The Valley, had all the cobwebs blown out ready for their homecoming.

Although I had promised I wouldn't take another holiday mid-season, Stuart the QPR fan talked me into going on a ten day tour of Europe together with a few other mutual friends. We suffered together, trekking through France, Luxembourg, Austria, Hungary, Czechoslovakia, Germany and Liechtenstein. We had a great time, but neither I nor Stuart the QPR fan were Happy Hectors when we heard on short wave radio that West Ham had lost 2–0 at Newcastle, and QPR had lost 1–0 at Chelsea. To make matters worse, we had Julian Dicks sent off, and David Kelly scored the second goal for Newcastle. Suddenly, stranded in the middle of Luxembourg, I began to panic. Two defeats out of three was relegation form. Perhaps we were heading for the third division? Somehow, I never really believed that. There had been an addition to the coaching staff that year, Harry Redknapp had joined as Billy Bonds' No.2. It soon became apparent that he was the tactical genius we had been craving. He also masterminded a few interesting transfer deals. He bought Peter Butler from Southend, a combative tough tackling midfield player, and Mark Robson on a free transfer from Exeter City. Robson was the fourth player of that name to play for the club, in recent years the previous three being Bryan ('Pop', that is, not the crap one who played for England), Keith and Stewart. Matty Holmes was the other new name, a young winger who came with Harry from Bournemouth. The other new arrival was a new sponsor. BAC Windows had obviously, like Avco Trust, had enough of being associated with total losers, and had given way to Dagenham Motors. It was better than we expected. We had almost expected Ken's Cafe to come in with a late bid. Unfortunately, we still had to wear shirts that looked like they had been designed by Stevie Wonder. On the debit side, West Ham let Stuart Slater go to Celtic for £1.5m. We sold him a season too late. At the end of 1990/91 he was one of the hottest properties in English football, and we could probably have got something in the region of £2.5m for him. After a totally barren season, we were lucky to get what we did. Frankie also went, of course. Our record signing went on a free transfer. The fans could only pray that Clive Allen wasn't past his sell by date, and that he could form a useful partnership with Trevor Morley.

My own personal hero, Jimmy Quinn had gone the previous season, to Bournemouth. I could never understand this. He had played and scored goals in every division except the top one. Why not let him have a go? If a donkey like Kerry Dixon could do it, why not Jim?

Depression thoroughly set in as we travelled through France, stopping at a motorway cafe to pick up an English newspaper to find we had only drawn 2–2 with Bristol Rovers in the Anglo-Italian Cup. Everyone mocked this new competition; mainly those who weren't involved, but I wanted to see us do well. After all, there was the chance of a day out at Wembley and I was prepared to take anything that was on offer. Dicks had scored both our goals. The newspaper failed to say that Steven Banks had made his first team debut in goal and made a total hash of it. It just goes to prove that being called Banks doesn't necessarily make you a great goalkeeper. Me and Steve are both living proof of that.

On returning home, Mike generously awarded me the Saturday off, and I took Dad to Upton Park to watch a 2–1 win against Watford.

Something must have clicked in the win over Watford because the next two away games not only produced two wins and eight goals but the manner in which they were achieved was a joy to the eye. We won 3–1 at Peterborough, coming from a goal behind. OK, I know it's only Peterborough, but at West Ham you have to grateful for what you can get. Then we trounced Bristol City 5–1 at Ashton Gate. Mark Robson scored his first goal and showed everyone just how much he loves the club, kissing his shirt and beaming all over his face. Trevor Morley and Clive Allen got two each – the start of something very beautiful.

Mitchell Thomas was far from beautiful, and far from talented. In fact, we could all have quite happily murdered him as he hit the ball against Ludo for an own goal against Derby. We managed an equaliser, but seemed curiously off form in front of the live TV cameras. The struggle continued in the Coca Cola Cup. (Yes, I know it's a stupid name for a football trophy, but then so is Milk, Littlewoods and Rumbelows, but that never stopped them. My guess is the next sponsor will be Willy Wonka.) We played Crewe at Upton Park and drew 0–0.

I should have been revising for my exam, but chose to watch our second live TV game of the season away at Portsmouth. We won 1–0 but it should have been five or six. Trevor Morley squandered enough chances to win a major cup tournament. I was coming down with a terrible cold. I had forty-eight hours until the most important exam of my life and I felt like death. I tried to ignore it, telling myself that it was merely my body rebelling against the pressure it was being put under. It didn't help. Drugged up to the eyeballs, I took the interview and the written paper in my stride; and failed.

It would be another year before I could take it again. So what?

Promised You a Miracle. . .

West Ham United 6 Sunderland 0 – 11.10.92

I wasn't to find out about my exam results until the end of November. That gave me a blissfully ignorant period of two months in which to enjoy what football I could and not feel guilty about it. After winning at Portsmouth, West Ham showed remarkable and unprecedented luck, when they beat Southend United 3–0 at Roots Hall. Nothing remarkable there, but it put us level with Bristol Rovers in the Anglo-Italian group stage, and we had to toss a coin to decide who went on to the international stage. West Ham won, believe it or not. The following Sunday, we were live on TV again, but unfortunately not in the LWT area. Central TV showed our 0–0 draw with Wolves, while we had to endure Millwall. Dicks got sent off again, and it seemed that things were slowly sliding down the toilet bowl once more. As if to confirm that supposition, we lost 2–0 at Crewe in the second leg of the second round. Again, I was just grateful that we were not in the Premier League. Outside of the top flight, it doesn't matter who you lose to, as far as the press are concerned.

Sunderland visited Upton Park the following Sunday in a comfortable mid-table position, enjoying the relaxed lifestyle that follows an FA Cup final appearance. I'm not sure if they were just over-confident, having come earlier in the year and beaten us 3–2, or if they were just crap. Whatever, we beat them 6–0. We were 3–0 up at half time with goals from Keen, Morley and Martin Allen, and in the second half Alvin Martin got on the score sheet, and Mark Robson added two more. To complete the day, Ludo saved a penalty. As is traditional in big West Ham wins, our main striker, Clive Allen, didn't get a sniff. When he was interviewed afterwards, the Sunderland manager, Malcolm Crosby said he thought West

Ham were six goals better than Sunderland. His honesty eventually cost him his job.

These things often turn out to be a flash in the pan, and normal service resumes. I fully expected a 0–0 draw at Bristol Rovers the following Saturday, but once again we were 3–0 up by half time. I was excited by the prospect of two consecutive 6–0 wins, but we had to settle for four. What a major downer!

The flash in the pan lasted two weeks, as opposed to the usual one. We lost at home to Swindon and had George Parris sent off. I couldn't believe my ears. Of all the players at the club, the one with the calmest temperament was 'Bruno'. He was an unsung hero at West Ham. There is always a lot of talk about players who give 100%. George always gave 120% and would sweat blood for West Ham. He scored more than his fair share of goals, too. In the Notts County debacle, he was the only player who seemed interested. When we lost 4–0 at Newcastle, he got some terrible stick from the home fans after injuring Paul Goddard in a tackle. George looked so upset, as though he was about to cry. He would never have done anything like that deliberately. He was a product of the youth policy, and had around 260 appearances under his belt when he was scandalously sold to Birmingham during mid-season. A more unappreciated player there has never been at Upton Park, proved by the pathetic attendance at his testimonial in 1995.

West Ham proved that while it is very difficult to sustain a winning run, it is child's play to sustain a losing one. We lost at Cambridge, a fact that the steering wheel of the Polo still bears the evidence of. Driving back from an appointment I heard the score and thumped it very hard. It was never quite the same after that. We then drew up at Grimsby, which actually wasn't a bad result. Grimsby had a good home record despite being lower mid-table and their midfield player Clive Mendonca had a kick on him like a mule. He put Grimsby ahead with a superb strike from way out. Morley equalised with an equally good goal and a point seemed fair.

We managed to halt the slide against Notts County. Our bogey team for the previous two seasons lay down in front of us and allowed Trevor and Clive to bag one each. It wasn't such good news on the road, however. We played Cremonese in Italy in the first of our Anglo-Italian Cup games. I seem to remember it kicked off at about five in the afternoon for some obscure reason. We lost 2–0, which meant that qualification for the semi-finals would be an uphill struggle. Having tasted the delights of Italy, we followed it up with an equally fascinating trip to Millwall. We lost again, 2–1 but Mark Robson scored one of the goals of the season, skipping past three defenders and lifting the ball over the goalkeeper. Magic.

We had three home games to try and pick up a bit of confidence, together with six points and an Anglo-Italian Cup win. We got both. We beat Oxford United 5–3 in a brilliant game. Oxford took the lead early on, but Clive Allen equalised, and Tim Breacker put us ahead with a shot on the run. Dicks then scored a wonderful brace of goals, both from well outside the area, which made you wonder why he didn't have a crack more often. Perhaps it was a mood thing. Then Oxford staged a comeback and got the score to 4–3, before Trevor Morley sealed it with a header towards the end. I was out of breath and I was only listening to it on the radio! I was told there was a possibility of the office closing on Saturdays – something I hoped would happen before the season ended. As it was, I had to make do with mid week affairs, like the game against Reggiana in the Anglo Italian Cup. Despite winning 2–0, I don't remember this game as being much to write about, so I won't. The next weekend I received the fateful news of my exam results. When life's being a total bitch, West Ham always seem to be there to pick up the pieces. We beat Birmingham 3–1 to put a smile on my face at the end of an emotionally difficult day.

I can't remember why I was in London the night we played Tranmere. I had been out the night before with Dobbo, a rare appearance after he had returned from Germany. We went out and got totally slaughtered on the Thursday, then he announced he wanted to go to Tranmere. I told him to go and wished him all the best. I remember tuning in my Walkman to get the final score; the game was played on a Friday night, the prerogative of Tranmere Rovers to avoid clashes with Everton and Liverpool, and all I heard was '. . .West Ham United 2'. Blinding! I thought.

We must have got at least a draw. Then I got home and rang

Clubcall. Oh dear. 5–2. At least we managed to salvage a bit of form and pride away in Italy again, Clive Allen scoring the winner against Cosenza in a 1–0 victory. Steve Jones, a young striker signed from non-league Billericay was making his debut and set up the goal for Allen. It was hard to understand exactly how we managed to hold on to third place in the table. We had already lost six games and we weren't even half way. Things were going to have to improve in terms of consistency. We suffered greatly from being brilliant one minute and totally and utterly crap the next. At least the clubs below us, Millwall, Swindon, Wolves, Leicester and Portsmouth, all appeared to be having similar trouble. Only Newcastle and Tranmere had shown us a clean pair of heels and were running away with it. After nineteen games, Newcastle were sixteen points ahead, which speaks for itself. We got three more points against Southend at Upton Park before failing in our attempt to qualify for the Anglo-Italian Cup semi finals by drawing 0–0 with Pisa.

I wasn't going to be duped into buying expensive prezzies at Christmas, especially for Karen II who was still keeping herself very much to herself, except for her legs, which she was showing off to everyone with the skirts she was almost wearing. It was very difficult for me. I had to sit opposite this goddess, showing off legs right up to her armpits and a body with more curves than a Formula 1 circuit. I had split up with Jenny in September. It was now December and I was getting a bit frustrated. Karen II wasn't helping. I bought her one of those dogs that barks and flips over. It was symbolic. It was what I did mentally in front of her every day. If she had given me the chance, I would have sat up and begged. She bought me a fountain pen. Thanks a lot.

It was at this stage in life that I began to write. I had been talking to Stuart the QPR fan who said he had read about a correspondence course that claimed it would refund your fee if you hadn't earned £180 before the end of the course. I checked it out and paid up for the course. I enjoyed it so much, if I'd had the money I would have bought the company. I found I didn't have to worry about getting off with Karen II or whoever was in my mind, because I could do it on my word processor, and I could do exactly what I liked without a hint of protest. I wrote an absolutely disgusting story, based on what I would like to have done with Karen II, and it was snapped up by a men's magazine which will remain nameless. Not only that, my tutor seemed to like my work. He gave me direction and helped me a great deal, but by the end of the year I was contemplating starting a novel and had written half a dozen short stories, sold two articles as well as my mucky little story and was spending every spare moment writing; churning out more rubbish than Jeffrey Archer on a good day. At last I had found my vocation. I always knew there was something wrong with me.

West Ham couldn't quite manage another victory in 1992. They drew at Brentford 0–0 and at Charlton 1–1 before the evil Luton visited Upton Park and came back from 2–0 down to draw 2–2. Have I told you recently how much I hate Luton?

The Land of Make Believe...

West Ham United 2 Portsmouth 0 – 16.1.93

The year began with an earlier than usual start to the FA Cup. A January 2nd date gave us a 2–0 win over West Bromwich Albion at The Hawthorns. Ossie Ardiles was putting a good side together that would eventually win promotion, but they were no match for West Ham on the day. Thoughts of an FA Cup campaign similar to that of 1991 sprang to mind, particularly as we were drawn away in the fourth round to either Barnsley or Leicester. We fancied our chances against either of them. Another live TV game followed at Derby. They had spent millions rebuilding their side following their relegation from the top flight, mainly with the money provided by benefactor Lionel Pickering. Derby had already lost seven games at the Baseball Ground when we visited, and made it eight. We won 2–0 with first half goals from Robson and Morley. Apart from the first ten minutes we never looked in danger. The momentum was starting to build. Tranmere had hit a sticky patch, and the win over Derby put us level on points with Tranmere, but ahead on goals scored. This was a new system employed by the Football League. Having become fed up with Goal Average, then Goal Difference, they decided it would be fun to put the emphasis on attacking play and make it the number of goals scored that was most important. If you scored forty and conceded sixty, it was deemed to be better than a team that had scored thirty and conceded ten. I still can't see the point. The only point at this stage was that we had scored one goal more than Tranmere. It was important that we had lost 5–2 at Prenton Park rather than 5–1. Portsmouth were creeping up on the rails. Creeping is the wrong word, they were storming. Guy Whittingham and Paul Walsh were one of the most potent strike forces in the division, but they lost when they visited Upton Park by 2–0. Morley and Foster scored in a morale boosting double win over our soon to be nearest rivals.

Something inexplicable happened at Barnsley in the fourth round of the cup. The match was played on a Sunday lunchtime and we got stuffed 4–1. I wondered if Janet's mum had got to the lads first with her Yorkshire pudding, tinned pears and custard. I could only put it down to the fact that it was Barnsley and we were destined never to get any change out of them, despite winning there on the opening day. That must have been a fluke. I used the age old excuse when faced with such a situation – we could now concentrate on the league. Three days later we completed another double, beating Bristol City 2–0 at Upton Park. This was disappointing after winning 5–1 at their place, but they were never likely to let that happen again. Robson and Morley scored the goals. Robson got on the scoresheet again the next Saturday at Filbert Street as West Ham came from behind to beat Leicester 2–1. Robson was turning into an excellent little player, with the emphasis on the word 'little'. He was so skinny he used to get food parcels sent to him from Somalia. His bony legs flapped about inside his shorts and the drag created by his shirt must have taken a lot of speed off him, but he was skilful on the ball, crossed well, scored a good few and proved he was no mug at heading either. To cap it all, he was a West Ham fan, having stood on the terraces probably around the same time as me, before joining Tottenham, and doing the rounds in the lower leagues before Billy and Harry gave him his big break. He accepted his chance gratefully and won over the fans immediately.

Barnsley came back to dish out more torture. They held us to a 1–1 draw, which was as good as a defeat, it hurt so much. Steve Jones scored his first goal for the club on his league debut, but Barnsley equalised straight away then shut up shop. The wobbles continued in the home game with Peterborough. Peter Butler scored his first goal for West Ham before Jones added his second. After beginning the game with beautiful flowing, attacking football, West Ham sat back and killed the pace. Peterborough scored a cracking goal and we had to bite our nails through the second half. If Julian Dicks had converted the penalty that Jones had won for him, things might not have been so tense, but West Ham love to put you through hell.

Newcastle had a day off league duty to lose at Blackburn in the FA Cup, so we had a chance to catch up a bit. After leading by nineteen points at one stage, Newcastle were only seven points ahead when we played Watford. The two wingers, Robson and Keen, gave us a victory and the gap was down to four, although we had played one game more. Newcastle's next game was against West Ham at Upton Park. A win for us would cut the gap to one point. Newcastle knew this of course, and cynically played for a draw. Our best chance was a Martin Allen shot from about twenty yards. Kevin Keen had a chance when he latched on to a loose back pass, but you would never bet on Keen in a one on one. Newcastle were well aware that a draw would put keep them four points ahead with a game in hand, whereas a defeat would have us breathing down their neck. I couldn't blame them for camping in their own half, but it did make the game about as interesting as a DIY catalogue.

Just as we were cursing our luck and feeling pretty bad about the whole situation, the club lost its most famous son.

Here Today. . .

Sunderland 0 West Ham United 0 – 27.2.93

I can't pretend that I remember Bobby Moore. I was aware of his presence in the 1975 Cup Final, but it wasn't until much later that I learned of the significance of the man to English football as a whole; not just to West Ham United. The only man to have lifted the World Cup for England, and the holder of a record number of caps, died on February 24th from cancer. There was a lot of debate about how long he'd had the disease, but that didn't matter really, did it? The fact was, he had been removed from our presence, and suddenly, despite never having seen him play for the Hammers, it seemed that there was a huge gap in West Ham's make-up. They showed the goings on at the main gates on the six o'clock news and I was moved enough to drive over and tie a scarf to the railings. It was a really weird feeling. Complete strangers were hugging each other and crying. This behaviour seems to occur at both ends of the emotional scale. The scoring of a goal, the winning of a trophy (so I've heard), and in the face of tragedy – people hug each other and cry.

The match at Sunderland was overshadowed by Bobby's death. A minute's silence was observed at every league ground, and at every league ground it was impeccably observed. The problems experienced later when Matt Busby died highlighted the esteem in which Bobby was held throughout the country. Love or hate West Ham, everyone loved Bobby Moore. Busby's death was equally tragic and sad, of course, but he never did anything for anyone outside the red half of Manchester. Was it surprising that Leeds fans objected to being asked to remember him? I'm not excusing their behaviour, just using the example to demonstrate the nationwide love for Bobby Moore. As a mark of respect, the No.6 shirt was suspended from the game, and

Ian Bishop played against Sunderland naked. Only kidding, he wore the No. 12 shirt instead.

If West Ham had any respect for Bobby they would not have commissioned the grotesque wreath in the shape of a No.6 West Ham shirt. It was the most hideous effigy ever to have appeared at Upton Park since Iain Dowie. When I saw it on TV I nearly threw up. It was a thousand times worse than those floral wreaths that spell out 'mum' or 'dad'. If any of my kids ever put one of those on my coffin, I'm coming back to haunt them; rattling chains, the lot. The dead should be afforded more respect than that trivialisation. Another minute's silence was impeccably observed, before a game took place which Bobby might well have played in himself thirty years previously. West Ham went 1–0 down against Wolves, but won 3–1 with goals from Morley, Dicks and Holmes.

It seemed that the rumours about getting Saturdays off were about to become reality. I was given a date: March 27th would be the last time I worked a Saturday. I saw us beat Grimsby 2–1 in an almost identical performance to the game against Peterborough, playing really well for the first twenty minutes or so, going 2–0 up, then letting them sneak one. It was OK, as long as we kept scoring twice. We failed to score at all at Notts County. Despite being five points clear in second place, our promotion back to the Premiership was by no means guaranteed. We still had to play Millwall and Leicester at Upton Park; both play-off contenders themselves, then Swindon away. Portsmouth were still charging up the league like a moon rocket. We needed to beat Tranmere Rovers at Upton Park to keep the momentum going. We did so with two Julian Dicks penalties. David Speedie made his debut on loan from Southampton. I never liked Speedie, right from the time he was with Chelsea, Coventry and Liverpool. He was nasty, arrogant and over the top; like a Scottish version of Paul Ince but without the skill. I wasn't happy about having him on our side.

That evening, Mike had a party for his fortieth birthday, and Karen II came in a rather fetching black cocktail dress that left very little to the imagination. I just came in my underpants. We had a few slow dances and thought I might be getting somewhere. I had something resembling the Blackpool Tower in my pocket, but it must have felt like a fun size Mars Bar to Karen II as she totally blanked me out after the party and leapt into a taxi to go straight home. 'Fine', I thought. Another one playing hard to get. I decided to get into Jenny-catching mode once again. This fox was not going to out-wit or out-run me. Everything comes to he who waits. If at first you don't succeed. Patience is a virtue. OK, I think you get the idea. I wanted her, and vowed to myself I would get her. Dramatic, isn't it?

In lusting after Karen II, I was experiencing the worst of all possible worlds. I had the Diana factor: working all day every day with someone who makes your groin want to explode. I had the Karen I factor: she was called Karen, and I had the Jenny Factor: she couldn't give a stuff about me. It all pointed towards a hideous disaster. Karen II was, and still is, a most beautiful woman. Part of the problem was that she was so gorgeous, my mouth used to dry up and I would go all nervous when talking to her. She made me look like a bit of an idiot. Actually that's not fair – she made me look like a lot of an idiot.

We lost at Oxford and missed the chance to make up ground on Newcastle, who were simultaneously losing at Watford. After completing my final Saturday at the office, I went along the next day to see one of our many Sunday games, against Millwall. I was proved right about Speedie. He missed as many chances as Morley had missed at Portsmouth earlier in the season. The difference was the score against Millwall was 2–2, not 1–0 in our favour. I cursed the man and vented a lot of pent up anger and frustration. Surprisingly I came away from the game feeling particularly good.

April 3rd may have been my first Saturday off since September, but it didn't mean I could go swanning off to Birmingham to watch West Ham win 2–1 with two goals in the last three minutes. Oh no. I had been knocked sideways with flu and was confined to bed. I had given Dad my orders for the Grand National, and after he had added his little tips the total stake came to £27. We were sure we would get a win somehow. We eagerly watched the race, only to see that the race was void. Fortunately for us, had the race been valid, we would have lost £27. I went to the bookmakers on Monday to get my stake back – my biggest ever collection on the Grand National. The shocking away form, punctuated briefly by the win at Birmingham, continued at Southend, where we lost 1–0. This Speedie character was really getting on my wick. If he was so brilliant, why hadn't he done something to prove it?

Against Leicester on Easter Sunday, he made a start. Two first half goals put the game beyond Leicester before Keen added a third. Perhaps I'd been a little harsh on him, but I still wasn't sending off my subscription to his fan club. Luton Town proved once again what a bunch of tossrags they really are. Instead of doing the decent thing and allowing us to cruise through to a win when visiting, they decided to get themselves caught up in a relegation dog-fight for a second season running and were facing the prospect of second division football. (That's the third division in English money.) We should have pulled out all the stops to condemn the little sods, but we gave in and let them win 2–0. Our generous gift was all very well, but Stormin' Portsmouth had nipped in front of us. While Luton sat back, safe in the knowledge they would have First Division football again, we faced the real prospect of dicing with the play-offs. Loaded guns, anyone?

I Can't Let Go. . .

West Ham United 2 Cambridge United 0 – 8.5.93

My eldest nephew expressed an interest in coming along to Upton Park. I should have done the kindest thing and told him to forget it, or shot him, but he was wearing the Hammers shirt I had given him for his fourth birthday, and had been nagging me for some time when I finally gave in. I bought two tickets for the family enclosure in the East Stand for the game against Brentford.

Things were looking a bit dicey. Portsmouth were ahead by three points and had scored three more goals than us which put them ahead, despite the fact we had conceded a lot fewer. Portsmouth had four games left, like ourselves. They had to play Notts County away, Wolves at home, Sunderland away and Grimsby at home. None of them looked a formality, and that was what we were counting on. We, meanwhile, had to play Brentford, Bristol Rovers and Cambridge at home, and Swindon away. While the three home games looked simple on paper, all three opponents were fighting a losing battle against relegation, and would spit and fight all the way down.

Brentford came first. They played well in the first half, with former West Ham man Alan Dickens running the midfield, but a Peter Butler header put us 1–0 up at half time. We knew it wasn't enough. We needed more goals. Portsmouth were drawing at Notts County: this was a good opportunity to catch them. In the second half we cut loose and scored three more, through Kevin Keen, Trevor Morley and Martin Allen. The news filtered through that Portsmouth had won 1–0 at Notts County and were still three points ahead, but level on goals scored. My nephew, Mark was hooked, and his enthusiasm rubbed back off on to me. I had been quite prepared at one stage to miss the last few games of the season, as I had already missed so many; but now I was back in 1986/87 mode – I didn't want to miss a kick.

The following week I took the opportunity to pay my last respects to another old friend we lost in 1993, the South Bank. Although it wasn't the last home game of the season, I already had West Stand tickets for the Cambridge game and therefore took the opportunity to say farewell. Bristol Rovers still had a chance of avoiding the drop if they beat us. They played with some purpose, going ahead in the second half, but Julian Dicks and that trash Speedie put us through with three points. Speedie was going to have to do better than that to impress me. Our two goal victory had been bettered by Portsmouth, who beat Wolves 3–1. We were back where we had started, one goal and three points behind.

Sunderland came to our rescue. They beat Portsmouth 4–1 at Roker Park, and we knew what we had to do. Now we were three points and two goals behind as we played Swindon at the County Ground; our final live TV appearance of the season. Somehow, we felt that a two goal victory would be too much to ask. If the game had been played on the Saturday, I don't think we would have won 3–1. It was only the fact that we knew what we had to do to overhaul Portsmouth that gave us the edge in the race for second spot. Trevor Morley scored the first goal, and both Clive Allen and Kenny Brown scored after coming on as second half substitutes. Jim Smith, the Portsmouth manager, was co-commentator on ITV and was very diplomatic, but inwardly he must have been cursing the TV schedules. Newcastle tied up the Championship at Grimsby, so there was only the one place available, and we occupied it as we went into the last game of the season.

The mathematics were relatively simple, once again. As long as we won, and won by scoring as many or more goals than Portsmouth, we were up. If we drew, we had to hope that Portsmouth drew or lost. The goals scored factor was throwing a real spanner in the works. It meant that if we drew 0–0, but Portsmouth drew 2–2, they would go up and we would have to take our chances in the play-offs. It was farcical. Nearly everyone in the ground had a transistor radio with them as Steve Potts deservedly won Hammer of the Year and the game kicked off. To say the atmosphere was tense would be like saying Duncan Goodhew needs a hair transplant. We made few chances, and Cambridge employed Wimbledon-type tactics, combined with a good degree of time wasting, shirt pulling and general bitchiness. The news came through from Fratton Park that Grimsby had scored. It lifted the crowd but did not transmit to the pitch; passes were going astray and tackles mis-timed.

Whatever Bill and Harry said at half time had the desired effect, and Speedie scored, barging Keen out of the way to fire a shot into the roof of the net. What a hero! I've always liked David Speedie; even when he was at Chelsea I thought he was a class act. Fickle git. Portsmouth equalised. It got tense again. If Portsmouth scored another, we would be level on goals scored and would have to rely on the fact we had conceded fewer. Cambridge had a goal disallowed, and a small sewage works emanated from the West Stand. A rumour went around that Grimsby had scored again, but it wasn't true. Whoever started that rumour was a gimp. I had my radio firmly up against my ear and was quick to quash the rumour as it reached us. Eventually, we heard that Portsmouth had scored and were looking good. We were in the doggy do. If Pompey got another one we were out of it. Cambridge were making life extremely difficult for us, but as the game wore on, aware of their own situation, they began to push forward and lost a bit of shape. Julian Dicks capitalised and set up Clive Allen for his easiest goal in a West Ham shirt. It may have been the easiest, but it was also the most important, and the most fervently received. The crowd spilled onto the pitch from the South Bank and held him, arms aloft. The referee managed to restore order and played the last couple of minutes, but you could see he couldn't wait to get off the pitch. The final whistle went. Aware of what had happened a couple of seasons before, I waited for the classified results on the radio before celebrating. Portsmouth had won 2–1. We finished level on points with them, but had scored one more goal. That 'goals scored' rule is so much better than goal difference, don't you think? It didn't actually make any odds. Our goal difference was vastly superior to Portsmouth's so we won on both counts.

I celebrated on the pitch with Tim and about 10,000 other friends.

Although we had again finished second, the disappointment wasn't as great because we had known since October that we were playing for second spot. We fought hard and won. It was very satisfying. In the back of my mind though, I saw pictures of 1991/92 and feared a one season stay in the top flight. As I leapt back over the wall into the West Stand, I saw the Cambridge supporters, some of them crying and some just with head in hands. I remembered how we had sent Manchester City down in 1987 and thought for a second of giving a few words of consolation. I then compared the two games mentally. Manchester City had come and played football with spirit and skill; we won an entertaining game 2–0. Cambridge came and kicked and scraped their way to a 2–0 defeat. Division two could have them – they deserved it. As I walked past I just said: 'Bad luck! You'll have to try playing football next season.' I think they got the point.

Summer Holiday. . .

West Ham United 0 Queens Park Rangers 4 – 28.8.93

I needed a holiday to compensate for the fact that Arsenal had won both the major Cup competitions. Despite the fact I had two holidays the previous year, and promised myself I couldn't afford one, I had obtained a credit card and they were always harping on about extending my limit, so I got them to put their money where their mouth was. Kevin and I went to Corfu for a week in July, together with two friends of his who I already knew socially, Stephen and Mark the Arsenal fan. Being an Arsenal fan, Mark was in smug mode most of the holiday, and I did my best to keep the conversation away from football, but it was difficult when there were four committed football fans living together for a week. Fortunately we all supported different teams so there was no danger of any ganging up.

The wonderful Helen had asked me to keep an eye on Kevin and make sure his roving eye didn't cause any trouble.

'I can't see it causing us any trouble,' I assured her.

'I don't mean for you,' she giggled. 'I mean for him!' Talking to the wonderful Helen was like flinging open a window and taking in two deep lungfuls of fresh country air. I had ignored her for so long, because of her involvement with my best mate, but nagging doubts were beginning to enter my head. I almost found myself encouraging Kevin to go for it on holiday in order that I could grass him up when we got back and I could ride off into the sunset with the wonderful Helen. Nothing terribly exciting happened the whole week, except for two occasions. Firstly, I went into Benitzes wearing my brand new West Ham shirt, manufactured somewhat appropriately, by Pony. I discovered that Benitzes was a northern stronghold and full of Newcastle, Blackburn, Manchester United, Leeds and Sheffield

Wednesday supporters. I was shitting bricks. You could have taken home some of the looks we got and still not been able to describe the feeling of utter humiliation.

The second exciting thing to happen, was blonde, Swedish and called Anna. She wasn't Karen II in the beauty department, but I wasn't in a position to be too picky. The other three had gone off to Mesonghi beach for the last day, but I decided to walk into Corfu town, buy presents and keep out of the sun. Both Mark the Arsenal fan and I had bought hats to keep the sun off our heads, but found that we both had trouble keeping them on. Even a brisk walking pace was enough to dislodge it. As I set off for Corfu town, my hat disappeared. I turned around to fetch it to find Anna holding it.

'I catch your hat!' she smiled. Her English wasn't very good, but it was a hell of a lot better than my Swedish. I asked her if she would like to catch something else, and we went back to the hotel for the afternoon. I'm not sure what I expected, but it was certainly a gratifying experience, I was surprised how easy it was to remember what to do. I can confidently state that what David Mellor has done for Chelsea, Anna has done for West Ham. By that definition, she is, at the time of writing, the last person in a West Ham shirt to score four times in ninety minutes.

Fully relaxed and refreshed, I returned home to find Karen II still indifferent, the wonderful Helen still wonderful, and another exam hanging ominously on the horizon.

Mark eagerly awaited the start of the season. He, too, sported a brand new Pony shirt and we strolled boldly into our first game, ergo, first defeat. West Ham pounded away at Wimbledon without effect, the only notable efforts coming from long range shots by Julian Dicks. Wimbledon inevitably took the lead. They were unbeaten in league matches at Upton Park, despite losing both cup ties played there. There was a hint of foul play about both the goals; don't ask me exactly what. There is something about Wimbledon's style of play which makes you believe they can't achieve anything without cheating. They were probably both perfectly legitimate.

Three days later, we were still pointless and goalless after losing 1–0 at Leeds. Things were looking bad. I listened to the commentary on the radio and heard nothing to give me the slightest bit of confidence. Stuart the QPR fan offered me the chance of a short break from the pressure. QPR were at home to Southampton the following Saturday; West Ham were away at Coventry. As our hoodoo over Coventry had been broken, I reasoned I should take the free ticket being offered and not trek miles to watch us lose again. QPR had also had a poor start, but at least they had scored a couple of goals. They had lost 1–4 at Villa on the opening day and 1–3 to Liverpool. Now we were back in the Premiership, it was goal difference that counted, not goals scored, and perversely, we were above QPR on goal difference. We weren't by 5.00pm. Although Dale Gordon had scored our first goal of the season, and we had won our first point, QPR beat Southampton 2–1 and automatically went two points ahead of us. The next Wednesday, West Ham displayed great grit and tenacity to overcome Sheffield Wednesday 2–0 at Upton Park. The Wednesday side included such big names as Chris Waddle, David Hirst, Mark Bright and Des Walker, so we all thought it was a fantastic win. Clive Allen scored two goals that proved to be his last for West Ham. They were typical Allen goals, the first a neat flick inside the six yard box, the second a brilliant dummy sold to Chris Woods, then squeezing the ball home from an impossible angle. We were filled with confidence for the visit of QPR – it turned out to be false optimism. We were not to know that Sheffield Wednesday were getting off to one of the slowest starts in their recent history, and anything but a victory against them would have been an injustice. QPR had been unlucky in their first two games, and had subsequently beaten Southampton, then lost at Chelsea. QPR were about to embark on another positive season though, finishing ninth. We were one of their victims. I had arranged for seats in the family enclosure for Mark, my dad and for Stuart the QPR fan. I was obviously hoping West Ham would win, just as Stuart the QPR fan was hoping for a Rangers' victory, but we both wanted it to be a narrow one. When Darren Peacock put QPR ahead in the first half there was little to suggest what would follow. Stuart the QPR fan sat on his hands with a sort of constipated expression on his face that made him pass quite easily for a Hammers fan. Mark was inconsolable as the fourth goal went in. He was convinced that he was a jinx because he had been twice so far in the season and hadn't seen us score a goal. I, on the other hand, knew that it was actually my fault. I had parked the car on Stuart the QPR fan's driveway – we always lost when I did that.

Mark's jinx continued during the home game with Swindon, but at least we managed a point from a 0–0 draw. The previous match had ended in an inevitable defeat by Manchester United at Old Trafford by 3–0. To our surprise, Mark Robson was sold to Charlton for £125,000. This was a move we couldn't quite understand. He had looked a little lightweight during his first two Premiership appearances, but then, so had everyone else. It was a bit of a rash move to off-load him like that, particularly so cheaply. As Kevin Keen had also left during the summer, it left us without the two players who had provided most of the goals for our strikers in 1992/3. Still, Billy and Harry knew best, didn't they?

I had arranged to go to the Munich Beer Festival with Foxy in about 1987. Every year since then we promised ourselves we would go, without quite making it. In 1993 he made the effort to actually sort out a booking and we were on. Three of us made the trip; myself, Foxy and his brother Martin. We took a coach from Victoria and soon found that of the seventy-six people on board, we were the only Englishmen. The rest were all Australians, New Zealanders and South Africans. We arrived for the opening day of the Beerfest and had a bit of trouble finding somewhere to park our bums. The rule was that you had to be sitting down at a table in order to be served. The Fraus serving the beer were as ugly as sin and had no sense of humour, so we had to make the best of it. They were bloody strong though, each one could carry five steins (each containing two litres of lager) in each hand. You try doing that at home and you will almost surely come a cropper. My mind was on other things as we polished off our third stein of the day. 'We'll just be kicking off at Blackburn,' I said to Foxy, who was already starting to go a bit fuzzy. 'Yeash,' he said. 'And Spursh will be playing Oldham. Hic!' There was nowhere on campus to get hold of the results. We had to wait until the following morning, when we all looked and felt our best, to get the results on the CNN channel in our hotel room. The Aussies in the next room didn't know quite what was going on as we both whooped with joy at the results.

Dig the New Breed. . .

Blackburn Rovers 0 West Ham United 2 – 18.9.93

Tottenham beat Oldham 5–0, so Foxy was pleased, but I was ecstatic. We had beaten the millionaires of Blackburn Rovers, and on their own patch, too. This was too good to be true. I assumed that Steve Jones had continued to play up front in the absence of Clive Allen, and as there were no more details on the TV, supposed that he had been involved in the goals. I was very pleased for him. I didn't think to phone Dad and try to find out more details, the result would keep me going until I got home on the Tuesday. It seemed silly to make a fuss when I was only away for a few days. Besides, there was some serious drinking to be done. We got chatted up by some South African girls. It's funny, but no matter how attractive a South African girl is, I am always put off by the accent. It's so aggressive; they might be the nicest people in the world, but they always sound as though they are about to rip you apart. We declined their offers and went in search of the Lowenbrau tent instead, ate half a chicken, smoked a very rich cigar then went on the roller coaster. Just thinking about it again makes me want to chuck.

When I got home, I phoned Dad, who gave me the somewhat confused details of the weekend. 'Dicks has gone,' he said. That was a downer. It had been on the cards, but it was still a massive downer.

'How much?' I said.

'Oh, we swapped him for, er, Thingy and Whatsisname.'

'Great!' I always admired Thingy. 'Think harder, Dad.'

'Burrows and Marsh.'

There was a silence of about twenty seconds, while I digested the information, and looked at the calendar to make sure it wasn't April. 'Are you sure?' If there were two players I could have named in the

Liverpool squad who I could not have imagined as West Ham players, it would have been Thingy and Whatsisname.

'There's more,' he said. 'With the loose change we bought Lee Dixon.'

'Now, come on Dad! This time you are joking!'

'Oh, not Dixon, Lee Chapman. He scored on Saturday.'

'Chapman? Yeeeessss!' Signing Lee Chapman was a dream come true for me. I had long been an admirer since his days at Sheffield Wednesday. He always scored plenty of goals and was, in my view, just the type of player we needed five years ago. I had even gone to the trouble of writing to John Lyall and pointing out the fact that Chapman was playing in France and was unhappy. We should make a bid for him. I wasn't to know that Chapman was involved in a tug-of-love battle between Robert Maxwell and Brian Clough, and that any other offers might have sent him do-lally, but I was very, very pleased that we had signed him at last. I dragged Dad down to Upton Park for the game against Chesterfield in the Coca Cola Cup, surviving a drenching in a thunderstorm on the way, to see West Ham win 5–1. Chapman could do no wrong. OK, this was third division opposition, but everything he touched turned to gold. He won a penalty for the first goal, deflected a Bishop shot into the net for the second, and won a free kick for Burrows to score the third. In the second half, he scored another and generally proved to be too much for the Chesterfield centre backs to handle. At last, a striker who would cause problems for visiting defences. To cap it all, he was married to the delicious Leslie Ash, so there was a chance of spotting her at the odd game or two.

Another new signing was Jeroen Boere, a Dutch under-21 player signed from Go-Ahead Eagles. I wasn't sure if it was such a good move to buy a player from a club with a name like that, but he had played well in reserve games, and I heard good reports about him, so I was pleased that at least Billy and Harry hadn't just tried to make the best of things. In conjunction with the board, they had made an effort to improve things, and it appeared to be working.

Mum and Dad had found a house they liked in Hastings and I was hired to go and carry out a structural survey; giving it a clean bill of health despite a few signs of woodworm. On the way back, the radio received a bit of a bashing as I heard we had lost 2–0 at Newcastle, and Boere had been sent off. Not the best way to start a new career. The good home form continued against Chelsea, winning 1–0 with a Trevor Morley goal. Dennis Wise was sent off for Chelsea; always an amusing situation. The Dutchman got onto the scoresheet at Chesterfield in the second leg of the Coca-Cola cup tie at Chesterfield, Martin Allen getting the other one on a 2–0 win, and we then drew 0–0 with Aston Villa, mainly because Mark came with me. By now I had abandoned the idea of parking my car on the driveway of Stuart the QPR fan. That, combined with the four recent signings, seemed to have turned things in our favour. While we played out a 0–0 draw with Norwich at Carrow Road, I watched QPR smack Coventry 5–1. You won't believe me, but I had predicted 5–1 as a scoreline, but didn't have the balls to put any money on it.

The following Tuesday, I faced my professional exam again. I went through it feeling much less nervous, having already been through the procedure before, and was helped a great deal by the fact that I saw many familiar faces in the exam room, friends from college. We went for a quick pint afterwards, and after discussing it all thoroughly, I felt reasonably confident that I had cracked it at last, and after nine years as a mere worker, I had finally made it as a professional. I still had to wait a month for confirmation of the results. Meanwhile, the next day, West Ham played at Nottingham Forest in the third round of the Coca Cola Cup. I decided to keep away from it totally and just watch the highlights on the late programme. Despite being a local TV show, they rated Sunderland v Aston Villa as being of more interest to London fans, and West Ham brought up the rear again. A 1–2 defeat was a little hard to take, particularly as Forest were not doing particularly well in the first division. The next day I sat down and wrote a 350 word piece about it for *90 Minutes* magazine in their 'Do the Write Thing' competition. I sent it off, again knowing that I would have to wait a month for the results. Unlike my professional exams, though, I forgot all about it.

It was pretty lonely up in the flat. I bought myself a cat – well, a kitten anyway. Kevin had said it was the only way I was going to get any pussy into my bedroom, and at that time, he was right. The little ginger ball of fluff was suitably named. I called him Ludo.

Ludo was going to be my lucky mascot, especially after we beat Manchester City 3–1 at Upton Park with goals from Burrows, Chapman and Matty Holmes. I had got into a mid-week game routine, meeting Tim in Canon Street for a couple of pints before the game and then jumping straight on to a District Line train to Upton Park. Again, I protest my innocence to those people who accuse me of being superstitious, but we always won when I went through this procedure, and Tim was more than happy to comply. It was so successful, we tried doing it on Saturdays, but it didn't work, because Canon Street station is closed on Saturdays. Certainly the lucky mascot powers of Ludo didn't last very long, as we lost 2–0 at Liverpool. While the game was going on, I was at Loftus Road watching Blackburn lose 1–0 with Stuart the QPR fan. Blackburn had just paid silly money for Tim Flowers, who was making his debut. We had to laugh.

At least Mark finally lost his hoodoo over games at Upton Park as we saw West Ham beat Oldham 2–0 the following Saturday. It was a game we expected to win; things really had changed! It was largely without incident, except for the fact that Oldham had a player sent off, then someone in the crowd blew a whistle. Mike Marsh thought it was full time and picked the ball up. The referee awarded a free kick to Oldham, and they sportingly gave the ball straight back to Marsh. It almost made up for the throw-in incident at Boundary Park a couple of seasons before. Almost, but not quite.

The game against Arsenal proved to be a turning point in more ways than one. It was the time when the team really arrived as a Premiership side. Everyone began to sit up and take notice after this 0–0 draw, which Arsenal achieved – we had always 'achieved' 0–0 draws until that stage. Now, teams were getting praise for getting a result at Upton Park. Of course, Arsenal only got that result by cheating. We had played them off the park, and when Marsh put Trevor Morley through late in the second half it seemed a certain goal. We hadn't reckoned on David Seaman committing the crime of the century, though. He wrestled Morley to the ground with his arm around his neck, just outside the penalty area. Seaman had to be sent off, the referee had no choice, but the punishment hardly fitted the crime. Arsenal were able to bring on their reserve goalkeeper, Alan Miller, by withdrawing Ian Wright, and the resultant free kick from David Burrows was cleared off the line. It had shades of Willie Young/Paul Allen in the 1980 Cup Final; the sense of injustice was just as great. I was so incensed after the game that I bought a couple of fanzines at Upton Park tube station and read them on the way home. The fanzines were *Over Land and Sea* and *Home Alone*. I read them on the tube and soon found myself having a little chuckle to myself. The humour was biting, the style clean and incisive. I wondered whether the editor might be interested in the article I had written about my life as a West Ham fan.

I had written the article initially for the magazine *When Saturday Comes*, but had received such a negative response from the editor I had decided not to punt it around anywhere else. I spent the next morning at work trying to find the article among my collection of floppy disks and amended according to the style of the fanzine. I put it in the post, more in hope than expectation, and a couple of days later, received a call from Gary Firmager, editor of *Over Land and Sea*. I was astounded. He loved the article and said it would be going in the next issue. It was such an ego boost to find someone actually liked something I had written. Even when I had sold articles and stories, no-one had taken the trouble to comment on the style and content of my work, or dish out praise.

I met Gary for the first time the next day as we played Wimbledon at Selhurst Park. He had given me a description of himself which meant I couldn't fail to find him.

To add to my big head, West Ham won 2–1 at Wimbledon with two goals from Lee Chapman. We were steaming up the table, and having already won 2–0 at Southampton, we sat in tenth place, our highest league placing for seven years. It was looking good. Of course, it was inevitable that someone would come along and burst the bubble. It was my own fault. I parked my car on the driveway of Stuart the QPR fan. We inevitably lost to Leeds United, giving away a goal a few minutes from time – a real sickener. My lasting memory of the game was that I was sitting among Leeds' fans, who were as good as gold throughout the game. At the end of the game they chanted 'There's only one Lee Chapman!' In later months, it was something that would ring around my head, and I had to force myself to believe it had been true. A few days later I saw myself in print for the first time in *OLAS*, as I took my dad to the game against Coventry City. We won 3–2, playing some of the best football we had seen for years. This was better than anything we had seen during the twenty-one match unbeaten run in 1990, and was certainly comparable with some of the football played in 1985/86.

Walls Come Tumbling Down. . .

Sheffield Wednesday 5 West Ham United 0 – 18.12.93

I failed my exam again. This time, it was terminal. Mike lost patience with me and I can't say I blame him. The day I got my results, he took me out to lunch and tried to soften the blow of redundancy with a bottle of red wine. I cannot describe the mixture of emotion I was experiencing as he outlined the reasons why I should leave. I didn't need to be told. I knew I had messed up and betrayed everyone's faith in me. The main reason for my upset was the fact that as a small company, and having been part of the team for two and a half years, it was almost as though we were a small family. It was like my dad coming to see me and saying 'Sorry son, we can't use you anymore. You'd better find yourself a new mum and dad.' Fortunately, Karen II had a day off and didn't see me in a state of distress. I made an excuse about having to go and feed the cat and went upstairs to the flat and had a good hard sob. I knew Mike had no choice; I faced a hard decision. He had been good enough to give me two months notice and therefore, I had two months to find another job, or, more in line with my thinking, a new career.

It was almost as though my examiners had sensed that I didn't really want to be a Chartered Surveyor. Ever since I had discovered writing, I had been determined to find a career that involved more use of the written word in a creative sense. As it was, I was already getting a bit too flowery with my business letters: 'Dear Mrs Jones, Thank you for your most eloquent epistle of the 18th. . .' It wasn't appreciated by anyone. I applied for thousands of jobs with newspapers and magazines and didn't get so much as an acknowledgement. It seemed that I was about to face a period of unemployment for the first time in my life.

Christmas approached, and West Ham were on a high as they faced Sheffield Wednesday at Hillsborough. We were only 1–0 down at half time. I listened to the game on the radio as I wrapped Christmas presents, and felt the physical pang of pain each time a second half goal went in. 5–0 was a terrible result and a huge knock to the confidence. I couldn't quite understand it, even seeing the goals on *Match of the Day* failed to provide any enlightenment.

Elaine held a Christmas party the same evening. I needed something to cheer me up, and the thought of spending some time with Karen II in a party atmosphere filled me with anticipation. She spent most of the evening dancing very suggestively with a real creep of a guy who I didn't know, and didn't want to know. There was some armpit encouraging me to go and ask her to dance. I felt like thumping him. It was obvious she wanted me to get the message that she wasn't interested. I decided to leave before they started getting physical or my head exploded. It was gut-wrenching. It seemed that everywhere I looked there were people slobbering over each other, and the only pussy I could look forward to when I got home had four legs and a name tag. I drove home despite being well over the legal limit, and didn't get out of bed until Monday. I was experiencing the same emptiness I had felt when Diana told me it was over. This time, I didn't even have the consolation of memories. I had nothing. No job, no woman, and no hope. Merry Christmas? Humbug!

West Ham didn't help. They scrambled a 1–1 draw at Ipswich and then the next day lost 1–3 to Spurs at Upton Park. I had paid £20 to a tout for a £9 terrace ticket and was not happy after the game. I couldn't wait to get back to work, to take my mind off life. At least I still had writing, but even then I had very few ideas and was relying on my course to provide me with inspiration and ideas. I was too choked up about Karen II to write anything emotional or romantic. Football writing took over.

On New Year's Day Kevin and I took my nephew, and the Wonderful Helen's two nephews, Miles and Luke to Ipswich to watch the game between Ipswich Town and Liverpool. Kevin had been starting to wind me up in a variety of ways. Mainly, it was his stubborn reluctance to accept that there was any other team in the country worth watching except Liverpool. It was such a pig headed, arrogant and boorish attitude, particularly as he had never been to Anfield in his life. Secondly, he regularly beat me at squash. I took the game very seriously, and he knew he was a better player than me, but used Liverpool-like arrogant tactics to demoralise me on court. These included only calling out the score when he was in front, stopping the game to tie up his shoe lace when I was in front, and taking a quick draw on his asthma drug when things got tight, giving him extra special physical powers. I would get so frustrated, I actually broke two racquets against the wall in my temper. I'm not a violent man by nature; but Kevin was bringing the worst out in me. To cap it all, he was living with the wonderful Helen, and candid conversations with her revealed that she wasn't at all happy and wanted to leave, but she had a financial stake in the house and it would prove tricky.

Watching the game at Ipswich didn't help the situation. Liverpool won and the trip home was a constant stream of 'Liverpool this and Liverpool that. . .' I just wanted him to disappear. At least West Ham won, 1–0 at Everton, with a goal from Tim Breaker. It was a sign of the decline that was to follow that a dire 0–0 draw with Sheffield United followed at Upton Park.

The FA Cup campaign began at home to Watford. I'd had a premonition, and felt that we would win 2–1 after Watford were leading 1–0 at half time. Unfortunately, I only put money on the score, which yielded a whole fiver. It was a poor performance. Chapman was beginning to play like a donkey and it was only the introduction of Steve Jones that provided any sort of shape and movement up front. Martin Allen and Mike Marsh scored, to give us a rather fortunate passage into the next round. We were drawn away at Notts County. I didn't see any reason to make plans for Wembley.

My piece on the Nottingham Forest game proved to be a winner. I had it published in *90 Minutes*, and received two tickets for the Coca Cola Cup final in March. At least I was due one Wembley visit.

Mum and Dad moved down to Hastings, and I spent the day lugging furniture around as we lost 1–3 at Villa. A few days later I had a job interview at a property management company based in Croydon by the name of Central Property Services. The managing director, Roy Woodman, appeared to be a charming man, who sold the company to me totally. They seemed to be progressive, used modern techniques, had a young complement of staff with forward ideas, and they were working towards a goal of wide expansion. I was taken on a guided tour of the office and felt confident that I had got the job. Surely, they wouldn't have bothered with the tour had they not been sure? My instincts proved correct and the next day, Woodman phoned and offered me a position as Management Surveyor, with an improved salary, a better car and a profit share. I was delighted – my initial disappointment at being made redundant by Mike ebbed as I looked forward to a new future. I could forget about Karen II and concentrate on qualifying at a company manned by professionals. There was a director at the company who I had been told I could work with to build up my experience for the professional exam, and my third attempt would be a formality. It all seemed too good to be true. Naturally, as you can no doubt guess, it was.

Still Crazy after All These Years. . .

West Ham United 2 Manchester United 2 – 26.2.94

Before starting work at Central, there was the small matter of a 3–3 draw at home to Norwich City, which tested everyone's patience and nerve. Ludo made two bad mistakes to deny us the win we deserved. Woodman had phoned me at work that day to confirm my appointment, and in a genial and friendly conversation, I told him I was going to Upton Park that evening for the game. He revealed that he was a Chelsea supporter. I should have smelled a rat at that stage, but as Mike had been a Chelsea fan too, I didn't see how it would cause any more problems than before. We managed to scrape a 1–1 draw at Notts County. Ludo made another error to allow Gary Lund to give County the lead, but Steve Jones equalised.

I started at Central on the first of February and during my first two weeks was made to feel most welcome, and had a relatively light workload. I was working with Jayne, who was due to depart a month later on maternity leave. Working with her, it was very difficult to make mistakes, and I didn't have to get too deeply involved. Within a few days of starting, people started to disappear. I was already aware from the number of names being bandied about, that there was a high turnover of staff. Someone would say 'Oh, Martin used to deal with that – he left a few weeks ago.' Or 'That's one of John's files – I've no idea how he used to organise things.' It was a recipe for disaster. There was little or no continuity. It appeared that staff lasted on average about eight months before moving on. I couldn't understand why; but I soon found out.

We played Notts County in the replay at Upton Park. It was one of the worst performances I had ever seen from a West Ham side, and that includes a number of defeats I could mention. It seemed that the tactics were totally wrong. Chapman was being targeted with long balls from the back, when I always felt his strength was getting on the end of crosses. Things improved when Steve Jones came on, but I have to place the blame for Chapman's demise on the shoulders of Billy and Harry, or whoever had the bright idea of using him as a target man. The crowd got on his back immediately and he became the scapegoat for an all-round poor performance. I was so pleased when he eventually scored the extra time winner. He had my utmost sympathy.

Things continued well in the new job. A new surveyor joined; David, who seemed like a good bloke despite showing tendencies towards Crystal Palace, and another new management surveyor, Peter, who had been built up by Woodman to be the best thing since the zipper. The new team, or Central Mark III, had been born. We all took in a deep breath, as Jayne left and I had to cope on my own. It was like taking the waterwings off in the kiddies pool then asking me to swim the Atlantic. It was apparent right from the start that the workload was far too much for one person. I sat tight, worked as hard as I could, and waited for the wheels to fall off. West Ham drew 0–0 at Manchester City, and still we awaited another league victory. It wasn't too serious, as we were drawing, not losing, but I was slightly concerned that the initial momentum created by the arrival of Burrows, Marsh and Chapman had been halted so easily by defeat at Sheffield.

I broke the bank and sent a dozen red roses to Karen II on Valentine's Day. They were anonymous, but she knew who had sent them, and phoned to thank me. I asked her to consider coming out for dinner – just as friends. She said she would – consider it.

We had a tricky fifth round tie away at non-league Kidderminster. They had rubbed us all up the wrong way by appearing to be disappointed when they were drawn against us. Ungrateful bastards. They all wanted Manchester United away. They should have looked on the bright side. At least this way they stood a chance of making the quarter-finals. Unlike Farnborough and Aldershot before them, Kidderminster decided to retain home advantage, and a capacity crowd of. . . wait for it. . .7,850 saw Lee Chapman score the only goal. I was grateful to have got through. I hate playing non-league sides.

When Manchester United came to town they were on a roll of something like thirty games unbeaten. The new stand at the old South Bank end was open to greet them and for the first time since the end of the previous season, there was an all-around atmosphere at Upton Park. The Paul Ince hate campaign had reached fever pitch. It wasn't just his misdemeanours which had increased his unpopularity. His general arrogance and attitude made him an object of hatred everywhere outside Manchester, but also, due to the fact we had been relegated twice and his 'injury' the last time Manchester United played at Upton Park, he had not actually appeared in front of us at home. That was rectified. Each time Ince got the ball, he was severely booed, and made to feel as welcome as a tax collector at Ken Dodd's house.

Tim was watching his last game with me before he went on a trip that he anticipated would take over a year. He wanted to make the most of the day, and we therefore met in London first for a few beers. Mark Hughes put United ahead after a mistake by Bishop put Roy Keane in a position to cross. We had enough chances to level it up before half time, but it was mid way through the second half by the time Chapman scored the equaliser. Three minutes later, Morley added a second and the crowd were in raptures. We only had to hang on for a few minutes before mouth almighty himself grabbed a late equaliser for United. It was yet another example of over-doing the barracking. It was a bad blow to have victory whipped away in the dying seconds, particularly as we would have enjoyed the kudos that goes with ending such a long unbeaten run, but it was not to be.

Lee Chapman made an error after the game, having a go at the fans for having a pop at Ince, intimating that there was a 'section' of fans at West Ham who tended to do that sort of thing. It was the same all round in the press. All the papers were very quick to leap to the defence of the 'innocent' Ince, and slate the racist and abusive West Ham fans. They really didn't know what they were talking about.

To compound the misery, we could only manage a 1-1 draw at doomed Swindon Town. Again it was a late show, an eighty-ninth minute equaliser for Swindon meant we had blown away a potential four points, and were slipping perilously towards relegation.

The memorial game for Bobby Moore took place the next Monday. It was also the official opening for the new stand, which had been named in his honour.

I arrived early that Monday night, almost an hour before kick-off as I quite fancied a seat in the new stand, but the queues put me off. As it was, I could quite easily have got a seat. Patience is a virtue. As a West Ham fan, I ought to know that.

I took instead, a seat in the East Stand, as I hadn't done so for a while, and waited for the events of the evening to unfold. I had an uneasy feeling as I sat high up in the stand, watching the sheets of rain come down against the white lights in the corner. It was reminiscent of televised winter nights in Belgium, *Jeux Sans Frontières* and Stuart Hall laughing his head off. I half expected to see a man with Ronald McDonald shoes and a rubber head come bowling out of the tunnel, but Lee Chapman wasn't playing. I was worried it might have got tacky. I needn't have. The 1964 and '65 cup-winning sides came onto the pitch and performed a short but sweet opening ceremony for the new stand. The opposition for the game were a Premiership XI managed by George Graham. The squad of twenty-two consisted of one player from each of the other twenty-one Premiership sides, plus Liam Brady. Tony Cottee, representing Everton, put them ahead, with a goal that brought tears to my eyes. It evoked memories of happier days, and sparked off the idea in a number of people's minds that it would be nice to see him back. Julian Dicks represented Liverpool, and sparked off the same emotions. He had only been away a few months, but we were missing him already. We won the game through goals from Clive Allen and Jeroen Boere, and everyone went away happy. It was like seeing an old lover on the street, stopping for a beer or two and realising that you are both still crazy after all these years.

The Stranger. . .

Aston Villa 3 Manchester United 1 – 27.3.94

Coca-Cola Cup Final, Wembley

Fate dealt a cruel blow as we drew Luton Town in the FA Cup quarter final. Of all the seven other teams left at this stage, Luton were the one team I wanted to avoid. The other options, Chelsea, Wolves, Manchester United, Charlton, Oldham and Bolton all seemed much more attractive compared to Luton. At least we were at home. The game was a complete farce. It had been moved to a Monday night to accommodate the TV bods, and I went along with Foxy, who despite being a Tottenham fan, was keen to try the facilities in the new stand. We had a definite penalty turned down, and Marsh hit the post in a 0–0 draw which as good as put us out of the cup. I knew we would never win at Luton.

The following Saturday, we were outplayed and outclassed by Newcastle, but I had the consolation of a dinner date with Karen II. She had finally accepted my invitation, having taken a month to weigh up the pros and cons, but made it clear that her acceptance meant nothing; it was just a friendly dinner, right? Right. Over dinner it was made clear to me that despite being divorced, she still hankered over her ex husband, who appeared, by all accounts, to be a complete villain. Something didn't quite add up. I wanted to ask her if that was the reason why she had got off with that hideous monster at Elaine's party, when if all she wanted was a seeing to, I was ready and waiting for action, with the added advantage that she would not have needed a paper bag for her boyfriend. I decided not to mention it, as it was clear from her body language that further attempts to win her affections would be futile. I still haven't given up hope though.

One day, she will realise what she has done. If you had ever met this woman, you would understand.

As a West Ham fan, you have to remain hopeful. I was hopeful that Karen II would see the error of her ways before I was too old to do anything about it, or, even worse, married. I was hopeful that my new boss, Woodman, was only joking when he told me I had to take on a new property with fifty-six tenants, when I was already up to my eyeballs, and I was hopeful that West Ham would shock me and win at Luton in the cup replay. All three proved to be nothing more than hopeful supposition. Despite Martin Allen putting us ahead, and Ian Bishop getting an equaliser, Luton were destined to turn us over right from the start of the first game when our penalty appeal was turned down. Scott Oakes scored a hat-trick for Luton. I watched the game on TV with a couple of mates and we all sat in silence. We had blown the chance of a visit to Wembley yet again. My only chance of getting there was to watch someone else play in claret and blue – Aston Villa.

Over the weekend of the Coca-Cola cup final, I stayed at Stuart the QPR fan's house. I invited Stuart the QPR fan to join me because he is the only one of my friends outside the fanzine who appreciates good football. Despite the fact I didn't think we would see any, I invited him anyway. I wasn't prepared to pay £25 to watch West Ham play Chelsea at Stamford Bridge, so I went with Stuart the QPR fan to watch Ipswich v QPR. On the Sunday, after reading about our 2–0 defeat at Chelsea, we set off for Wembley in my new company car. As we were guests of the sponsors, we were invited to a pre-match reception, which began at 1.00pm. Kick-off was at five, so we aimed to get there for about 1.30, so as not to out-stay our welcome. I never had any doubt that I should wear my West Ham shirt to Wembley. Stuart the QPR fan was of similar mind and proudly wore the blue and white hoops. We got a lot of strange looks throughout the day. You would have thought we had both stood on chairs and yelled 'Buy Pepsi!' Mainly, the stares were from disgruntled Villa fans. I was told I was wearing the right colours, but not quite in the right way. One Villa fan was a bit more blunt and merely asked 'What the fuck are you doing here?' Nice girl, she was.

'Supporting Villa,' we replied. She had no answer to that. The toilet facilities at Wembley leave a little to be desired. I had to wade, ankle deep, in Villa fans' urine, to the next available set of urinals. They were all pouring beer down their throats like there was no tomorrow, and letting it out the other end into any available receptacle: sinks, plastic cups, coat pockets, or Manchester United fans.

We had narrowly avoided having the car towed away, due to the fact that we had parked in a bay marked 'P Free.' We returned to the car an hour before kick-off to find that the sign had miraculously changed to 'Resident Permit Only' and my Rover was half way up the back of a tow truck. I said something that rhymes with tow-truck, but was slightly concerned to note that not only were the vehicle removal unit in attendance, but also a policeman and an ambulance. It appeared that the traffic warden, shortly after hitching my car on to the back of the truck, had fallen from the cab and damaged her back. While trying to suppress our laughter, we realised that we had a chance of getting the car back, if we spoke nicely to them. Stuart the QPR fan was at his most diplomatic and managed to negotiate a deal whereby we got the car back, on the condition that we took it elsewhere for the afternoon and paid the £30 parking fine. It had to be worthwhile. The alternative was a £170 release fee at the depot. We apologised to the lady traffic warden for causing grief, but were silently fuming at the changing of the sign. I'd had a few free pints at the Coca-Cola reception and waited for the copper to go before driving off to find another space to park. A breathalyser test was the last thing I needed. I wasn't exactly on good form when it came to passing tests.

The episode with the car was a bit of a downer, but we still thoroughly enjoyed seeing the treble snatched away from Manchester United. Fortunately, the majority of fans around us were Aston Villa supporters, and we stayed to watch Kevin Richardson lift the trophy, but nothing more than that. We had felt like intruders all along; gatecrashers at a family do. Complete strangers. We beat a hasty retreat. I was just grateful to find that the car was still in one piece.

I had to write another short piece about the cup final, along with the other winners of the competition, with the final prize being a trip to the Cup-Winners' Cup final in Copenhagen. I did this as I listened to West Ham going 2–0 up at Sheffield United. I was so pleased with the piece I had written, I immediately phoned Stuart the QPR fan to read it to him. He liked it too, but during the time I was on the phone to him, West Ham leaked three goals. Maybe it was Stuart the QPR fan who was the jinx, not just his driveway?

Things Can Only Get Better. . .

Tottenham Hotspur 1 West Ham United 4 – 4.4.94

It took three months to register our first league win since New Year's Day. It came against Ipswich Town at Upton Park, Matthew Rush and Trevor Morley scoring the goals in a 2–1 win. It was just the boost we needed before facing Spurs at White Hart Lane. Spurs had another terrible season at home, having failed to win a league match there since October. I wasn't fooled by that. I knew they would probably beat us. West Ham were used to breaking barren runs, after all. I couldn't go. I couldn't get a ticket. I have to say I didn't try particularly hard to get one, as the events of the Ray Clemence Testimonial game were still fresh in my memory, and I was convinced we were going to lose, but Foxy was going and promised to buy me a programme. He didn't speak to me for a few weeks afterwards. I was astounded by the result. The commentary had been on the radio, but I had tried to avoid it as much as possible, particularly after Spurs had pulled back to 2–1. I feared another Sheffield United and went to bed, burying my head under the pillow. I tuned in again at full time to hear the marvellous news. We won 4–1, two goals from Trevor Morley and one each from Steve Jones and Mike Marsh.

The confidence boost of a six-point haul over Easter should have sent us rocketing back up the table. Instead, we contrived to lose to Everton at Upton Park, Tony Cottee scoring a goal which proved vital in Everton's relegation fight. A team which didn't quite make it in that battle were Oldham Athletic. I cried for ages when I heard they had gone (once I had stopped laughing.) My stomach muscles ached for days. We contributed to their downfall by winning 2–1 at Boundary Park and ensured our own safety in the Premiership.

I felt right from the start it would be a mistake to invite Kevin along to Upton Park for the game against Liverpool. Although I was confident of a result, this game has an awful habit of pulling your trousers down in front of your best mates. A group of seven of us attended the game. Apart from myself and Kevin were the two nephews of the wonderful Helen, Mark the Arsenal fan, my nephew, and Stephen, who had come to Greece with us the previous summer and had been able to wangle free tickets, as he worked for the company that insure the stadium and all the players at West Ham. Before you ask, no – he can't get cup final tickets.

I had written an article in *OLAS* bemoaning the fact that we hadn't beaten Liverpool in the league since 1982 and that we had never had such an opportunity to beat them. I was filled with hope when Martin Allen scored in the first minute, and as Kevin was only two seats away, I took every opportunity to show him how pleased I was. Robbie Fowler equalised for Liverpool, but I still felt we had the edge. Towards the end of the game, I started to get annoyed with Kevin, as he was always claiming to be such a big fan of Liverpool, but he hadn't uttered a word during the match. I told him he ought to show his support in a more vocal fashion. As I did so, Tony Gale under hit a back pass, and Rush nipped in to score Liverpool's winner.

'All right then,' he said. 'Yeeeeeessss!!!' Bastard.

After the game, he tried to put on his mock diplomatic voice. 'I think a draw would have been a fairer result.' He said in his most irritating, condescending way. My reply was simple and to the point.

'Fuck Off.'

During mid-week, I was forced to miss the home game against Blackburn Rovers because of my boss. He was desperately trying to dig himself out of another hole, and, of course, it was my fault that he couldn't. As I was around, I helped him. 'Have you got to go?' he said, looking at his watch at about seven o'clock. It was too late for me to get to Upton Park anyway, so I said no. A colleague may have mentioned the fact to him that I missed a home game to help him out, but I don't suppose he really cared. He was, and still is to my knowledge, a complete pile of shit.

Missing the Blackburn game, which was a 1–2 defeat anyway, was more than compensated for by the 2–0 win at Highbury the following

Saturday. Again I missed it, as I was in France buying up a few duty frees, but the result came through just as we were rolling off the ferry. Mark the Arsenal fan had been with me, and having witnessed the display against Liverpool, was sure Arsenal would at least score a goal or three. I hit the roof of the car with my hand when the score came over, and the bruises took ages to go down. Stuart the QPR fan obliged with a ticket for the game at Loftus Road. I was obviously hoping for a bit of revenge for the 4–0 mauling we had received at home at the start of the campaign, but I was more than happy with a 0–0.

The final game of the season was at home to Southampton. They needed to win to be sure of avoiding the drop, but as it turned out, it didn't matter, all the other results sent Swindon, Oldham and Sheffield United down. Trevor Morley won Hammer of the Year – unexpectedly but not totally without merit. An end of season spectacular ended 3–3, with Danny Williamson scoring on his home debut, Martin Allen and a Ken Monkou own goal provided our other scores. I missed it. I had been into the office to try and catch up on my backlog and lost track of the time. By the time I got to Upton Park the North Bank gates were locked and it was ticket holders only. I had vowed that I would rather die in the fires of hell than use a tout again. Even Gary couldn't help me, and so I had to slope off home, tail between legs. It had been an entertaining season of highs and lows. There was a World Cup to look forward too, sceptically, as it would be without England or West Ham players of any description. The only straws we could grab were the fact that the Republic of Ireland squad included former Hammers Ray Houghton and David Kelly.

If I had thought that supporting West Ham was a bit of a struggle at time, I was to face an even tougher battle over the summer: with my dictatorial employer at the prison camp.

Summertime Blues. . .

Mexico 2 Republic of Ireland 1 – 24.6.94

Joining Central, or Cuntral as David had christened it, turned out to be the biggest mistake since Allen McKnight pulled on a pair of goalkeeping gloves and said 'Hmm. . . these feel comfy.'

Had I turned the job down, I could have waited for a more suitable job to come along, and in the meantime, been entitled to full benefit as I had been made redundant. Woodman, or Darth Vader as he was unaffectionately known at the Death Star, had sold the company so well that I would have been a fool to turn it down. The job itself was pressure enough. I had 1200 tenants all of whom had a death wish. They all had a problem of some sort which needed dealing with, and needed dealing with yesterday. Identifying the priorities was impossible, as yet another memo from Darth landed on the desk demanding immediate response. I didn't mind keeping the managing director informed of progress on various matters, but what I did object to, was the way he would treat us all like nursery school children, threatening juvenile punishments if we failed to 'revert by' certain dates, or if we transgressed the unwritten law. As the unwritten law was, by definition, unwritten, how were we to know when we were going wrong? We all tried hard to make it work, but Vader's liking for humiliation tactics and piling on the guilty conscience proved too much. Despite the fact I knew I had nothing to go to, I told him to stuff the job.

Matters had come to a head on the day Ireland played Mexico in the World Cup. I had made it clear I wanted to be away dead on 5.30pm in order to be home in time to catch the second half. I NEVER left the office dead on 5.30pm. My workload was such that I was generally lucky to get away before 7pm. To aid my day, I had made a list of priorities which consisted of some fifteen items. For various reasons, mainly linked to our beloved black-helmeted leader, I was unable to even start the list and didn't leave the office until 6pm. By the time I got home, I had missed the game, and the video had failed to work, because my electricity meter had run out of credit. I sat down and considered my position. I wrote a long memo to Darth explaining that I could no longer work under the present conditions at the Death Star, and that both me and Han Solo were extremely pissed off. Han Solo, or David, was of the same opinion, and, if anything, was getting even more grief than I was. We decided to resign together, to maximise the impact. During our time at the company, starting in February and March respectively, we had lost no fewer than seven colleagues. That might not sound very many, but the company only employed sixteen in the first place. David and I made it nine, and Peter, not liking things to be uneven, made it a round ten a few days later.

We all took all the holiday that was due to us. David took a few more off sick as well, and I helped him convalesce by going fishing with him. We had a brilliant day down by the lakes, caught loads of fish. It was wonderful just to relax out by the water and let our troubles float off into the reeds. We had often joked that our associate director was a bit of a fish out of water, so when Dave caught a particularly large specimen, he held it firmly and asked it how things were going at Central.

While I still had the car I took the opportunity to do as many miles as possible and tried in vain to try and land another job before the old one ran out, but to no avail. To my astonishment, when the DSS were told the full story surrounding my departure, they fell over themselves to give me some money. They called it constructive dismissal. Had I known they would do that I would have left two months earlier, and saved myself a lot of booze. I was very disappointed to have to leave Central, my colleagues were real diamonds, and I thoroughly enjoyed the office atmosphere, but it was a question of extremes once again. The good times were brilliant, the bad times made me suicidal.

The wonderful Helen was causing me trouble. For her birthday, I had composed a short story, parodying her situation, and including characters she could easily recognise and identify with, but setting it in an abstract American background. My birthday followed a few weeks later, and she phoned me to wish me a happy birthday. As Kevin was away on holiday with Stephen and Mark the Arsenal fan, it was her first opportunity to discuss the story and its significance – to us. We spoke for over three hours, and the next Friday, we spoke for over four hours. At the end of it all, I was just a little confused. I didn't want to barge in on her relationship with Kevin, but it seemed I was being given a license to do so.

The club made some interesting signings in Joey Beauchamp and John Moncur. I had seen Beauchamp play for Oxford and had been impressed, but I hadn't been so impressed by his attitude when the club had tried to sign him just before deadline day in March. He had opted to stay with Oxford rather than take the opportunity to play for a bigger club in the Premiership. This was to the dismay of his manager, Denis Smith, who had been banking on getting £1 million in the coffers before the end of the season. Beauchamp showed at that stage, his unerring capacity to piss people off. The warning signs were there when he finally did put pen to paper in June. No sooner had he signed than he started whingeing. You all know the details; I need not go on. Moncur was also an exciting prospect. I had seen him play in the play-off final against Leicester and rated him then as a top quality midfield player. Not only that, but we had whipped him away from Chelsea. I just prayed that it wouldn't backfire on us.

I got the chance to see the pre-season friendly at Portsmouth. It's quite a long way from Hastings, about ninety miles, in fact, and it took nearly three hours to get there, ploughing through traffic on the A27. Still, it was worth it wasn't it, Dad? No, I know it wasn't. We drew a pathetic game 1–1. If Ludo hadn't been in such sparkling form we would have been crushed. Beauchamp was on the subs' bench and was getting cat-calls every time he warmed up. Bill and Harry didn't play him, which was hardly surprising.

A few days later came the bombshell that rocked us all. Bonds resigned. My interpretation of his departure (and it's purely supposition) is this: Harry Redknapp was offered a position at Bournemouth which was extremely tempting, being that of manager, plus a financial stake in the club. West Ham, noticing that it was Harry who was pulling the strings and not Billy, told Harry not to accept the position at Bournemouth and they would sort something out that was better for him at West Ham. In doing so, they totally messed up, by offering Bonds a position as director of coaching on the board. They might just as well have put him up against a wall and shot him. It would have been a lot kinder. If Billy Bonds resigned, then why did the board pay up the rest of his contract? Billy was made an offer that was designed to be refused, and he walked. This was not, as I saw it, through choice.

I was devastated. The man had been at the club longer than I had been alive. I had never known West Ham United without Billy Bonds. It was like losing my dad. Having said that, there can be no denying that Bonzo's greatest days at the club were as a player. As a manager, his attitude was totally the opposite. He had gone from a man who would break a leg rather than see West Ham lose, to a man with a rather weak 'It's only a game' type of attitude. Redknapp was also one of the family, and to keep it in the family he brought in his brother-in-law, Frank Lampard, as his no.2 and after the initial shock of losing Billy, the fans, myself included, sat back and awaited a good start to the season.

We should have known better. Leeds came to Upton Park and destroyed us. It was the most fortunate 0–0 I have ever seen in my life. Gary had been in touch and suggested that I join the OLAS gang for the trip to Manchester City. I was flattered by his offer, but as it transpired, the game was being shown on live TV screens at Upton Park. Gary decided to stay at home and sell OLAS at Upton Park. The offer was still open though, for the game at Norwich the following Saturday. I gratefully accepted; it was like being called up to play for England. I had read all about the exploits of the OLAS team on their away trips and now I was part of it. In the car that day apart from Gary, were John the Seller and Richard Ryan. I had to earn my ride, and did my first bit of fanzine selling outside Carrow Road. It made the game a bit more interesting, which was just as well, because it was another dire performance. After losing 3–0 at Man. City, we added another 1–0 defeat. Goalless and with only one point, Harry said at the press conference afterwards that he was looking to buy new strikers, but, in his words, 'If you buy cheap, you get cheap.' I attended the press conference, and couldn't believe that I was actually there. The words – the quotes you see in the Sunday papers – coming straight from the horse's mouth. I had a taste for it. I wanted more.

The Things We Do for Love. . .

West Ham United 1 Newcastle United 3 – 31.8.94

The story reads like a catalogue of disaster right from the very scoreline. If the truth be known, the whole day was a bit of a cock-up. It made the *Hindenburg* look like a shaving cut. By the time I got home in the evening and settled down to a slice of toast and a cup of coffee, I found myself wishing that I could just turn the clock back twenty-four hours and do things differently. At least if we had won things might have been a little easier to bear.

The day started badly. The wonderful Helen telephoned to say that Kevin was convinced the two of us were having an illicit affair, and he was on the warpath. To make matters worse, my so called friend, Mark the Arsenal fan, had poured petrol onto the fire by reminding Kevin that I had once said in a drunken haze on holiday in Greece that 'Kevin should get his act together and let someone else have a go at Helen. . .' I can't believe I would ever have said anything like this, particularly about Helen, but then, we did have a lot of ouzo that night. It made her sound like a Nintendo. The crux of the telephone call was that I was being told stuff I shouldn't really know, and that if Kevin phoned, I was to act innocent. He may have phoned later that day, I don't know – he always did find my answering machine a little difficult for his limited intellect. He is a solicitor, after all.

I checked my bank balance to find that I had been paid short for my final month at The Death Star. I checked with Dave to find that the same had happened to him. What were we going to do about that? Sod all, really. We could hardly launch an attack in our X-wing fighters, could we?

The phone was red hot. It rang again and I fully expected it to be Harry Redknapp asking me if I could play on the right side of midfield tonight, as things were a little tight and he had to 'shuffle the pack' as it were. I love that expression, don't you? It doesn't matter how many times he shuffles the pack, he still ends up with eleven jokers on the field. It wasn't Harry, it was Gary. 'Want to earn yourself a tenner tonight?' he asked. I momentarily thought that he had started pimping, but then cottoned on to his line of thinking. I looked out of the window and made a silent prayer that it wouldn't rain, before accepting, and realising that if I didn't leave pronto, I wouldn't get there on time. I should have known things were not going to go well when I got as far as the end of my road before noticing that I was missing one vital factor – my match ticket.

Talk of an end to the rail dispute turned out to be just a rumour. I got on a train at Elmers End, knowing full well that it was probably being driven by a no-hoper who had consumed twelve pints of Guinness at lunchtime, and that the signals were being operated by the cleaning lady. Despite this, a twenty minute service was operating, and I arrived at Upton Park in good time. I excused myself from selling duties for a while, as I explained to Gary that I had to go to the ticket office to flush some more money down the toilet. Gary grinned in cheerful and resigned acceptance of the fact that we would probably be doing so for the rest of the season.

By the time we got selling I was feeling better. Spotty Herbert at the ticket office had accepted the fact that I was unemployed merely on production of a UB-40. I claimed that I had not been able to join the Irons Club as I could not afford two passport sized photographs. He took the reduced rate anyway. Result. Having guaranteed vantage points for the forthcoming games against Aston Villa and Arsenal, I took up my position with Scott and stood around for a while watching the world go around. As an inexperienced seller, I felt very self conscious about shouting out aloud when there was no-one around. Bill Clinton would have been proud of the way we provided mutual aid for each other: '*Forever Blowing Bubbles*!' I yelled. 'The brand new West Ham fanzine from the writers of *Over Land and Sea*! Pound mate. Cheers.'

Scott replied: '*Over Land and Sea*, West Ham's number one fanzine from the truly EXCELLENT writers of *Forever Blowing*

Bubbles...!' A seller from *On The Terraces* joined us briefly, but as the rain started to come down, he sought a more sheltered spot. Conscious of the fact that we have a good pitch, Scott and I remained, and were drenched. Five minutes before kick-off, we dumped our bags and unsold books with Gary and ran round to the Bobby Moore Stand. Scott disappeared in a watery haze, continuing round to the East Stand, while I desperately tried to decipher the writing on my soggy ticket. I got to my seat a few minutes into the game, hating myself for making everyone stand up as play was in progress. I know how much I hate having to do that myself. Once all the tutts had subsided it appeared that West Ham were actually making a go of it. Don Hutchison was making his debut and appeared to lead the line quite well, although in my mind he was never the player we required.

It all went wrong, of course, as it inevitably does. Andy Cole, scoring sensation of the decade (but totally crap when playing for Bristol City and Arsenal) went round Alvin as though he wasn't there, and seeing that he did not have an angle for a shot, played the ball cleverly against Steve Potts' legs to rebound into the goal. That was his version, anyway. My view was that Alvin slipped allowing Cole to get to the by-line, he tried to score from an impossible angle, and Potts, running in on goal, could do no more than score only the second goal of his career. Rumours abounded that he was desperate to score, having done so only once in 240 games. He didn't have to go that far.

Robert Lee was always going to have an influence, as he was desperate to play for West Ham, but we couldn't find the money to buy him when Charlton sold him to Newcastle in 1992. Having just been called into the England squad for a friendly against the USA, he was determined to book his place in the starting eleven. He would have done so, had it not been for injury, as he slotted home the second goal, and West Ham's defence was carved open again. I buried my face in my hands and prayed for half time. A steady second half, but I always felt that if we did manage to sneak one, they would race up the other end and get another, and that's exactly what happened. Having hit the bar and been totally frustrated, the referee finally took pity on us and awarded a penalty, which Hutch converted, somewhat tentatively. There were no fans behind the goal as the stand was being re-built, and it took a while for the fact to register that the ball had actually gone over the line. The cheer that went up was somewhat muted, the biggest cheer having been for the winning of a corner – against the run of play as well! Just as I had thought, Newcastle sprinted out of the blocks, and as we committed more men forward looking for an equaliser, Mathie scored such an easy goal even Lee Chapman could have tapped in.

Beaten, but not totally depressed, I headed for the tube station and considered my route home. I knew there would be no trains from Charing Cross, so I decided to give Victoria a whirl. After all, nearly every train in the world calls at Clapham Junction or East Croydon, and I could get a bus from either of those places. Unfortunately, there were no trains whatsoever from Victoria that night. 'No problem,' I thought to myself. There is a bus station here the size of Lake Michigan. There must be a bus going to. Beckenham from here. I checked the map. Night bus N3 left in twenty minutes from stop 'V' I searched high and low for stop 'V' finally locating it in the upper reaches of Buckingham Palace Road. By now the rain was becoming annoying. My hush puppies had taken on the consistency of wet papier-mâché and gave me all the grip and control of roller-skates on Teflon. Stop 'V' showed no signs of being a pick up point for an N3 bus. Should I wait? I still had ten minutes. I skated back to the bus station, only to notice to my horror that the stop 'V' it referred to was at Trafalgar Square. Balls. I searched in vain for a bus that would take me to see Nelson, but they were all going to such exotic places as Peckham and Lewisham. Not via Trafalgar Square. I just had time to get a tube to Embankment before Victoria station closed. By now it was 11.15pm and I was starting to become annoyed, tired and tetchy not to mention damp.

I found the illusive stop 'V' and an N3 duly arrived ten minutes late. I showed the miserable sod of a driver my pass, but it wasn't valid on night buses, so I had to stump up another £2 for the privilege of sitting among a bus load of people who all looked as though they were about to vomit. I guess it's no worse than sitting in a crowd of 20,000 people who all look as though they are about to vomit.

Anyway. The bus finally pulled away, and I relaxed, settled back and tried to read my book. Just the other side of Trafalgar Square, the bus pulled in at Whitehall, when BANG! Another bus already in the stop decided to pull out and smacked straight into us. The drivers had a stand up argument over whose fault it was, failing to tell us whether we should stay put, get out, put our heads between our legs, paint ourselves white, or what. Eventually the driver got back on the bus and took out his cash box. 'We ain't going any further,' he muttered.

The rain was now coming down so hard it was bruising. I went back to my newly adopted spiritual home, stop 'V' only to see that the next bus had already gone, and the one after that was only going as far as Crystal Palace. Another hour to kill before the bus I needed. I slid off to find something to eat at Piccadilly Circus, and had my second opportunity of the day to earn a tenner. He didn't look my type. God! What must I have looked like? I thought about going to the public toilets in Leicester Square to look at myself in the mirror, but decided against it as I would probably have got more unwelcome advances. The rain eased off and I went in search of shelter, but the only available establishments either had red lights outside or would have cost £10 for a beer and a fat tart to come and talk to you. I'd rather die of cold.

I've never been so pleased to see a bus as I was when the N3 finally turned up at five to one on September 1st. Not sure of the route it would take, I kept a watchful eye out of the window, at the same time keeping my carrier bag close by as it offered protection against the threat of an impending puke attack from the bloke sitting next to me. That would have rounded the evening off nicely, would it not? The bus meandered its way across Lambeth Bridge, through Brixton, Herne Hill and Crystal Palace before dumping me ten minutes walk from my front door. That wouldn't have been so bad if the rain hadn't started up again, but by now I didn't care. I was within striking distance of a towel and a cup of Nescafe.

I crossed my doorstep at a quarter to two. Straight to the bathroom, I discovered that I was, quite literally, soaked through to the skin. Coffee and toast followed, and I checked the messages on my answering machine. There was a message from the wonderful

Helen. She had exchanged contracts on the flat. Kevin could shove his jealousy up his backside. She was sorry for all the trouble: Did I fancy lunch tomorrow? I looked at the clock. 'I think you mean today,' I said, to myself. I wasn't going to have lunch with the wonderful Helen. I decided to wait until she had left Kevin for good. I didn't want to get cited in despatches. On the other hand, I thought, munching on a piece of cold toast, I could give Karen II another call and see if she's changed her mind. . .

That wasn't the end of the disasters for the day. In my hurry to go to sleep, I forgot to take out my contact lenses, and awoke next morning with eyes like billiard balls. While I peeled the lenses from my stinging eyeballs, the radio played that old 10cc hit: 'The things we do for love.' I agreed with the sentiment, and tried to work out a way whereby this sort of thing never happened again. It called into question the whole rationale behind being a West Ham supporter, and messing around with women such as Diana, the wonderful Helen and Karens I & II. I drew up a list of four possibilities, which would in theory alleviate my problems:

a) Support Crystal Palace – only twenty minutes walk from home
b) Move home to any stop on the District Line
c) Stop going to football
d) Ignore women for the rest of my life.

As in Australian elections, I was forced to make a choice. Having had twelve hours to get over the initial discomfort, I went for e) None of the above and if I'm honest about it, I probably always will. There is nothing else in life to get excited about, after all.

The End. . .

West Ham United 1 Manchester United 1 – 14.5.95

You don't have to be a West Ham supporter, or even a football fan in general, to realise what this book is all about. Life is God's way of telling you that he hates your guts. If he had an ounce of sympathy for the human race, he wouldn't have allowed the Eurovision Song Contest to be invented. As occupants of a reasonably wealthy first world country, we spend the majority of our time waiting to die. In many ways, we would be better served struggling to survive; then you wouldn't have anything else to worry about, like careers, relationships, the size of your wedge or West Ham United.

During season 1994/95, West Ham had very little else but survival to worry about. The Ethiopians of the Premier League searched long and hard for their next basic meal which might deliver them from the disease and pestilence that prevails in the Endsleigh League. It was a struggle, but they eventually managed to haul themselves out of the relegation scrap. Had we been told that in August 1994, after taking just one point from the opening four games we would have laughed heartily. But then, if I had been told what would happen to me during the course of season 1994/95 I would have laughed too.

In many ways, season 1994/95 encapsulated everything that had gone twenty years before it within one nine month period. Success, failure, optimism, despair – and not just on the football pitch. That being the case, it seems superfluous to describe the season in detail, as you will have read it all before, particularly if you buy *Over Land and Sea*. . .

The feature of the season for me, was not that I managed to attend forty-seven league and cup matches, (including three not involving West Ham) more than any time since 1986/87, but the way in which

I attended them. Virtually everyone I used to go to football with had gone from the scene. Dobbo, Barney, Close, and Stain Tooth had nearly all moved away or weren't interested any more. Tim from college was in Aussie land, so I was delighted when Gary Firmager asked me to join the fanzine team on away trips.

I made a total of eighteen trips away with the gang, which often involved the use of a press pass to get into areas I had previously only dreamed of, access to players and the chance to write about our experiences for the fanzine. The *OLAS* crew had as many if not more characters than the team itself, and in that respect, made it a wonderful group of people. Gary was our leader; chief arm twister and blagger, Phil Daniels, expert writer but whingeing pain in the bum. Kevin Williamson totally devoted to West Ham and a most fluent and talented writer. Jim & Bill Drury and Liam & Sean Tyrrell, all talented writers. The very funny yet strangely anonymous Jughunter. In addition, the non-writing sellers, John, James, Young Mark and Little Rob. Heroes all, but ahead of anything else, committed West Ham fans. There were other talented writers too numerous to mention who didn't travel with us, but that chemistry made *OLAS* the best West Ham fanzine, and continues to do so.

As well as the league and cup matches, we made several other trips including a jaunt down to Exeter in September to see Eamonn Dolan's testimonial game. Eamonn invited us to the reception afterwards and we rubbed shoulders with all the players. I was in a different league.

I saw Jenny one Saturday night and asked her out again. She said yes, which called my bluff a bit, and after six days I realised why I had knocked it on the head the first time around and had to repeat the dose. Mr Popular strikes again.

Meanwhile I remained jobless. I passed the time by writing a book and going to football. Oh yes, and the occasional bit of job hunting. I must admit it was a bit of a struggle having to get up at nine in the morning to go and sign on – what a liberty. I was looking for work in the media, and had limited success, but eventually, out of the blue, a job landed at my feet – albeit a temporary one. Dealing with council tax appeals in Streatham was not my idea of heaven, but the pay was good and I wasn't in a position to complain. They were a good bunch, and it gave me the opportunity to play football once a week too, in a local lunchtime league. I was aware, however, that something more permanent was required.

The weekend before I started with the Valuation Office, West Ham re-signed Julian Dicks, having already retrieved Tony Cottee. That day, we beat Southampton 2–0 at Upton Park and reached the dizzy heights of twelfth position. After our dreadful start to the season, it seemed we would breeze through as long as we continued in the same vein. The heroes of 1993/94, Burrows, Marsh and Chapman all disappeared. Burrows for Cottee, Marsh to Coventry and Chapman to Ipswich. A successful October gave way to a dreadful November, yielding nothing but a 1–0 win over doomed Leicester and a dismal Coca-Cola Cup exit at the hands of Bolton. From the height of optimism, we sank to the depths of despair.

We signed two international players on loan in December. Marc Rieper from Danish side Brondby, and Michael Hughes, an Ulsterman from Strasbourg. Hughes made his debut in the 2–1 defeat at QPR. I sat and watched the game with Stuart the QPR fan, and neither of us was impressed. Of the *OLAS* crew, only Gary and I made the trip to Leeds to see Rieper make his debut. Pottsy's only mistake of the year gifted Leeds their second goal, but the team showed fighting spirit and fought back to 2–2. The following game saw Cottee back on top form with a hat-trick against Manchester City in a 3–0 pre-Christmas demolition. It was so typically West Ham. Having shown such courage at Elland Road, and swept City aside, we let a 1–0 lead slip against bottom side Ipswich and could only draw. We allowed Wimbledon only one shot on target, but it was enough to win the game 1–0. Then we beat third placed Nottingham Forest 3–1. What the hell was going on? We were brilliant one minute and laughable the next – as I said, so typically West Ham United.

I had an endowment policy mature in November. My Co-op agent came to see me and I fully expected to be sold another policy, or a pension, or something of the like. I didn't expect to be offered a job, but by January I had left the valuation office; left all trace of property valuation behind and started a new career in insurance. My life was even less predictable than West Ham's form.

We travelled up to a bitterly cold Blackburn to see the boys play outstanding football and take a 2–1 lead, only to succumb 4–2. Gary, Phil and I wandered about on the pitch and wondered if simply playing good football would be enough – it had never guaranteed results before, and certainly wasn't doing us any favours this season. It did enough to get us past Wycombe Wanderers in the FA Cup, but a run of six defeats in eight games saw confidence hit the floor so hard it knocked itself out. QPR knocked us out of the Cup, 1–0 at Loftus Road, a result which left both myself and Stuart the QPR fan somewhat confused and disappointed. Home defeats by Tottenham and Chelsea were hard to swallow, particularly as we went in at half time with a 1–0 lead after playing the opposition off the park. Sheffield Wednesday sneaked three points when referee Danson sent off Alvin Martin and Tim Breacker for no apparent reason. The only points gathered came in a 2–1 win at Leicester and a 2–2 draw against struggling Everton. Not good.

The wonderful Helen finally escaped the clutches of the evil Kevin, who by now had become my sworn enemy. He had the impression that I had something to do with the wonderful Helen's departure, when in fact nothing could have been further from the truth. Despite the fact that I love her very much, our conversations led me to believe that I would never be anything more than a friend to her; but I was happy to accept that privilege. I was having nil success on the female front, and decided not to try any more. I sent more red roses to Karen II, but this time she didn't even have the courtesy to acknowledge them. She and her exquisite legs had their wish – I gave up.

Everything, they say, comes to he who waits. So I'm just waiting. One of these days one or both will come to their senses.

Something amazing happened. From being unable to win, West Ham suddenly could not lose. Of the final thirteen games of the season, we lost only twice – predictably at Newcastle, and not so predictably at Crystal Palace. We beat Arsenal at Highbury and Aston Villa at Villa Park, and enjoyed home wins over Wimbledon, Blackburn and Liverpool, drawing against Norwich, Southampton, Forest, Ipswich, QPR and, most significantly, Manchester United, a result which enabled Blackburn to lift their first title for eighty years.

As the final whistle went at Upton Park for 1994/95, I took time out to reflect. From almost being in a position to send West Ham out of my life for good, I was now more involved than ever, and finding to my delight that after twenty years of support, they were still as irritating and infuriating as ever. If we ever did win the title it would be a huge disappointment – that mystique would go. Fortunately, I don't think anyone will have to worry about that in my lifetime.

A season that began with relegation a safe bet and myself out of work had ended with a safe fourteenth place having outplayed league leaders Blackburn twice. The addition of five new quality players to the squad had also raised hopes for next season. Meanwhile I had a new career with prospects. All that remained was success in a relationship. The relentless search goes on. It is at least some consolation that the worst thing that can happen is nothing. (Second only to drawing Luton away in the third round of the FA Cup.)

If life and West Ham's form really are a mirror for each other, I shudder to think where I will be this time next year. I might be in a different job, I might have a different car, I might be living in Scotland. I might have written my last word. I might even have found Miss Perfect. On second thoughts, that's a bit farfetched; if I went to live in Scotland I wouldn't be able to watch West Ham. Only two things are certain; I will still love West Ham, no matter what they do, and I will still have an irrational hatred of Luton.

Epilogue: You Are Not Alone. . .

West Ham United 5 Burnley 3 – 28.11.2009

It is July 2010. I am running through New Cross at 6.30am. There is the usual strong smell of drains and rotting vegetables but that is only because the local dogs have not yet been allowed outside to open their unattended bowels in the centre of the pavement.

I am wearing my new West Ham away shorts and I flick an obvious 'V' sign at the site of the Old Den, as I do every morning as I run this route to work. It's facile and it's childish, but it amuses me. As I run through the Greenwich foot tunnel I am overtaken by a blind cyclist. At least I assume he is blind, otherwise he would see the big signs saying 'no cycling'. I think about complaining but realise that I am turning into Victor Meldrew and that my complaint will have more impact it I wait until he has knocked over a small child or killed an elderly lady. As I emerge on the north side of the tunnel I feel the fresh air of East London and as Mr Churchill once said I continue my journey into broad sunlit uplands.

Running every morning gives me time to think. Not just about life but where to go and what to do next. When An Irrational Hatred of Luton *was first published in 1995 I had no idea it would prove so popular and spawn two more books. I had no idea I would move north and live away from London so long. And no idea that I would eventually come back and find a job I love, meet a girl I adore and find an inner peace I probably haven't experienced since I was 11.*

That has been achieved despite having a season ticket at West Ham for 2009/10 and renewing it this year. It was my first season ticket since 1999/2000. Things have changed a bit since then. But as things change so the desire to remember things as they were becomes stronger. Witness the popularity of the retro shirt. We have to face the fact that we are unlikely to achieve much as a club in terms of silverware. Much better to reflect on past glories. They cannot be taken away. They cannot flatter to deceive. They cannot be sold to Tottenham. Irrational was retro in 1995. It starts its story in 1975. It still starts in 1975 so now it's retro retro.

I did start to write a fourth book but decided against it a short way in. There were three main reasons for this. The first is that it would cover a period from November 2003 to date, when apart from last season I saw only a handful of games in person and was living 200 miles away. Hardly grounds for serious and incisive comment on team matters. The second is that I could not possibly have written as freely and openly as I did in Irrational. Even had it not been for threats of legal action, it would not have been possible to tell it like it was. I think that was what made Irrational so popular, my naive willingness to bare all and call a spade a spade. The years have naturally tempered that naivety and now I find myself questioning every sentence in terms of the damage it could do. The third is that despite the fact that I think West Ham 'til I Die and The Legacy of Barry Green are written better, Irrational is my first born and my favourite. So when the opportunity came to share it with some new readers I jumped at the chance.

I have picked out one chapter from the book that never was and would like to share this with you if for no other reason than to prove that it doesn't matter how many internationals you put into the team, how many new stands you build, how many rich owners you have. Nothing really changes. At West Ham, in football, in life or in the world.

*

After the euphoria of snatching a draw against Arsenal, the loss of a 2–0 lead at the Stadium of Light had somewhat tempered the enthusiasm by the time Aston Villa arrived at Upton Park. By now, the superstitions between myself, Mark and Sam were becoming frankly ridiculous to the point where I, a grown man of 41, was refusing to wear the home shirt because I was convinced it was a jinx.

Not quite as stupid as it sounds – I had bought the shirt moments before the first defeat of the season against Spurs. I hadn't owned it when we won at Wolves on the opening day – we hadn't won since. Football fan logic told me it was time to ditch it. Mark, Sam and Jamie persevered. As I had been at work I opted for a collar and tie.

Working at Canary Wharf being fair and reasonable made it easy for me to get to Upton Park and meant I could work until 6.30, jump on the Jubilee Line to West Ham and then the District Line to Plaistow, where I got off and met the others at the Prince Albert.

The atmosphere in the STBU was subdued, but we did have the bonus of not being kicked in the back every fifteen seconds and we had some humour in the stand around us. Sam started a new tradition for us, a new superstition. Brad Friedel had the ball on the edge of the six yard box. There was a deathly silence. Sam yelled 'Wanker!' at the top of his voice and I am convinced it put Friedel off for the rest of the game. Zavon Hines won a penalty and Mark Noble despatched it with more than a little nervousness. His last penalty had not been so well taken and the relief when it went in was tangible. I was sure that Brad Friedel was still trying to work out who had been questioning his personal habits. The penalty came in first-half injury time and the second half had barely got under way when the ginger Pele himself happened to be standing underneath Manuel Da Costa when he re-entered the earth's atmosphere after a freakishly high jump. Unbelievably, referee Steve Bennett gave a penalty to Villa.

Rob Green had not had to endure anyone suggesting that he liked to pull his own pudding (that would not happen until 11 June 2010), so was able to concentrate and pull off a great save from Ashley Young, but was caught napping a few minutes later when Young curled a shot from an impossible angle into the top corner. The silence was deafening. You could almost hear 30,000 heads drop in simultaneous acknowledgement that the first home win was not going to happen tonight.

Resigned to another draw at best and disappointing defeat at worst, the crowd took matters into their own hands – literally, refusing to return the ball to the Villa players at throw-ins, only throwing it back once a replacement had already been provided. Childish – but brilliant.

Diamanti warmed up tantalisingly on the touchline but Zola decided Jiminez was the man for the job. I wasn't so sure. Villa had Faye sent off for having a girl's name. Hines popped up with an unexpected but welcome winner in injury time and I decided never to wear the replica shirt again.

The relief was obvious and suddenly everyone was buzzing again and Everton at home on Sunday suddenly didn't look so tricky after all – three points there, an nice rest for the international break then a tidy win at Hull and whipping boys Burnley at home would make November the month when it all turned around and we could make that assault on the top six, right? Wrong. Everton was a disaster. They had two shots on goal all afternoon and won 2–1. I prepared to console myself with a trip to Doncaster.

I hired a car for the drive north. With business to attend to with the house I had contacted Daniels to see if the Keypoint gang fancied a night out on the Friday and I could also take the chance to go back to my old, happy, stamping ground. I also took the opportunity to ask Stephanie out and she readily agreed but I had reluctantly accepted by this point that a pint, a curry and a good chinwag would be the extent of it. Yet there were still highly flirtatious undertones in her texts that led me to believe more might be on offer. I had to check it out to satisfy myself. And if there was nothing doing, I could still go back to my hotel room and satisfy myself.

Beth had been flirting with me outrageously on Facebook. When I told her I had booked a hotel in Doncaster things progressed although I couldn't be sure if it was real or tongue-in-cheek. We had arranged to meet in my room after everyone had left on Friday. She was amazed that I fancied her. I was amazed that she would even contemplate seeing me. With her being married I felt pangs of guilt but they were fleeting. After all, this was the reason I got divorced – to spread my wings again.

I drove up on the Friday afternoon through torrential rain and got texts from Beth checking I would be there. I confirmed. As the afternoon wore on, though, it became apparent she would only be able to pop in for a drink as she was being dragged to a party by her husband. Part of me felt that knowing deflated feeling that comes with a half-expected disappointment, usually experienced after a home defeat to one of the big four. It had looked like it might be achievable. But in the end reality kicked in and normal service was resumed.

She did turn up for a drink and she did have a wicked look in her eye, and, I sensed, a hint of despair and regret that she couldn't make it. I decided to give her the benefit of the doubt. Maybe she really was being dragged away against her will and on another occasion things might have been different. Or maybe she had just been teasing me. Either way I decided married women were now off the agenda.

The evening was great fun – Daniels was on top form, as was Daniels junior, but at 11pm I made my excuses and headed for my room as the drive had left me exhausted and I was keen to experience a good long sleep the like of which I had not known for some time. I left Shaun and Richard to their final pints and went to my room, wondering if maybe Beth had been pulling my leg and would be waiting for me with a glass of rosé and a cheeky grin when I opened my door. She wasn't. I slept, but not before I'd had a good long think about the way my life was going to develop from here.

On Saturday I pleased myself after driving to Bradford and back to see the estate agent and sign the papers. A bit of shopping. Lunch in the pub, a long sleep in the afternoon. England v Brazil on TV. Part of me was telling me this was how I wanted to live my life, with only myself to answer to. Another part was telling me I was in danger of becoming a sad cunt. Like the dog who chases the car with no knowledge of what he would do if he actually caught it, I took Stephanie out and had a great time, but despite the body language saying 'I really like you but I don't want to sleep with you' I still invited her back to my room for 'coffee'. My invitation was politely declined. I apologised the next day and considered what shiny car I might chase after next. The David Gray concert was looming but surely Elaine was out of my league?

Hull City should have been out of our league but somehow

managed to finish as equals after 90 minutes of changing fortunes at the KC stadium. I'd been into work for a morning of fairness and reasonableness and Mark had given me a lift home. When I left his house we were 2–0 up. By the time I got home we were 3–2 down. It would take a good long run to sort this one out, and it did, Da Costa poking in an equaliser. For the second away game in succession we had thrown away a 2–0 lead and the omens were not good. I reasoned, though, that we were at least taking a 2–0 lead and if we hadn't done that we would have lost the last two games 2–0 and 2–1. It doesn't work like that, though – confidence is a fragile thing in football. Most professional snooker players, for example, can clear the table in a single visit during practice. Most professional golfers can be on the green in three on a par five. It's what happens when you are under pressure that counts. It's how you react to circumstances you may not be used to. The very best football teams, historically, don't lose matches very often. They would rarely go 2–0 down or lose a 2–0 lead. But West Ham, historically, are not a very good football team. So why are we so surprised when we draw or lose from 2–0 up? Search me.

The following Monday I met Elaine at London Bridge and we travelled on the tube up to Highbury and Islington to see David Gray at the Union Chapel. The tickets had not been cheap – £40 each, but I reckoned it was for a good cause. Mine. On the Northern Line she was pressed against me, through necessity rather than desire, but I looked down at her and valiantly succeeded in resisting the temptation to kiss her. She looked amazing. It would not have been a good move. We had a decidedly second-rate Italian meal, widely available in Islington, and watched a very good David Gray concert, supported by Lisa Mitchell and the Low Anthem. At various points I chanced an arm around her, a touch of the knee. She didn't flinch or slap me. My confidence grew. I was probably 2–0 up at this point and wondering when it was all going to collapse. I'd asked Bob to come and pick us up as I couldn't be sure of the timing and the trains and I wanted to be sure Elaine got home OK. He turned up in the limousine.

Dressed in his bouncer gear and dripping in bling, Bob opened the door to an astonished Elaine, and I had the presence of mind to go along with it, as though I had planned it all along. As we climbed into the back seat of the limo, I spotted the chilled bottle of champagne. As Bob drove us to Elaine's I took her champagne glass and put it on the rack and kissed her. She kissed me back. Thank you God. In my mind I was 5–0 up and heading for added time.

Burnley arrived at Upton Park with a wretched away record and things did not improve for them when Collison, Stanislas and Cole put West Ham into a 3–0 lead.

The STBU made a telling contribution again by distracting the opposing goalkeeper. The usual five-year-olds in the row in front had been replaced by a group of lads steaming drunk, but very funny. At every opportunity when Burnley goalkeeper Brian Jensen got the ball they would shout 'Jensen, you're rubbish!' This was repeated every few seconds. It could have been very annoying, but it caught on. Very soon, everyone in the STBU was shouting the mantra 'Jensen, you're rubbish!' and the hypnotic, subliminal effect meant he was believing it and he was he was proving it.

Burnley were so poor they even let Jonathan Spectator get into their half. Not only that, they were daft enough to let him into their penalty area and naive enough to foul him. Cole didn't come out for the second half but we thought nothing of it as Franco and another penalty, this time from Jiminez, put us 5–0 up. I said to Mark I wanted a clean sheet – that I would have settled for 3–0, that I would have preferred that to 5–1. Confidence. When Roger Federer is 5–0 up in the third set, he doesn't lose three games in a row. When Phil Taylor can smell blood, he finishes off his opponent. When Tiger Woods is driving. . . OK, bad example. My point is, we were not high on confidence, and being 5–0 up was a bit of an alien experience.

I wasn't too concerned, we were playing well, but it was clear we would not keep a clean sheet. It didn't take Shelley von Strunckel to predict that Burnley would score at some point. And they did, and again, and again. With Franco off we had no focal point up front and the shape of the team collapsed like a deck of cards. In the end we were begging the referee to blow for full time. Ridiculous, but typical.